Stopping Child Maltreatment Before It Starts

SAGE SOURCEBOOKS FOR
THE HUMAN SERVICES SERIES

Series Editors: ARMAND LAUFFER and CHARLES GARVIN

Recent Volumes in This Series

Stopping Child Maltreatment Before It Starts

Emerging Horizons in Early Home Visitation Services

Sage Sourcebooks for

the Human Services

Neil B. Guterman

Sage Publications, Inc.
International Educational and Professional Publisher
Thousand Oaks ▪ London ▪ New Delhi

For information:

Sage Publications, Inc.
2455 Teller Road
Thousand Oaks, California 91320
E-mail: order@sagepub.com

Sage Publications Ltd.
6 Bonhill Street
London EC2A 4PU
United Kingdom

Sage Publications India Pvt. Ltd.
M-32 Market
Greater Kailash I
New Delhi 110 048 India

Printed in the United States of America

Library of Congress Cataloging-in-Publication Data

Guterman, Neil B.
  Stopping child maltreatment before it starts: Emerging
horizons in early home visitation services / By Neil B. Guterman.
    p. cm. — (Sage sourcebooks for the human services; v. 42)
  Includes bibliographical references and index.
  ISBN 0-7619-1311-4 (cloth: alk. paper)
  ISBN 0-7619-1312-2 (pbk.: alk. paper)
    1. Home-based family services—United States.   2. Child abuse—
United States—Prevention.   I. Title.   II. Sage sourcebooks for the human
services series: v. 42.
  HV43 .G87 2000
  362.76'7'0973—dc21   00-009212

01 02 03 04 05 06 07 7 6 5 4 3 2 1

Acquiring Editor:	Nancy Hale
Editorial Assistant:	Heather Gotlieb
Production Editor:	Nevair Kabakian
Editorial Assistant:	Victoria Cheng
Typesetter:	Tina Hill
Indexer:	Molly Hall

For Stacey, Maor and Noa . . .

Contents

PREFACE

In a free society, some are guilty and all are responsible.
quoted in A. J. Heschel, 1996, p. xxiv

A jury needed only two and a half hours yesterday to convict
Tabitha Walrond of criminally negligent homicide for the fatal
starvation death of her infant son but acquit her of second-degree
manslaughter, a more serious charge. Ms. Walrond, who was 19
when the 2-month-old son she was breast-feeding died in August
1997, wept quietly as she heard the verdict in State Supreme Court
in the Bronx. The conviction carries a maximum sentence of 4
years in prison. . . . The trial, which lasted more than three weeks,
focused on whether the death of the boy, Tyler Walrond, could have
been prevented, and who was responsible for failing to save him.
(Bernstein, 1999b, p. B1)

Who is responsible for failing to save Tyler and the countless other
children suffering abuse and neglect at the hands of their parents?
Although by legal definition, the culpability for physical child abuse and

neglect rests with the parents of maltreated children, one of the most clear patterns emerging from the last several decades of research is that the social contextual "nests" in which parents are embedded and sustained bears a heavy burden of responsibility for the unfolding of physical child abuse and neglect. The existing system of child protection in the United States, which places the onus of the problem on individual parents, does not square well with this expanding scientific consensus concerning the power of ecological contexts to shape and provide potential solutions to the problem of child maltreatment. From both a scientific and moral standpoint, although some parents may be guilty according to legal definition, all are responsible for the presence of child maltreatment in our society.

Fortunately, an emerging nationwide movement is under way to promote within local communities the necessary supports and services to aid families who are struggling to parent their children. This movement aims for nothing less than the prevention of child maltreatment *before it ever starts.* The rapidly developing field of early child maltreatment prevention, most commonly delivered through the vehicle of early home visitation services, provides a beacon of hope as our nation strives to turn the tide on the problem of child abuse and neglect. Although not a novel service vehicle, early home visitation services offer an innovative strategy by delivering services during the sensitive perinatal period, aiming to promote a positive start in parenting in order to avert potential child maltreatment down the road.

Although the promise of early home visitation services remains alluring, this rapidly developing field continues to be fluid, fraught with uncertainty about its future and challenged by the complexity of efforts to realize the dream of preventing child maltreatment before it ever takes place. Indeed, ongoing scrutiny of research findings on early prevention efforts provides grounds for both optimism and some caution. Clearly, the growing early prevention movement holds great potential and is eminently sensible. Yet, the movement also presents unanswered questions, which, if unaddressed, threaten to derail progress toward reducing the incidence of child maltreatment in the United States. Most assuredly, the early home visitation movement is at a crossroads.

This book's purpose is twofold: First, it aims to introduce the field of early home visitation, presenting practice strategies and the contexts from which they have developed. Second, the book aims to evaluate early home visitation services on the basis of supporting scientific evidence.

In light of this evidence base, I will point out future directions necessary for the early prevention movement to thrive and advance beyond its present limitations. It is hoped that by explicating what is known and still to be known and tested, *Stopping Child Maltreatment Before It Starts* will serve as a map that may be relied upon to help reorient professionals in the field about our present location, identifying important next steps in this tough and dark terrain of child abuse and neglect practice. It is my modest wish that this book will serve as one useful vehicle to advance us away from the human darkness of child maltreatment and toward more supportive and healthful rearing of children in our society.

ACKNOWLEDGMENTS

Although the cover of this book notes only a single author, the work between the covers is drawn from the efforts of countless concerned parents and families, professionals, and academics. I have been fortunate to collaborate in the field of early prevention with many talented scholars and practitioners. Ann Reiniger, executive director of the New York Society for Prevention of Cruelty to Children, first established the Best Beginnings program in New York City, with which I continue ongoing study. Liz Anisfeld has proven a wise and generous collaborator in our study of the Best Beginnings program. Best Beginnings and its community-based anchor, Alianza Dominica, are filled with dedicated and creative practitioners whom I wish to acknowledge for their contributions to families and the community, as well as to the larger field of early home visitation services. I wish to especially thank Milagros Batista, Sobeira Guillen, and Moises Perez for their compassionate and dedicated work and insights, Lesbby Estrada-Nadal for her solid and conscientious management of the evaluation efforts, and Alisa Land for research assistance. The other members of the Best Beginnings directorate, Nick Cunningham, Mathilde Irigoyen, Wanda Lay, and Mary McCord, remain a supportive and empowering executive committee sifting through and applying important changes in the home visitation field. I also wish to acknowledge Mel Schneiderman, Vincent Fontana, Michael Garber, and Sister Carol Barnes of the New York Foundling Hospital and Len Walsh and Kathleen Collins of St. Vincent's Hospital in Manhattan, who have shown the foresight to support and test some of the innovations proposed in this text.

Several individuals at the national level have aided in invaluable ways in making sense of and advancing early home visitation services as a field. The collegial interchanges I have had with many, most notably with Deborah Daro and John Landsverk, have helped me to keep on my toes in this rapidly developing field. Deborah, in particular, deserves special appreciation not only from myself, but I believe from the larger field of child maltreatment prevention.

As in many books, the ideas in this volume would not have flowered without a fertile academic soil in which my work has been rooted. There are many individuals to thank here. Ed Mullen, the director of the Center for the Study of Social Work Practice, a collaboration of Columbia University School of Social Work and the Jewish Board of Family and Children's Services, provided early support to kick-start my efforts in early child-maltreatment prevention. Ron Feldman, my dean, and Alan Siskind, an executive at the Jewish Board, have both made tireless efforts at developing the infrastructure for practice and evaluation research on behalf of children and families. Peg Hess, Brenda McGowan, Sheila Kamerman, Jane Waldfogel, and Mary McKay have provided their own critical doses of encouragement and belief in this project and its larger mission for children and families in the United States. Rob Schilling, Nabila El-Bassel, and the Social Intervention Group at Columbia University also deserve special acknowledgment for their critical support, which led to the first pilot-testing of the Parents Together program.

Over the years, many colleagues have provided more general guidance and wisdom in the rigors of scholarly practice research, and they deserve thanks: David Bargal, Betty Blythe, Charles Garvin, Siri Jayaratne, Armand Lauffer, Denise Bronson, and Eric Bermann. Charles and Armand, the co-editors of the Sage Sourcebooks series through which this book is published, have maintained their faith and enthusiasm throughout, and their wise editorial support has shepherded this book to print. Also, Nancy Hale, Sage's editor, has been a delight to work with. Caitlin Adams, Sheryl Sodohoue, and Lisa Cammett provided editing assistance along the way. Most especially, I wish to express thanks for those who have read and commented on various portions of this book, including Liz Anisfeld, Stacey Gordon, Jane Waldfogel, Mary McKay, Andrew Hamid, Hyeouk Hahm, and Sobeira Guillen.

Last, it is the author's privilege to offer profound thanks to the most influential people of all in this enterprise, my precious family: my wife, best friend, and trusted adviser, Stacey; our children, Maor and Noa (the most direct and unquestionable proof of the successes of early "in home" supports); my brothers, Mark, Larry, and Bruce; and everyone in the larger extended family, especially Martin and Lee. I offer unending gratitude to my parents, Monty and Dora, z'l. B"H.

—Neil B. Guterman

Chapter 1

THE DARKNESS OF MALTREATMENT, THE RAYS OF LIGHT IN PREVENTION

A local child protective services department fielded a call from a hospital reporting suspected child abuse against a 5-month-old white infant, Baby G, by the infant's 27-year-old father, Mr. L. Upon medical examination, Baby G exhibited a number of likely signs of physical abuse, including red round lesions resembling burns on his stomach, a skull fractured in three locations, a detached retina, a collarbone that had been broken and later healed, marks on his arm that looked like bites and possible squeezing, and a round burn mark on the bottom of his foot.

Mr. L claimed that he found Baby G choking on a bottle and rushed him to the hospital. Hurrying into the hospital entrance, Mr. L stated, he ran into the automatic doors, which hit the baby in the head. Mr. L claimed the baby's burns were received from chemicals in the backyard pool, and the bite marks came from the baby's two older brothers. Mr. L's story largely coincided with that of Baby G's mother. Protective services did not charge the family with child abuse but referred them for 6 weeks of intensive family preservation services.

An anonymous caller to child protective services alleged that K, an 8-year-old African American girl, and her five siblings, ranging in age from 11 months to 10 years old, were not adequately fed and were living in a garbage-strewn and rat-infested household. The caller stated that their mother was regularly high on heroin and that, in addition to the six children and the mother, at least four other adults lived in the home part-time, using and selling drugs. The caller asserted that there was little furniture in the home and no beds for the children to sleep on, as the adults had been known to sell the children's belongings to purchase drugs. The older children were reported to have poor school attendance and performance. After investigating the home, the protective services worker reported that there was not enough evidence to substantiate child neglect.

Protective services had ongoing contact with the D family since 2-year-old J was reported by his mother as being "abused" by her husband. Child abuse was not substantiated at the time. One year later, a local hospital reported J to protective services, and again, abuse was not confirmed. At this time, however, a case was opened on the family, and the protective services worker visited the home monthly to monitor and manage the case. Throughout this period, J was brought several more times to the emergency room for bumps and, later, for a scratched cornea and a round lesion on his chin that appeared to be a burn. Later, J was treated in the emergency room for a bloody nose, a boxed ear, and bruised shoulders. Shortly before J's fourth birthday, J was brought to the emergency room in a coma, resulting from months of intracranial bleeding. Doctors also discovered bruises covering the boy's body. J emerged from surgery permanently paralyzed and profoundly retarded, requiring institutional care for the remainder of his life. (Reidinger, 1988)

Although the wounds that maltreated children suffer differ in variety and severity, all abused and neglected children confront the reality that those who take care of them are also those who harm them. The wounds left by child abuse and neglect are, thus, not only physical ones but also ones that disturb the souls of developing and vulnerable children. Might the lives of Baby G, the K children, and J, like millions of other children in the United States, have taken different paths, free from parental abuse and neglect? Those concerned with the problem of child abuse and neglect and familiar with youngsters such as these often face a gnawing question: Could we have prevented their maltreatment from occurring? *Can we stop child maltreatment before it ever starts?*

Sadly, we cannot turn back the clock for those children already harmed by maltreatment. For such children, ongoing intensive efforts are necessary to ameliorate the effects of their maltreatment, to protect them from future harm, and to give them the best chance of developing into whole and healthy functioning adults. However, for those children not yet maltreated but facing the possibility in the future, can we prevent their personal catastrophes from occurring and, in so doing, also avert the damaging and often long-term consequences that result?

This book's premise, as its title pronounces, is that child maltreatment *can* be stopped before it starts. Preventing child abuse and neglect before it occurs has long remained a hope of many who work with children at risk. Over three quarters of a century ago, for example, Christian Carl Carstens, the first director of the Massachusetts Society for Prevention of Cruelty to Children and later founder of the Child Welfare League of America, exhorted concerned professionals to work toward "the prevention of cruelty and neglect, and not merely the prevention of its recurrence" (quoted in Antler & Antler, 1980, p. 202). Although the ideal of preventing child abuse and neglect before it happens has engendered great hope, it is nonetheless a goal that has never yet been adequately realized.

Recently, however, advances in early intervention research have reignited the hope of stopping child abuse before it starts (Guterman, 1997a; Olds & Kitzman, 1993). Selected interventions under careful study and specific conditions have shown that the onset of child maltreatment can be averted. Inspired in part by such findings, a national movement has been spawned promoting the establishment of neonatal support programs for families facing special challenges in raising their children. Although we cannot turn the clock back for those children already abused and neglected, the current evidence suggests that the potential trauma for other children facing similar circumstances may now be preventable.

The unfortunate reality is that, since you started reading this chapter (likely just a few minutes ago), and if this is a typical day in America, another several dozen children—roughly enough to fill several hospital neonatal nurseries or a school classroom—have been identified by authorities as abused or neglected. An additional untold number are being maltreated but are not known to the authorities. If you continue reading through the end of this first chapter, it is likely that another 100 children or more across the United States, roughly the equivalent of a sizable preschool filled with children, will have been identified by official sources as having been abused or neglected. Each one of these children faces heightened risk for a variety of health and psychosocial problems, including physical injuries, cognitive and academic delays, depression, substance and alcohol abuse, increased aggression, and involvement in later criminal activity (see Chapter 2). Perhaps most disturbingly, those victimized in childhood are more likely to perpetuate a cycle of victimization against others, both in the present and into future generations (e.g., Rivera & Widom, 1990; Widom, 1989a, 1989b). The consequences of child maltreatment, thus, transcend individual children and families and entail a spreading circle of damage to the wider social fabric. It's been said, "the day is short, and the work is great" (*Pirke Avot* Chapter 2, Mishna 15). The problem of child maltreatment in America is extensive and requires urgent attention.

Our nation's response to the problem of child maltreatment to date can at best be characterized as inadequate, or perhaps more realistically, as a valiant failure. Discovery of the "battered child syndrome" in the late 1950s and early 1960s spurred a flurry of activity across the nation, leading to state and federal legislation establishing child protective services systems across the country. Today, child protective services systems in the United States remain the nation's major institutional framework entrusted with "fixing" the problem of child abuse in America. Evidence indicates that child protective services systems, for reasons that will be examined, have yet to make a dent in the problem of child abuse and neglect in the United States. Indeed, since the establishment of child protective services systems in the United States, the problem has by all measures worsened. In 1997, approximately 3 million children in the United States were the alleged victims of child abuse and neglect (U.S. Department of Health and Human Services, 1999a). These figures represent a dramatic increase in the number of children known to have suffered child maltreatment since national data collection efforts were first initiated over three decades ago.

One of the first national studies of the incidence of child maltreatment found that 8.4 per 100,000 children were reported for physical abuse in 1967, with about an additional third of reports representing other forms of child maltreatment including child neglect, sexual abuse, and other nonintended cases of victimization against children by their parents and caregivers (Gil, 1970b). Studies since that time have documented an upward spiraling of child maltreatment, leveling off in just the last several years. For example, protective services data analyzed in the 1997 Annual Fifty State Survey conducted by Prevent Child Abuse America (formerly the National Committee to Prevent Child Abuse) estimated a rate equivalent to 4,700 children per 100,000 reported for child maltreatment. These figures represent an increase in child abuse and neglect reports of more than 400-fold over the three decades that national data have been collected.

Likely a substantial proportion of this increase is due to increased public awareness and willingness to report maltreatment cases to authorities. However, the rise in child maltreatment reports cannot solely be attributed to increased awareness; rather, it is likely due to an actual increase in the phenomenon itself. For example, through the late 1980s and into the 1990s, after the dramatic rise in public attention to the problem had leveled off, official statistics continued to report a steady rise in child maltreatment reports. Data collected by Prevent Child Abuse America during the 10 years from 1988 to 1997 indicate a steady rise in suspected maltreatment reports, from 35 per 1,000 children to 47 per 1,000 (a 34% increase) over the decade post-dating major policy developments that encouraged an increase in child abuse and neglect reports (see Figure 1.1).

Similar upward trends are reported by the National Child Abuse and Neglect Data System or NCANDS, which notes increases in maltreatment from 40 per 1,000 children in 1990 to 42 per 1,000 children in 1997 (U.S. Department of Health and Human Services, 1999a; National Center on Child Abuse and Neglect, 1994) and by the three National Incidence Studies, or NIS, which reported increases of harmed and endangered children from 22.6 per 1,000 in 1986 to 41.9 per 1,000 in 1993. Regardless of the varying reported statistics and study methodologies employed, it is clear that the problem of child maltreatment continues largely unabated, despite the efforts of the nation's protective services systems.

Child protective services, by design, intervene in families' lives only after child abuse or neglect has been uncovered. By this point, chil-

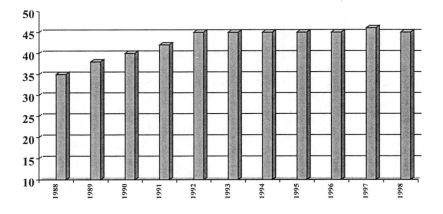

Figure 1.1. Estimated Number of Children Reported for Child Maltreatment in the United States From 1988 to 1998 (per 1,000 children)
SOURCE: Wang & Harding, 1999; Wang & Daro, 1998.

dren have already been placed squarely in harm's way, often suffering destructive consequences, and family problems have most commonly reached a severe and entrenched phase. At this point, family members are unlikely to be receptive to involuntary and stigmatizing intervention that holds the threat of child separation. In reality, many families aim to banish protective services from their lives, ironically to "protect" their family from breakup. Thus, even well-intentioned intervention at this point is often "too little too late." Protective services intervention burdens struggling families with the paradoxical dilemma of having to cooperate with coercive intervention that can sever family ties in order to maintain those family ties. Child protection professionals, at the same time, face the unsavory no-win burden of being the arbiter of family breakup or the preserver of families in a high risk state.

The dark realities presented by child protective services have pressed professionals to search for alternative solutions to the problem of child maltreatment. In this context, some of the promising findings supporting early preventive interventions have shed hopeful rays of light. Applied to the problem of child maltreatment, early prevention represents "an ounce of prevention as worth a pound of child protection." To avoid later child protective intervention, early prevention programs aim to intervene soon enough and powerfully enough that the parent-child relationship trajectory will be altered away from a future of maltreatment toward more positive and responsive interaction patterns over the long term. Knowledge recently developed in prevention science, early childhood, and parenting studies has underscored that a window of opportunity may open during early childhood providing the potential for early preventive intervention to leverage long-lasting changes on behalf of the developing child and family.[1]

Although a variety of approaches to preventing child abuse before the fact have been reported, *early* or *perinatal home visitation services* have received the lion's share of attention. Early home visitation programs show some variation, yet all provide in-home support to families with very young children, seeking to promote child and family functioning during a vulnerable and opportune period, with the aim of improving their longer-term developmental trajectory. Early home visitation services most frequently begin providing services perinatally—that is, shortly before, during, or after the birth of a child—and have traditionally targeted a broad array of concerns young children and families face during early childhood. Some programs specifically seek to reduce low birth weight and its consequences or to promote cognitive gains for later childhood. Others aim to promote a broader spectrum of infant and maternal health and psychosocial outcomes. Although all early home visitation services form "sister" programs, of special concern in this text are programs that explicitly aim to prevent physical child abuse and neglect by supporting the development of positive parent-child interaction patterns that may last into the future.

Emerging scientific knowledge has underscored the promise of early home visitation services. Based on selected early findings from reported studies, the U.S. Advisory Board on Child Abuse and Neglect in 1991 adopted as its single most important recommendation the phase-in of a nationwide system of neonatal home visitation services to address the problem of child maltreatment. In 1992, Prevent Child Abuse America launched the Healthy Families America initiative to foster the development of early home visitation programs in communities throughout the United States. More recently, key organizations such as the American Academy of Pediatrics, the National Research Council, and Zero to Three have issued reports highlighting the importance of perinatal home visitation in support of vulnerable families. Recent special issues of key journals such as *The Future of Children, Journal of Community Psychology, Zero to Three,* and *Family Futures* have focused on home visitation services, contributing to a remarkable acceleration of interest and activity promoting early home visitation services across the United States.

Parallel to these developments, an increasing array of outcome studies evaluating the effectiveness of home visitation services has revealed that, although promising, such programs are, nonetheless, no panacea. These studies have revealed, in fact, that home visitation in and of itself is unlikely to be effective if program services are not appropriately configured and delivered (Gomby, Culross, & Behrman, 1999; Guterman, 1997a, 1999; Olds & Kitzman, 1993). Indeed, the available studies in early home visitation services have long reported a complex variety of outcomes—some positive and some mixed—resulting from program services. A recent special issue of *The Future of Children* has highlighted limitations in the design and implementation of home visitation services (Gomby et al., 1999), sounding a precautionary note to this rapidly expanding movement. The field, thus, faces both a promising and uncertain future in the search to proactively avert child maltreatment on a broad and realistically attainable scale.

It is at this juncture that the present text aims to "revisit" home visitation services with a fresh and careful eye. As a number of highly controlled studies have demonstrated that such services can, indeed, reduce maltreatment risk, this text is less concerned with the largely resolved question of whether home visitation programs can be effective. Rather, at issue is what kinds of home visitation practices and strategies, under what conditions, and with what populations provide the greatest chances of leveraging positive preventive outcomes.

Some program models have already attempted to identify "best practice" strategies believed to maximize the likelihood of delivering beneficial services to families. For example, derived from the Hawaii Healthy Start program, the nationwide Healthy Families America initiative, with which over 330 early home visitation programs in the United States are currently affiliated, has developed a list of critical elements believed essential to implement a sound program with a meaningful impact across sites. However, large-scale programs such as Healthy Start, from which such best practices are derived, have rarely had the luxury to step back and scientifically test which program elements are empirically linked with positive outcomes. Thus, program components identified as best practices or critical elements often lack the benefit of careful scientific scrutiny, and run the risk of application in the field as "model" strategies, promoting a large-scale codification of untested and possibly suboptimal practices. Implementing untested best practices, although it may be expedient and may even reduce uncertainty for program developers, nonetheless jeopardizes the impact of a program in the long run and even the viability of home visitation services as a field if such practices later turn out to be ineffective. A secondary risk of following established yet untested best practices is that they often have a tendency to drift over time as new views supplant older ones regarding what may be ideal practice strategies. Such shifts may be an appropriate and natural means of program evolution in accordance with changing circumstances. Yet, best practices are not programs but rather *ideal practice principles* serving as guides for programmatic decision making and entire fields of practice, independent of context-specific conditions or changes. As such, shifting best practices, like shifting sands, become slippery ground on which to establish and expand solid and efficacious efforts on a fieldwide scale.

What is necessary, then, is scientifically tested information shedding light on fieldwide practice principles, population needs, and conditions, as well as the intertwining role they play in child maltreatment risk reduction. Fortunately, although individual studies afford little opportunity to test a broad menu of best practices for the field, early home visitation programs have now collectively undergone enough varied study so that practice principles can be discerned by comparing variations across studies along with their associated outcomes.[2] This synthesis of programmatic patterns linked with outcomes across a wide body of studies provides one essential source of scientific information from which evidence-based best practices can be derived (e.g., Evidence-Based Medicine Working Group, 1992; Sackett & Rosenberg, 1995; Simpson & Knox, 1999). A second essential source of scientific information from which to build a best practices scientific knowledge base can be found in etiological studies illuminating the processes that lead to future physical child abuse and neglect. This widening knowledge base provides an essential theory template against which practice principles can be evaluated as to the degree to which they hold the capacity to interrupt causal pathways leading to maltreatment. Given a complex and widening knowledge base in both these domains, this book takes a bird's-eye view of the present state of the science and knowledge of early home visitation services, highlighting practice strategies that are scientifically undergirded, offering the best chances of reducing child maltreatment risk.

This book, thus, moves beyond a "one size fits all" approach to early home visitation services and, rather, provides a multidimensional view, highlighting best practice principles that transcend any single home visitation program model. For application purposes, emphasizing best practice *principles* rather than whole program models enhances flexibility for programmatic adoption while minimizing overly prescriptive information that might constrain adaptation to specific needs and contexts. Furthermore, an emphasis on practice principles over models avoids an unnecessary polarization that often accompanies comparisons of competing program models available in the field. To facilitate application, this text then profiles specific program exemplars to illustrate the ways they embody best practice principles, noting the empirical support each has garnered. The home visitation field is currently experiencing a number of controversies over what constitutes the "best" approach. This text addresses such controversies by referring to the available empirical findings as landmarks from which to navigate this increasingly complex and rapidly diversifying field.

Early home visitation services have come to vogue, they have tended to drown out other reported non-home visiting approaches to early prevention that may hold key lessons for stopping child maltreatment before the fact. Therefore, this text steps outside the box of the home visitation model, aiming to encourage reconsideration of early prevention pathways, particularly in light of the known etiological processes in the unfolding of child abuse and neglect. Although a natural tendency exists to jump on the bandwagon of early home visitation services, advancing the cause of child maltreatment prevention will be best served by carefully and even self-consciously examining intervention strategies in relation to the known etiology of physical child abuse neglect. In what ways do home visitations services interrupt etiological processes heightening child maltreatment risk? How might such services more efficaciously accomplish this purpose? Are there etiological pathways that home visitation services have yet to adequately address? How might home visitation services be reconfigured to optimally fit the needs of families facing child maltreatment risk? Underlying these questions is the view that home visitation services represent a substantial advance toward addressing the problem of child maltreatment, and yet they themselves must yet be advanced in several critical domains to more effectively interrupt several of the most potent etiological influences known to breed physical child abuse and neglect. Without such steps forward, the field of early home visitation faces the prospect of continuing to evidence mixed outcomes in reducing child maltreatment, jeopardizing its potential to expand and significantly contribute to child maltreatment reduction on a large scale. This book, thus, aims both to orient readers to the field and to reorient the field in ways that promote the overall goal of realizing meaningful child maltreatment prevention before the fact.

It is important to note here that the focus of this book is on the prevention of physical child abuse and neglect, parenting practices that place a child at substantial risk or directly cause harm to a child and that are outside the norms of parenting (adapted from National Research Council, 1993). Although child sexual abuse, as well as emotional and educational maltreatment, remain difficult and important forms of child maltreatment, this book's primary focus is on the prevention of physical abuse and neglect for several reasons. First, the field of early prevention largely embodied by early home visitation approaches has, as yet, not addressed the problem of child sexual abuse through the content of its interventions or in the outcomes assessed. This is not surprising, given that the majority of child sexual abuse occurs later in childhood, whereas early home visitation, by design, intervenes in the earliest years of childhood. Second, child sexual abuse, although showing some overlapping etiological elements, also presents a distinct set of etiological dynamics that the field of early home visitation is as yet largely unequipped to handle, both theoretically and practically. Thus, this text will remain focused on prevention of physical child abuse and neglect, involved in over 80% of the cases of child maltreatment reported to child protective services systems in the United States (U.S. Department of Health and Human Services, 1999a).

This book aims to critically examine the early prevention of child maltreatment in a series of steps. The first segment of this book (the first three chapters) will examine the contexts of early prevention services historically, theoretically, and empirically. First, the nature and etiology of physical child abuse and neglect in early childhood will be examined, pointing out a window of risk and opportunity for intervention in the early childhood years (Chapter 2). In this light, then, child protective services and early home visitation services will be examined to assess the mechanisms they have traditionally adopted to address the problem of child maltreatment (Chapter 3). The mismatch between the design of child protective services and the etiology of physical child abuse and neglect will be highlighted as one important reason why the nation's child protection system has been characterized as in "a state of collapse" (U.S. Advisory Board on Child Abuse and Neglect, 1990). The recent rapid advancement of early home visitation services will be detailed in response, highlighting in particular the two most visible programmatic approaches at present in the United States, the Perinatal/Early Infancy Program reported by David Olds and colleagues (Olds, Henderson, Chamberlin, & Tatelbaum, 1986; Olds et al., 1999) and the Hawaii Healthy Start model adapted and promoted via the Healthy Families America initiative of Prevent Child Abuse America (Breakey & Pratt, 1991; Daro & Harding, 1999). With this background in place, the present state of early home visitation services will be examined, providing a detailed inside tour of best practice principles that have been empirically linked with positive outcomes in families (Chapters 4 and 5). Several key intervention issues in the field will be examined, surfacing intervention strategies that have received empirical support across a wide variety of early home visitation program models.

The book's focus then steps back from the rapid advances of early home visitation services to revisit its underpinnings and dominant strategies and, most especially, to examine three critical domains that require substantial further development in light of what is known about the origins of child maltreatment. In particular, Chapter 6 examines ways early home visitation services may more adequately address the problem of family substance abuse in reducing child maltreatment risk. Chapter 7 examines ways home visitation services may more effectively attend to social network and community influences—a key struggle in substantially reducing families' child maltreatment risk. Finally, Chapter 8 addresses the broad role of parental powerlessness in child maltreatment risk and suggests pathways that early home visitation services may take to empower parents to reduce their child maltreatment risk. Whereas the early portions of this text highlight the promise of early home visitation services and their rapid ascent, the latter portion seek to reorient the field in ways that can stimulate still further forward movement toward realizing the promise of meaningful child maltreatment reduction in the United States. It is hoped that highlighting emerging horizons in early prevention will serve to map future pathways by which early prevention services can continue to better assist families to raise children in abuse- and neglect-free environments. Although early home visitation services at present are no panacea to the problem of physical child abuse and neglect, they nonetheless represent a first real step toward realizing the dream of stopping child maltreatment before it ever starts.

NOTES

1. Despite recent polemics, which have attempted to portray the importance of early childhood for later development as a myth (e.g., Bruer, 1999), overwhelming evidence in neurobiology, developmental psychology, and ethology has demonstrated that key developmental processes become set in motion in the early years, predictive of later psychosocial development (see Chapter 2).

It is also important to point out at this juncture that prevention science often distinguishes between primary, secondary, and tertiary prevention, or the more recently applied terms, *universal, selected,* and *indicated* preventive intervention strategies (e.g., Mrazek & Haggerty, 1994). Such terms concern the timing of an intervention in relation to the development of a problem (e.g., before a problem occurs, during the first foreshadowing or initial indications of the development of a problem, or after a problem is identified), as well as the target, goals, and design of the intervention. Applied to the field of child maltreatment, this book clearly concerns before-the-fact prevention, most often labeled primary or secondary prevention, or otherwise universal and selected intervention. However, such labels, drawn from medical and public health models, become somewhat artificial and imprecise in their application to the problem of child maltreatment. As Chapter 2 will highlight, child maltreatment is better viewed as a manifestation of an unfolding parent-child process over time, rather than as a discretely discernable disease state. As in much of the work in this field, then, this text applies the term *early prevention* to connote intervention before the parent-child interaction is identifiable as abusive or neglectful and to emphasize that the onset of intervention occurs very early in the parent-child interaction. Chapter 5 will revisit the targeting process in the design of early prevention services, often viewed as a critical issue in determining optimal levels and types of preventive strategies.

2. By outcomes, this text concerns itself with child maltreatment-related outcomes as well as intermediate outcomes related to families' response to program services. Given that physical child abuse and neglect are extremely difficult to directly assess, well-controlled studies in early home visitation have typically measured child maltreatment-related outcomes via official reports to child protective services systems or via proxy measures of child maltreatment, such as parenting attitudes or behaviors that may be indicative of abusive and/or neglectful parenting. Intermediate outcomes that may assess families' responsiveness to services are infrequently reported in the literature. Among the most consistently reported and readily available data in this regard are programs' engagement and retention rates, which may serve as indicators of the degree of families' involvement in services (see Chapter 5). Thus, this text focuses on findings in both these outcome domains and other closely related domains reported in the literature to discern best practice strategies garnering empirical support.

Chapter 2

CHILD MALTREATMENT
AND EARLY CHILDHOOD

A 21-year-old Brooklyn woman was charged yesterday with killing one of her three small children, a bruised and battered 2-year-old girl who apparently had borne the brunt of her mother's secret abuse for a long time until Sunday night, when she fell unconscious after another beating and died, city officials said. . . . Neighbors and a sister of [the mother] Ms. Clarke in a rundown, four-story walk-up . . . were stunned over the child's death and the mother's arrest. They said Ms. Clarke seemed a devoted if frustrated mother, pregnant with a fourth child and apparently overwhelmed by the problems of single parenthood and poverty. . . . "We had no indication that this woman ever abused her children," Ms. Falk [a spokeswoman for the city's protective services agency] said, "only that she had perhaps neglected them by leaving them with someone incapable for caring for them."

"She had three kids and she was pregnant with another," Ms. Johnson [a neighbor] said. "I think she was overwhelmed taking care of her kids, and with another on the way it may have been too much to handle. She didn't have a husband or a mother who could help her. It could send someone over the line." (McFadden, 1999, p. B3).

Early childhood represents an especially critical phase of life for families, holding both the potential for great growth and heightened risk for child abuse and neglect. The transition to parenthood and the initial months of parenting involve many unique adjustments and challenges. If not well prepared in the early months, parents may become quickly overwhelmed. At the same time, the hopeful possibilities and in-the-moment pleasures of parenting an infant present glimpses into the future, opportunities for living life afresh with a new family member.

Those who have experienced the early days of parenthood may understand why this phase of life has been termed a "sensitive period." In addition to the profound growth and change occurring in the child's life, a parent's struggles to adjust to a new role and identity raise deep but sometimes inchoate questions. Who will this little person be? Who am I as a parent? What am I supposed to do? Can I handle this? What relationship will I have with my new son or daughter? Accompanying such fundamental questions is a mounting set of often unfamiliar challenges and pressures such as

- The need to develop an ongoing repertoire of skills and knowledge in parenting a new child
- The task of responding to the infant's immediate and quickly evolving needs
- Possibly chronic sleep deprivation
- Biological changes accompanying the pregnancy, birth, and healing, as well as possible lactation
- Reduction in autonomy
- Increased financial and material stresses
- Decreased time and energy for other relationships
- New social influences and messages in parenting and alterations in significant relationships as a result of the new role

The perinatal phase from pregnancy through early childhood is also marked by a great deal of plasticity, whereby an infant's development and the parent-infant relationship are characterized by a malleability that can stabilize over time and hold predictive influence over future development. Given this, the sensitive perinatal period and the time shortly afterward have been viewed as holding heightened responsiveness to external influences and thus receptivity to intervention that may promote lasting effects. This chapter examines the early years of childhood as a window of both opportunity and risk, a key transition period presenting special considerations for preventive intervention, particularly in light of the known etiology of physical child abuse and neglect.

A WINDOW OF OPPORTUNITY

The period *in utero* and the first 3 years of a child's life are uniquely characterized by remarkably rapid development in neural and physiological systems as well as in emotional, cognitive, and social competencies (Dawson, Hessl, & Frey, 1994; Zeanah, Boris, & Larrieu, 1997). Neurons, for example, generate at a rate of 250,000 per minute during the second trimester of pregnancy and through the first several months after birth (Casaer, 1993; Johnson, 1997). These building blocks for the nervous system quickly differentiate, develop fatty sheaths of myelin around neural pathways, and—most notably from birth through the second year of life—form synaptic connections through which they communicate to one another. These synapses are genetically programmed, "primed" to receive and become shaped by environmental input. Stimuli from the environment selectively activate neural pathways, which then become stabilized over time, leaving unused pathways to become "pruned" away. Over time, as neurons become myelinated, they lose some of their plasticity, paralleling a loss of plasticity in other elements of the nervous system, such as in the cortical vascular system (Anastasiow, 1990; Greenough et al., 1993).[1] Overall, neural proliferation and synaptic overproduction begin to level off through the second and third years of life (Aylward, 1997). From birth to 4 years of age, the brain approximately quadruples in weight, reaching about 80% of its eventual adult size (Spreen, Risser, & Edgell, 1995).

The early sensitive years of neural development are paralleled in the infant's psychosocial development, highly reliant on mutual transactions with the environment (Sameroff, 1993). Evidence suggests that development proceeds through predictable sensitive stages whereby the infant is temporally primed, both biologically and psychologically, to master specific developmental tasks, after which behavior patterns stabilize and change may become more difficult to achieve. The first 3 years of life remain remarkable for the dense set of biobehavioral stages forming the building blocks for later life tasks. Mastery of life competencies typically occurs in such foundational areas as learning to habituate to environmental stimuli, to communicate in linguistic and nonverbal ways, to self-regulate emotions, to form attachments and relate to other human beings, and to locomote (cf. Zeanah et al., 1997). During such phases, the environment may serve to support mastery of these tasks or, in the face of impoverishing or traumatizing contexts, to alter not only behavioral trajectories but even brain structure and chemistry itself (Fox, Calkins, & Bell, 1994).

The perinatal and early childhood phases for parents (especially first-time parents) have also been characterized by rapid change and transition, marked by alterations in roles, stresses, life concerns, and relationships (Michaels & Goldberg, 1988). Parents' primary responsibility in developing a relationship with a new infant is nested within a variety of new challenges. For primiparous (first-time) mothers, the physiological changes associated with pregnancy, birth, and postpartum recovery also are accompanied by a transition to the uncharted territory of parenthood, a role for which few have been actively prepared.

The transition to this new role often involves increases in daily household responsibilities, decreases in time available for leisure activities, restrictions of freedom, alterations in relationships (particularly spousal or immediate familial relationships due to new demands), and disrupted patterns of partner or marital intimacy, often leading to increased conflict and declining partner satisfaction (Belsky, Sanier, & Rovine, 1983; Cowan & Cowan, 1988; Crohan, 1996; Nitz, Ketterlinus, & Brandt, 1995; Steffensmeier, 1982). Increasing economic demands brought by increased family size can provoke changing work patterns, greater economic dependencies, and, for parents with marital or long-term partners, a more pronounced division of labor and increased tension in the relationship (Belsky, Lang, & Rovine, 1985; Crohan, 1996; Sanchez & Thomson, 1997). Becoming a parent for the first time also often provokes increased questions about one's identity and competency in the new role (Belsky, 1994; Diamond, Heinicke, & Mintz, 1996). For parents, then, it is clear that the perinatal and early infancy period is marked by dynamic change and reorganization, providing opportunities for supportive intervention to make a notable difference.

In the midst of such dynamism, a parent-infant attachment forms and ultimately serves as a major foundation stone for the development of social competencies and relationships later in life. Early classic research by John Bowlby (1969) and Mary Ainsworth (1967; Ainsworth, Blehar, Waters, & Wall, 1978) served to reorient thinking about human development, revealing the central importance for later-life adjustment of primary attachments, those lasting affectional ties that transcend distance between infants and their primary caregivers. Attachment theorists

Bowlby and Ainsworth drew from the work of Konrad Lorenz (1965) and Harry Harlow (1958), who identified bonding processes in animals. Lorenz's classic studies, for example, documented the biological "hardwiring" of ducklings at birth, which operates to imprint on the first moving object they witness after leaving the eggshell, propelling ducklings to seek proximity to it as their primary caregiver. Harlow's classic studies revealed a biologically hardwired drive for comfort, reporting that infant rhesus monkeys sought out a cloth-covered surrogate mother over one that was not comfortable but that nonetheless delivered food. Such early work served to reveal the biological importance for the infant in forming a protective and nurturing bond with a caregiver. The work of Ainsworth, Bowlby, and later attachment theorists demonstrated that the developing affectional tie between an infant and caregiver is a reciprocally evolving one.

Studies have discerned that in humans, the development of the parent-infant attachment is one primed by biological mechanisms in both the infant and mother at birth. For example, neonates show rooting and sucking reflexes that are unlearned and in place at birth, whereby the newborn will turn and "root" for a nipple and then, once latched on, will initiate sucking. During this same initial period after birth, mothers' breasts become engorged, and studies have found that nursing a newborn stimulates the release of oxytocin, the same neurotransmitter that causes nipples to become erect during lovemaking and that plays a role in pair bonding and other affiliative behaviors in mammals (e.g., Keverne, Nevison, & Martel, 1997; Nelson & Panksepp, 1998). Furthermore, infants' crying, also biologically hardwired, serves to elicit a physiological and behavioral response on the caregiver's part, forming a basis for a reciprocally evolving interactional pattern of attachment (Acebo & Thoman, 1995; Bell & Anisworth, 1972; Crockenberg & Smith, 1983; Donovan, Leavitt, & Walsh, 1998).

Primed by biological processes, the development of reciprocal interactions between caregivers and their infants may evolve into an enduring affectional attachment across distances. Ainsworth's work, in particular, has highlighted that key in predicting an infant's attachment security to a primary caregiver is the sensitivity and responsiveness of the primary caregiver to cues, such as crying and eye contact elicited by the infant (Ainsworth, 1967). The infant's security of attachment can be assessed via the infant's degree of confidence in exploring the surrounding environment, as well as the infant's response when confronted with a separation from the primary caregiver, for example, through clingyness and/or inconsolability.

Bowlby noted that from such early experiences in the infant-primary caregiver interaction, humans develop internal working models or internal *schemata* composed of cognitive representations of self and others (Bowlby, 1969). These internal working models are organized representations of earlier experiences. They function by filtering present experiences in ways that accord them understanding and that guide an array of behavioral responses to environmental events, particularly those that are deemed stressful or threatening (Shaver, Collins, & Clark, 1996). For example, when an infant's cues provoke inconsistent caregiver responses, or when the environment provides chaotic or unpredictable communications about meeting an infant's basic needs, the infant is likely to develop an anxious-ambivalent internal working model of attachment. This kind of internal representation serves to organize memories of primary caregiver interactions in ways that orient infants toward demonstrating vigilant and preoccupied behaviors with their primary caregivers, becoming quick to cry and anger and more difficult to soothe (e.g., Sroufe, Carlson, & Shulman, 1993). Once established, such internal representational structures (related to what social psychologists term *cognitive schemas*) appear to stabilize and become resistant to change.

Recent findings have extended attachment theory, highlighting the importance of the infant's own temperament (e.g., Kochanska, 1998), the possibility of developing multiple secure attachments within a cultural context of multiple primary caregivers (cf. Tronick, Winn, & Morelli, 1985), and the relevance of attachment theory to understanding later developmental phases and other relationships, such as those between peers or romantic partners (e.g., Field, 1984; Kobak & Sceery, 1988). However, the fundamental construct of attachment theory in understanding the developing person and the trajectory for later life competencies has nonetheless remained remarkably resilient.

For example, attachment patterns, especially the security of attachment found in infancy, have repeatedly been demonstrated as important predictors of later psychosocial competencies and adjustment. Studies have shown that early attachment security predicts a wide variety of youngsters' social interactions and competencies in preschool. These include children's ability to accurately read social cues, their degree of self-confidence and industry, their levels of empathy, their degree of aggression toward others, and even their own victimization by others

(Kestenbaum, Farber, & Sroufe, 1989; Renken, Egeland, Marvinney, & Mangelsdorf, 1989; Shulman, Elicker, & Sroufe, 1994; Sroufe et al., 1993; Suess, Grossmann, & Sroufe, 1992; Troy & Sroufe, 1987). Attachment patterns in infancy have been found to predict later peer competencies, aggression, distractibility, and capacities to cope with stress and middle childhood (Carlson, Jacobvitz, & Sroufe, 1995; Lyons-Ruth, Alpern, & Repacholi, 1993; Main & George, 1985; Shulman et al., 1994). Studies have even identified early attachment patterns as a predictor of psychopathology levels in young adulthood (Warren, Huston, Egeland, & Sroufe, 1997; Ogawa, Sroufe, Weinfield, Carlson, & Egeland, 1997) and (through retrospective studies) the security of the parental attachment mothers eventually develop with their own infants (Main & Goldwyn, 1984). Such findings may help to partially explain observed intergenerational patterns of child maltreatment (see also Egeland, Jacovitz, & Sroufe, 1988; Zuravin, McMillen, DePanfilis, & Risley-Curtiss, 1996).

Collectively, this widening set of findings about the tremendous density of milestone events occurring in the first three years of life has served to fuel rapidly expanding U.S. interest in enhancing supports during early childhood. Foundations, governments, policies, and programs have begun to increasingly focus on the importance of "developmentally sensitive" services during these early years, and not only with respect to early child-maltreatment prevention (Duerr Berrick, Needell, Barth, & Jonson-Reid, 1998). The federal government has substantially expanded its support for such early childhood supports as day care as well as Head Start in the earliest years, and an increasing number of private foundations have reoriented their interest and support provided during this window of opportunity in early childhood (Marchetti, 1998).

A WINDOW OF RISK

Although the earliest years hold the potential to shape positive developments for later life, they can equally pose special risks for troubling developments, particularly, for the parent-child relationship to become characterized by physical child abuse and/or neglect (e.g., Hegar, Zuravin, & Orme, 1994). Several sources of national data shed light on maltreatment risk in the early years. NCANDS data for 1997 show that the first 6 years of childhood account for nearly half of all substantiated child maltreatment victims; in contrast, the years 12 to 18 account for

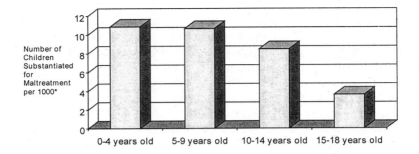

Figure 2.1. Rates of Children per 1,000 of Substantiated Child
Maltreatment in the United States by Age, 1997
Note: These numbers are derived from 40 of 50 states reporting data to the NCANDS system in 1997,
and thus, they underestimate the overall incidence rates nationally for that year.
SOURCE: U.S. Bureau of the Census, 1999; U.S. Department of Health and Human Services, 1999.

only about one quarter of child maltreatment victims. NCANDS data for
1997 on physical child abuse and neglect only (excluding medical
neglect, sexual abuse, and emotional abuse) indicate that 29.1% of victims substantiated for physical child abuse and neglect are age 3 and under and that 57.2% are age 7 and under (U.S. Department of Health and
Human Services, 1999). Figure 2.1 depicts the declining relative risk for
physical abuse and neglect across age, based on substantiations reported
in 1997 to the NCANDS system, compared against U.S. census data for
that same year (U.S. Bureau of the Census, 1999; U.S. Department of
Health and Human Services, 1999a). The data suggest that the highest
substantiation rate for child maltreatment occurs in the earliest years of
childhood, a rate that remains relatively stable even into early school
years.

The Third National Incidence Survey (NIS-3) reported similar findings, with an upward trend in the rates of both physical child abuse and
neglect from birth through the early school years (6 to 8 years old), followed by steadily decreasing incidence rates as children grow older.
Extrapolating from these findings, which represent data from official
reports and from mandated reporters of child maltreatment, it is likely
that the years prior to school entry are in reality characterized by higher
rates of maltreatment than the first years of schooling for several reasons. Community professionals mandated to report child maltreatment,

including school personnel such as teachers and nurses, face greater difficulties monitoring and therefore reporting younger children to protective services systems (English, 1999; Sedlak & Broadhurst, 1996). Once
children enter school, maltreatment that may have been hidden from the
scrutiny of such professionals becomes more easily known, providing a
probable explanation for the slightly higher increase in maltreatment
reports during the earliest years of schooling in the NIS-3 survey. Furthermore, very young children are less developmentally capable—
verbally and behaviorally—of revealing their maltreatment experiences
to outsiders likely to file an official maltreatment report.

Perhaps the most profound and less controvertible evidence that early
childhood presents the highest risk period for maltreatment are data
available on severe child maltreatment. About one in four children entering foster care placement due to child maltreatment are under 1 year of
age (Duerr-Berrick et al., 1998; Wulczyn, Harden, & Goerge, 1998), and
studies have consistently indicated that child fatality rates are disproportionately higher in the earliest years of childhood. Studies have shown
that the younger a child is, the higher the risk for severe or fatal child maltreatment (American Association for Protecting Children, 1987; Hegar
et al., 1994; U.S. Department of Health and Human Services, 1999;
Wang & Harding, 1999). For example, data reported to the NCANDS
data system in 1997 found that about 77% of child maltreatment fatalities
concerned children 3 years old and under. Furthermore, data from the
1998 Annual Fifty States Survey conducted by Prevent Child Abuse
America reported that 39% of all child maltreatment fatalities occur
among children under 1 year of age (Wang & Harding, 1999). Figure 2.2
shows the severe overrepresentation of officially reported child fatalities
due to maltreatment in the earliest years of life, as indicated by data
reported to the NCANDS data system in 1997 (U.S. Department of
Health and Human Services, 1999). Although these data are startling,
they, in fact, most likely *under*estimate the proportion of child maltreatment fatalities in the earliest years, given evidence indicating that early
childhood fatalities are frequently misclassified (Herman-Giddens et al.,
1999; McClain, Sacks, Foehlke, & Ewigman, 1993). For example, findings indicate that substantial proportions of early childhood fatalities classified as accidents or as "sudden infant death syndrome" are
most accurately attributable to incidents of child maltreatment (e.g.,
Ewigman, Kivlahan, & Land, 1993; Meadow, 1999). Although the number of fatalities due to maltreatment in infancy remains somewhat imprecise, it is clear that such fatalities are egregiously disproportionate when

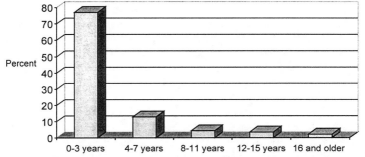

Figure 2.2. Proportion of Fatalities Due to Child Maltreatment in the United States by Age, 1997
Note: These data are derived from 41 states reporting data to the NCANDS data system in 1997.

compared to those occurring at other ages. It remains shocking that despite the underestimation of these fatalities, child maltreatment still represents the leading identified cause of injury-related death for children under 1 year of age (Waller, Baker, & Szocka, 1989).

DEVELOPMENTAL SEQUELAE FOR MALTREATED CHILDREN

For children surviving physical abuse and neglect, the effects of such experiences will likely vary according to the nature of the maltreatment experiences, the child's age, the available supports and resources, and other ongoing life stressors. Studies have, nonetheless, discerned an array of medical and psychosocial sequelae associated with experiences of abuse and neglect. Numerous studies have found child maltreatment linked to a broad array of immediate and longer term sequelae. These include

- Physical injuries such as subdural hemorrhages, retinal hemorrhages, burns, or bone fractures (Bonnier, Nassogne, & Evrard, 1995; Lancon, Haines, & Parent, 1998)
- Delayed physical growth (Drotar, 1992; Money, 1977)
- Neurological damage (Bonnier et al., 1995; Dykes, 1986; Lewis, 1992; Perry, Pollard, Blakeley, Baker, & Vigilante 1995; Perry & Pollard, 1997)

- Problems with social relationships, developing trust and attachments (Carlson, Cicchetti, Barnett, & Braunwald, 1989; Cohn, 1979; Dodge, Pettit, & Bates, 1994; Egeland & Sroufe, 1981; Kaufman & Cicchetti, 1989; Kinard, 1979; Main & Solomon, 1986; Okun & Parker, 1994; Schneider-Rosen, Braunwald, Carlson, & Cicchetti, 1985)
- Problems with self-regulation of emotions (Cicchetti, Toth, & Lynch, 1993; Shields, Cicchetti, & Ryan, 1994)
- Aggression, externalizing behavior problems, and later criminal activities (Aber, Allen, Carlson, & Cicchetti, 1990; Cummings, Hennessy, Rabideau, & Cicchetti, 1994; Dykman et al., 1997; Herrenkohl & Herrenkohl, 1981; Hoffman-Plotkin & Twentyman, 1984; Main & George, 1985; Maxfield & Widom, 1996; Polansky, Chalmers, Buttenwieser, & Williams, 1981; Salzinger, Kaplan, Pelcovitz, Samit, & Krieger, 1983)
- Depression, low self-esteem, and increased risk for suicidal ideation and behavior (Allen & Tarnowski, 1989; Gaensbauer & Mrazek, 1981; Kazdin, Moser, Colbus, & Bell, 1985; Oates, Forrest, & Peacock, 1985; Okun & Parker, 1994; Silverman, Reinherz, & Giaconia, 1996)
- Symptoms of posttraumatic stress disorder (Dykman et al., 1997)
- Increased risk of substance and/or alcohol abuse in later life (Malinosky-Rummell & Hansen, 1993; Widom & White, 1997)
- Cognitive and language deficits (Allen & Oliver, 1982; Allen & Wasserman, 1985; Azar, Barnes, & Twentyman, 1988; Cicchetti & Beeghly, 1987; Fantuzzo, 1990; Hoffman-Plotkin & Twentyman, 1984; Kolko, 1992; Perry, Doran, & Wells, 1983)

It is an unfortunate fact that the younger the victim, the more devastating the consequences are likely to be. In addition to facing heightened risk of fatality, very young children are at inordinate risk for such profound problems resulting from maltreatment as nonorganic failure to thrive, shaken baby syndrome, mental retardation, impaired growth and dwarfism, brain injuries, blindness, or injuries to other parts of the body (Frank, Zimmerman, & Leeds, 1985; Mrazek, 1993; National Research Council, 1993). Advances in neurological assessment technology have documented a sobering variety of neurological sequelae that may particularly result from child maltreatment in early childhood, including brain contusions, intracranial hemorrhages, brain atrophy, and alterations in the development of the limbic system of the brain linked with memory, emotions, and basic drives (Cheah, Kasim, Shafie, & Khoo, 1994; Frank et al., 1985; Ito, Teicher, Glod, & Harper, 1993; Teicher, Ito, Glod, Schiffer, & Gelbard, 1996). Consistent with a "use dependent" theory of brain development, recent work has suggested the possibility that brain

Schiffer, & Gelbard, 1996). Consistent with a "use dependent" theory of brain development, recent work has suggested the possibility that brain chemistry and organization may be altered permanently by exposure to physical abuse and neglect in the first 3 years of life (Ito et al., 1993; Perry et al., 1995; Perry & Pollard, 1997). For example, a number of studies have documented cortical atrophy and decreased brain volume in severely abused and neglected children (Bonnier et al., 1995; De Bellis et al., 1999; Frank et al., 1985; Perry & Pollard, 1997).

Studies of children maltreated in early childhood have also consistently documented disturbances in children's ability to form attachments and develop relationships with others in a more generalized sense (e.g., Egeland & Sroufe, 1981; Schneider-Rosen et al., 1985), heightening risk for multiple later life problems. Although the evidence is not yet conclusive given the difficulty in executing longitudinal studies of maltreated children, early maltreatment appears to especially heighten risk for such later problems as juvenile delinquency and crime, depression, school failure, and substance or alcohol abuse (National Research Council, 1993).

ETIOLOGY OF
EARLY CHILDHOOD MALTREATMENT

Why is it that children face their greatest risks for maltreatment, particularly in its most lethal and damaging forms, during their most vulnerable years? To fathom this, it is important to examine what is known about both the etiology of physical child abuse and neglect, as well as the developmental unfolding of the parent-child relationship. One of the most carefully studied areas concerning child abuse and neglect is its etiology. Studies beginning in the 1960s, during the rapid development of protective services systems, and continuing up to the present have carefully examined profiles of maltreating parents to discern the origins of child maltreatment. Such studies have uncovered a great deal of information about the factors predicting the likelihood of child maltreatment. At the same time, child maltreatment studies are necessarily naturalistic, most often involving parents already identified as maltreating, and given this, researchers have faced great challenges in designing studies that isolate and observe an unfolding set of factors that directly lead to abusive or neglectful parenting. At present, although a good deal is known about correlated risk and protective factors, the current empirical base does not yet adequately depict the dynamic developmental chain of events that result in child maltreatment.

In spite of this, mounting evidence across several decades of research has continued to paint a multileveled, transactional, and developmental picture of the problem of child maltreatment, one that has often been organized within an ecological framework. First applied to the problem of child maltreatment by James Garbarino (1977) and Jay Belsky (1980), an ecological view highlights that physically abusive and/or neglectful behavior derives from the complex set of transactions within and between

- The *microsystem* representing the parent and child and their interactions
- The *meso-* and *exosystems* in which the parent-child dyad are embedded, including the settings, networks of relationships, and institutions in which the parent and child socialize and are sustained
- The *macrosystem* composed of overarching social structural elements within which the meso- and exosystems are themselves lodged (Belsky, 1980; Bronfenbrenner, 1977, 1979; Garbarino, 1977)

In the microsystem, a number of parental characteristics have been associated with heightened risk for physical abuse and neglect, including parental depression, external locus of control, poor coping skills, negative attitudes toward pregnancy, history of past victimization, and abuse of alcohol or drugs (cf. National Research Council, 1993, for a review). Studies also have noted that in abusive and neglectful families, parental discipline is often harsh, inattentive, and inconsistent (e.g., Crittenden, 1981; Stringer & LaGreca, 1985). Within the microsystem of the parent-infant dyad, several studies have pointed out that characteristics of the infant, such as prematurity or difficult temperament, although not viewed as causal, may heighten parental stress and create greater demands on parents challenged to cope in the parenting role (e.g., Meisels & Plunkett, 1988; Parke & Collmer, 1975).

Particularly during the perinatal phase, families may face unique burdens complicating the stresses experienced by parents. Among the most immediate challenges are mothers' own hormonal and biological changes, which accompany pregnancy, birth, and postpartum adjustment. Mothers may not only need to contend with a variety of biomedical concerns associated with pregnancy and birth including potential postpartum depression, birth after-pains, bleeding, or recovery from medical procedures such as a cesarean section or episiotomy. They may simultaneously face learning how to live with and care for a newborn, including coping with chronic sleep deprivation and night waking, the physically draining aspects of breast-feeding, and responding to the crying of an infant who is still incapable of verbalizing needs or discomforts (e.g., Eisenberg, Murkoff, & Hathaway, 1991; Zelkowitz & Milet, 1995). In instances where an infant is born prematurely, with medical complications, with a positive toxicology indicating psychoactive substance exposure *in utero,* or even simply exhibiting a "colicky" or "difficult" temperament, parents also face especially heightened challenges in attempting to settle the child and to wrest the few positive experiences of a happy and cuddly baby (e.g., Minde, 1993; Zuckerman & Brown, 1993).

Within the mesosystem, research has discerned a key role for life stressors in neglectful and abusive parenting (e.g., Browne, 1988; Hillson & Kupier, 1994; Kolko, Kazdin, Thomas, & Days, 1993; Kotch, Browne, Dufort, & Winsor, 1999; Rodriguez & Green, 1997). Studies across age groups have documented that stressors such as material deprivation, unemployment, family strife, multiple life events, or geographic moves are associated with heightened risk for child maltreatment. It is important to note that despite their importance in the maltreatment equation, most studies and theoretical formulations underscore that stressors are best viewed as contributors to but not direct causes of maltreatment (e.g., Chan, 1994; Crittenden, 1998; Egeland, Breitenbucher, & Rosenberg, 1980; Justice, Calvert, & Justice, 1985; Straus & Kantor, 1987). Many families facing a high degree of stress do not maltreat their children.

One of the central stressors identified in maltreatment risk is that of family poverty. Studies have found that families reported to child protective services systems are more likely to be single mothers, have unemployed fathers, receive public assistance, and/or live in poor neighborhoods (e.g., Ards, 1989; Coulton, Korbin, Su, & Chow, 1995; Drake & Pandey, 1996; Hampton & Newberger, 1985; Zuravin, 1989a). Several sets of studies, as pointed out by a report of the National Research Council (1993), have further found that child maltreatment, especially child neglect, is concentrated in the "poorest of the poor" (p. 133). Clearly, the pervasive stresses of life in poverty, the relative lack of options and material supports, coupled with a likely greater scrutiny by public authorities, can pose inordinate challenges for families struggling to rear children.

At the same time, the fact that large proportions of impoverished families are never identified as maltreating suggests that the stresses of poverty, like other stresses, cannot be viewed as a direct cause of maltreatment. This requires us to look at other factors and processes to better understand the causal links to maltreatment.

Social networks are one mesosystemic factor carefully considered for their potential to alter the relationship between stressors experienced and parenting behaviors. Research spanning three decades has consistently discerned important links between problematic aspects of families' social networks and heightened child maltreatment risk (e.g., Adamakos et al., 1986; Altemeier, O'Connor, Vietze, Sandler, & Sherrod, 1984; Altemeier et al., 1979; Chan, 1994; Coohey, 1996; Elmer, 1967; Garbarino & Sherman, 1980; Gaudin, Polansky, Kilpatrick, & Shilton, 1993; Gaudin & Pollane, 1983; Kirkham, Schinke, Schilling, & Meltzer, 1986; Lauer, Ten Broeck, & Grosman, 1974; Newberger, Reed, Hyde, & Kotelchuck, 1977; Salzinger, Kaplan, Pelcovitz, 1983; Smith, Hanson, & Noble, 1974; Straus & Kantor, 1987; Straus & Smith, 1990; Young, 1964). For example, although there is some variation in the findings owing to the complexity of measuring social networks, studies have tended to report that, when compared with nonmaltreating families, maltreating families have smaller, less dense social networks with whom they enjoy less contact and reciprocal exchanges (e.g., Corse, Schmid, & Trickett, 1990; Crittenden, 1985; Elmer, 1967; Kotelchuck, 1982; Lovell & Hawkins, 1988; Salzinger, Kaplan, Pelcovitz, et al., 1983; Young, 1964). Social networks may play both a direct and an indirect role in how parents manage the stressors they face. Social networks can directly aid parents by shaping their self-esteem and efficacy, altering their internal capacities to manage stressors that may come their way. Indirectly, social networks can serve in ways that respond immediately to specific stressors themselves, for example, through the provision of child care and material or informational aid (see Chapter 7; Cohen & Wills, 1985; House, Umberson, & Landis, 1988; Thompson, 1995).

The consistent correlational evidence linking child maltreatment risk with broader contextual factors such as impoverishment and social networks also highlights the importance of incorporating other meso-, exo-, and macrosystemic factors in understanding the etiology of physical child abuse and neglect. Recent work has documented that community-level disorganization and lack of cohesion, as well as degree of instability and community violence, are significantly linked with heightened child maltreatment (Coulton et al., 1995; Korbin, 1994; Osofsky,

Wewers, Hamn, & Fick, 1993; Richters & Martinez, 1993). In addition to economic impoverishment, "social impoverishment" has long been viewed as an important contributor to maltreatment risk. Under such conditions, neighborhood life is characterized by fewer community resources and associations for parents and children, and neighbors feel less connectedness and identification with one another around common concerns (e.g., Coulton et al., 1995; Garbarino & Sherman, 1980; see also Furstenberg, 1993; Sampson, Raudenbush, & Earls, 1997). A number of scholars have also emphasized that in the macrosystem, social structural forces and cultural ideologies about children and child rearing, as well as dominant historical influences that lead to the devaluation of children, may condone parenting behaviors that heighten the likelihood of maltreatment (Gelles & Cornell, 1983; Gil, 1984; Zigler, 1979).

Although a highly complex issue, cultural influences have been underscored for some time as a key consideration in the child maltreatment equation. The role of culture has most frequently been considered in the means by which cultural messages convey norms of parenting behavior, along with sanctions and allowances for a variety of parenting practices (Finkelhor & Korbin, 1988; Korbin, 1987, 1994). Wide variation has been noted across cultural contexts regarding culturally accepted and normative supervisory arrangements, the number and nature of caregivers, and medical practices employed with children (e.g., Fischler, 1985; Korbin, 1994; Ritchie & Ritchie, 1981). Likewise, corporal punishment, which may appear to be physical abuse within some cultural contexts, may be wholly acceptable and defined as normative within other contexts (Solheim, 1982). Given this, what may be accepted as normative child-rearing patterns within a specific cultural context may be misconstrued across cultural boundaries as child maltreatment, especially in situations where professionals must enact child protection laws and policies derived from a majority cultural value system (e.g., Gray & Cosgrove, 1985).

It has been argued that these reasons partially explain the over-representation of non-majority group families in studies using official child protective services data (e.g., Jason, Amereuh, Marks, & Tyler, 1982; Lauderdale, Valiunas, & Anderson, 1980; Spearly & Lauderdale, 1983). Data from child protective services reports and from official mandated reporters, however, are limited in their capacity to tease out cultural influences on actual child maltreatment, given biases likely present in professional reporters' own child-rearing values and reporting patterns (e.g., Ards, Chung, & Myers, 1998; Carr & Gelles, 1978; National

Center on Child Abuse and Neglect, 1981). Also troublesome, some studies drawing from protective services data have failed to parcel out the effects of low socioeconomic status, which inordinately affects non-majority culture families. For these reasons, the few available studies that use nationally representative samples and are not reliant on protective services data can be particularly instructive in helping to tease out the role of culture and minority group status. Their findings are somewhat inconsistent. Some studies have reported significant relationships between minority group status and physical child abuse (Cazenave & Straus, 1979; Connelly & Straus, 1992) and neglect (Chaffin, Kelleher, & Hollenberg, 1996), whereas others have reported no discernable relationship between minority group status and physical child abuse (Chaffin et al., 1996). It is clear that the interaction between ethnicity and class must be more carefully teased apart. For example, findings reported by Cazenave and Straus (1979) appear to indicate that minority group status may become more important as a predictor of child maltreatment only under conditions of increasing economic deprivation (Garbarino & Ebata, 1983).

DISEMPOWERMENT AND PARENTAL CONTROL IN THE UNFOLDING OF CHILD MALTREATMENT

The strength of an ecological understanding of early child maltreatment is its capability to locate and organize multiple etiological factors, from micro- to macrosystemic. However, although an ecological view provides a helpful snapshot inventory of risk variables, it does not well depict dynamic process over time, explaining *why* such factors might lead to maltreating parenting. Perhaps part of this limitation is due to the relative paucity of longitudinal studies following families over time, which might trace such processes leading to maltreatment. Garnering such causal knowledge remains critical for preventive intervention work, which must consider how and when to intervene to interrupt the developmental chain of events that leads to later abusive or neglectful parenting.

To aid in understanding such causal processes, and given these limitations in existing empirical knowledge, it can be instructive to look at causal models of human behavior drawn from allied problems and fields. One such set of theories especially relevant to how and why ecologically based factors operate to cause physical child abuse and neglect are those concerning personal control and powerlessness. Although not often emphasized as a key element in an ecological understanding of maltreatment, early theoretical work by Garbarino and others (Garbarino, 1980; Garbarino & Gilliam, 1980; Wolff, 1983) attempted to infuse an ecological model with a dynamism by offering the notion of "life out of control." For example, Garbarino and Gilliam noted in 1980 that although stress is a key element leading to maltreatment, "it is the *unmanageability* [italics added] of stress which is the most crucial factor" (p. 35).

Theories about personal control and stress have highlighted the importance of individuals' perceptions of environmental events as manageable and within their control (e.g., Folkman, 1984; Gecas, 1989; Greenberger, Strasser, Cummings, & Dunham, 1989; Thompson, 1981). Research has consistently found that those life situations viewed as uncontrollable are especially prone to elicit less effective coping responses and more negative psychosocial outcomes (e.g., Brosschot et al., 1998; Goldberg, Weisenberg, Drobkin, Blittner, & Gotestam, 1997; Lefcourt, 1992; Pearlin, 1999; Peeters, Buunk, & Schaufeli, 1995). Martin Seligman's (1975) classic work on "learned helplessness," for example, has illustrated that when individuals exert efforts to alter or escape aversive situations, which then remain unresponsive to those efforts, they tend to "learn helplessness," developing beliefs that they are incapable of influencing the negative outcomes they experience (see also Abramson, Seligman, & Teasdale, 1978). In turn, they withdraw, becoming apathetic and passive. The cognitive schemas developing out of such experiences facilitate hopelessness, reduce motivation to act, and have been linked with depression, substance abuse, and other psychosocial problems (e.g., Kiefer, 1990; Peterson & Seligman, 1984; Sherman, 1998). Other researchers have shown that when individuals perceive an environment as aversive and not within their control, they may as well respond in a hostile and angry manner, even engaging in illicit activities in attempts to regain control (Folkman, 1984; Taylor, 1983; Thoits, 1983).[2]

Pointing out the benefits of personal control, research conducted by Albert Bandura (1977, 1997) has documented that when individuals experience events as within their control—that is, when environmental stimuli respond to individuals' efforts to achieve their desired aims— perceptions of self-efficacy become enhanced. As a result, expectations about their own future capacities to shape the course of events rise, increasing motivation to act and promoting still further efforts to advance their goals. In simple terms, efficacy beliefs are shaped by environmental responses, and in a potential spiral, the success or failure feedback garnered from such experiences shapes subsequent choices, further altering or reinforcing those environmental realities. Although Bandura's (1997) work acknowledges the role of environmental opportunities in shaping such a spiral, the focus of self-efficacy theory lies predominantly in the development of self-perceptions and their influence on subsequent behavior.

Theorists studying empowerment and powerlessness, in counterpoint, have emphasized the potency of the social environment in shaping individuals' cognitive schemas about personal control (e.g., Gaventa, 1982; Riger, 1993; Wallerstein, 1992; Zimmerman, 1990). Empowerment theorists underscore the critical role of macro-, exo-, and meso-level structures and processes in shaping the immediate environment within which individuals exert and judge their efforts to attain their aims (e.g., Sennett & Cobb, 1972) . Larger macro- and exo-systemic structures that promote social stratification and competition, and that obstruct individuals' efforts to attain their goals, can undermine individuals' self-efficacy by increasing perceptions of failure, promoting a downward spiral toward learned helplessness (Gaventa, 1982; National Research Council, 1993; Wallerstein, 1992). Emphasizing social structural elements trapping young mothers of color, Patricia Collins (1990), for example, has pointed to a "matrix of domination" within the fabric of American culture serving to undermine the women's efforts to achieve success whereby "race, class, and gender conspire in a network of ways leading to exclusion and oppression, creating a collective lens of powerlessness" (pp. 225-226).

From the vantage point of control and power theories, it becomes clearer why ecologically based risk factors promote a trajectory of parenting that leads to physical abuse and neglect, especially in early childhood. In line with the learned helplessness paradigm, ecologically based factors identified with maltreatment risk can directly heighten parents' exposure to aversive experiences, while also conveying to parents a sense that the environment is unresponsive to their efforts. Within the microsystem, parents of very young children not only struggle to handle multiple immediate concerns threatening their sense of control, such as responding to an infant's needs with little prior life preparation and in the throes of sleep deprivation or the challenging physiological changes experienced by mothers during the perinatal period. Increased demands on parents' time, energy, and resources simultaneously heighten the likelihood of interpersonal conflict and constrain opportunities for positive social interactions, particularly those whereby parents may receive "success feedback," critical to the development of self-efficacy. An infant's crying and/or inconsolability also may be perceived as aversive, especially if the parent has developed cognitive schemas from earlier nonresponsive or aversive relationships and if parents perceive they have fewer opportunities for support (Main & Goldwyn, 1984; Pederson, Gleason, Moran, & Bento, 1998).

Mesosystem stressors and social network problems can directly expose parents to additional aversive experiences while also constricting access to needed resources, information, or skills, undermining parents' options as they seek to manage the daily challenges of parenting. Social networks influence parents' views about their worth, their capacity to manage stressors, and the availability of social resources in times of need, directly shaping their perceptions of efficacy (Pierce, Baldwin, & Lydon, 1997; Sarason, Pierce, & Sarason, 1994). If parents are engaged in coercive interactions with significant others (a frequently co-occurring problem in cases of child maltreatment; see Chapter 7), cognitive schemas about inescapable and painful realities become concretely reinforced, further deepening parents' feelings of helplessness. From this viewpoint, social networks hold the potential to act as webs of support and sustenance during challenging times or, conversely, as webs in which parents feel themselves trapped in coercive and undermining relationships from which they have learned to see no escape.

Parents' relational schemas are also shaped by earlier life experiences, and memories of such experiences serve to orient individuals when they are appraising new interactions and choosing responses. Thus, both current and past relationships are important in shaping parents' response repertoires, their actual coping behaviors in the face of environmental challenges, and ultimately their control perceptions and responses in the parenting role. For example, key findings regarding the intergenerational transmission of child maltreatment appear to indicate that it is not merely that violence begets violence per se, but rather that parents' views of the ongoing quality and responsiveness of their primary relationships shape whether parents will later behave in abusive and/or neglectful ways (e.g., Egeland et al., 1988; George, 1996; Widom, 1989; Zuravin et al., 1996).

Exo- and macrosystemic influences such as parental and neighborhood impoverishment, community violence and disorganization, and minority group status can directly increase aversive experiences while minimizing opportunities to access resources necessary for managing important personal or parental challenges (Umberson, Anderson, Glick,

& Shapiro, 1998). Within a competitive society stratified by ethnic and economic groupings and that simultaneously promotes an ideology of equality and opportunity, individuals with low objective power may resolve a cognitive dissonance created by such disparities by labeling their own personal efforts as failures, internalizing a sense of powerlessness and promoting immobilization (Gaventa, 1982; National Research Council, 1993). Studies have, indeed, reported that parenting behaviors appear to be shaped by social structural variables such as poverty through their influence on parents' self-efficacy beliefs and depression (Elder, Eccles, Ardelt, & Lord, 1995; Gecas, 1989; Lyons-Ruth, Zoll, Connell, & Grunebaum, 1986).

In sum, ecological contexts appear to heighten child maltreatment risk in the ways they undermine parents' perceptions of power and control—through aversive, coercive, or stressful experiences, by constricting parents' life options and opportunities, and by leaving few venues for support, skills, information, or resources to cope. Nested within such disempowering contexts, parents face caring for an infant or young child whose own responses to the parent may provoke still further parental out-of-control feelings. In line with this analysis, maltreating parents have consistently reported "feeling out of control" and holding greater external loci of control than nonmaltreating parents, reflecting their view that events in their lives are beyond their capacity to manage and rather are shaped by external forces (Ellis & Milner, 1981; Gynn-Orenstein, 1981; Nurius, Lovell, & Maggie, 1988; Stringer & LaGreca, 1985; Wiehe, 1986).

Such control and power struggles become inextricably interwoven into parents' interactions with their children. When parents perceive they have low power, they tend to act in coercive ways toward their children *in an effort to regain control* or, conversely, behave tenuously or withdraw in response to their perceived precarious state of authority. As Daphne Bugental et al. (1999) state,

> There have been continuing suggestions that individuals in a nominal position of authority—when they are unsure of their actual power—are more likely to demonstrate coercive tactics in their attempts to influence others. That is, *loss of control serves as a motivator to establish or regain control* [italics added]. At the same time, those who see themselves as powerless also reveal their uncertainties or apprehension in their communication style. Ultimately, they present a picture in which it is unclear what emotion they are feeling and what level of power assertion they are attempting. (p. 214)

This pattern, particularly in cases of physical abuse, has received consistent empirical support. Studies have found that maltreating parents tend to be more directive, controlling, coercive, and rigid in asserting their power over their children (Chilamkurti & Milner, 1993; Engfer & Schneewind, 1982; Mash, Johnston, & Kovitz, 1983; Oldershaw, Walters, & Hall, 1986; Schellenbach, Monroe, & Merluzzi, 1991). Such a pattern has been shown to hold at different levels of socioeconomic status (Trickett, Aber, Carlson, & Cicchetti, 1991), indicating that power struggles linked with maltreating parenting operate independent of the stresses of poverty alone.

Bugental et al. (1999) and others, such as Gerald Patterson and colleagues (Patterson, 1982; Reid & Patterson, 1989), have further shown that such problematic power assertion by parents tends to provoke aversive or insecure responses from children, reinforcing in a cyclical fashion parents' own precarious and unsatisfactory control in relation to their children. Parents are likely to respond with still further dysfunctional attempts at parental control, promoting a downward spiral toward physical child abuse.

Parents may as well respond to low feelings of power in the face of aversive child behaviors by learning helplessness—that is, by withdrawing, becoming apathetic and depressed, or by making attempts to psychologically escape, for example, through the use of substances that "anesthetize" the aversive experiences (Murphy & Rosenbaum, 1999; Sherman, Saunders, & Trinh, 1998). Such learned helplessness responses to powerlessness—especially parental depression and substance abuse—have long been identified as key predictors of child neglect (Burns, Melamed, Burns, Chasnoff, & Hatcher, 1985; Kelley, 1998; Kelly, 1999; Marcus & Nardone, 1992). Consistent with a profile of learned helplessness, depressed mothers appear more apathetic and less engaged in parenting, demonstrating decreased responsiveness and sensitivity to their infants' cues (Donovan, Leavitt, & Walsh, 1998; Murray, Fiori-Cowley, Hooper, & Cooper, 1996). In turn, their infants tend to display a depressive style, exhibiting fewer attempts to engage their mothers (Field, 1992), and often show "dysregulated" behavioral patterns through intensified and demanding behavior or through excessive crying (Cox, Puckering, Pound, & Mills, 1987; Field, 1998). Such dyadic patterns can also spiral downward over time: An infant's unregulated or depressive style may be experienced by a parent as aversive or unresponsive or a combination of both, further exacerbating the parent's feelings of inefficacy and disengagement, leading to even less responsive and engaged infant behavior. Recent studies have shown that such a downward interactive spiral can begin very early. Findings by Field (1998), for example, indicate that a dyadic depressive, potentially neglectful interaction may have biochemical substrates and may appear at birth or even *in utero* (Field, 1998). Other evidence suggests that postpartum depression is linked with adverse infant behavior, and such may potentially serve to instigate an early downward progression (Bor et al., 1997).

In short, theories of personal control and powerlessness can provide a meaningful integrative lens explaining why ecologically based factors such as economic impoverishment, minority group status, social isolation, and multiple stressors—although perhaps not direct causes of maltreatment—may heighten risk. Each may serve directly or indirectly to challenge parents' sense of control and power by restricting opportunities to fulfill personal needs and aspirations and by increasing painful life experiences, thus dampening parents' beliefs in their capacities to overcome and function effectively. Such factors, although not directly causing maltreatment per se, may heighten risk by engendering in parents a sense of powerlessness.

An ecological model of child maltreatment, one that incorporates a dynamic understanding of the role of parents' control and power in the parent-infant dyad, highlights sources of maltreatment as deriving from aversive, unresponsive, and out-of-control environmental experiences, from microsystem to macrosystem. Such an analysis also points out that child abuse and neglect are, in fact, rarely discrete incidents or events but rather the results of an unfolding developmental process of transactions among the child, the parent, and the social contexts in which they are embedded.

Given an American legal and ideological backdrop that has historically rested on individual rights and family privacy, families with young children face the daunting task of bearing the sole responsibility for child rearing during their most vulnerable and difficult years. Rather than providing families with supportive "nests" that bolster parents' control and capacities to effect these responsibilities, the larger institutional and dominant cultural framework is oriented to stand apart from those that most need supports—that is, except at the point when parents are at their nadir in feeling out of control, demoralized, and powerless. When specific events are revealed to others that threaten the safety of their children, intervention has been institutionalized in a social services system that, by its design, exacerbates parents' struggles to efficaciously parent their children, and this system has been called child protective services. Attention will now be turned to the development of child protective services and early home-visitation services as venues to address the problem of child maltreatment.

NOTES

1. However, it is important to note that studies have also documented that neural systems retain some degree of regenerative and reorganizing capacity through adulthood (Pons, 1995; Stiles, 1995).

2. Interestingly, a neurobiological substrate to this pattern has been discerned, whereby learned helplessness appears causally related to disturbances in serotonin neurotransmission in the brain (Neumaier, Petty, Kramer, Szot, & Hamblin, 1997; Wu et al., 1999), a process that has been identified in both human aggression and depression (Kroetsch & Shamoian, 1983; Valzelli & Bernasconi, 1979; Van Praag, 1982).

Chapter 3

THE PARADOX OF CHILD PROTECTION, THE PROMISE OF HOME VISITATION

The idea of preventing child abuse and neglect before it occurs is a not new one, nor is the venue of home visitation services. Both share overlapping origins in the United States, yet only relatively recently have the two converged again on a broad scale. Whereas home visits have been provided on a continuous basis for health care purposes in the United States and parts of Europe since their inception, intervention approaches to the problem of child maltreatment have had a varied history in the United States. This chapter examines the historical contexts out of which the movement grew to prevent child maltreatment through early home visitation. In particular, it reviews the historical origins of the tension between child protection and prevention and considers, from a prevention and an ecological perspective, the paradoxes of child protective services in effectively addressing the problem of child maltreatment. In response to these paradoxes, this chapter examines the spawning of the early home visitation movement in the United States as a promising alternative means to address the problem of child maltreatment.

THE ORIGINS OF HOME VISITATION AND CHILD MALTREATMENT EFFORTS

Home visitation services date back at least as far as Elizabethan England in the form of "outdoor relief" for the poor (Fink, Wilson, & Conover,

1963) and in the pioneering work of Florence Nightingale. Nightingale's work has been credited with first encouraging the development of specialized nurse training in visiting the sick poor in their homes and in promoting non-nurse health visitors for poor mothers living in rural settings (Wasik, Bryant, & Lyons, 1990). In 1892, the first specialized training for nurses in home health visiting was formally launched, and by the turn of the century, home health visiting was provided by virtually every local authority in Britain (Kamerman & Kahn, 1993). (See Table 3.1 for a capsule history.)

In the United States, home visitation and public concern over the problem of child maltreatment have intertwining origins, both arising with the increasing urbanization of the late 19th century. As Heather Weiss has noted,

America's first relatively large-scale experiment with home visiting occurred in the late nineteenth century when private charity organizations dispatched friendly visitors to the homes of the urban poor to transform their character and behavior, and thereby to attack the growth of urban poverty, class antagonism, and social disintegration. In the 1890s, more than 4,000 volunteer middle- and upper-middle class women were regularly visiting poor families in the tenements of major cities to provide guidance and to serve as models of how to live right. (Weiss, 1993, p. 115)

In 1874, a home visitor named Mrs. Etta Angell Wheeler discovered the abuse of "Little Mary Ellen," spurring action that led to the development of the New York Society for the Prevention of Cruelty to Children (SPCC), the world's first child protection organization. Influenced by a prosecutorial approach that formed the primary method of Societies for the Prevention of Cruelty to Animals, the New York SPCC adopted case investigation, filing of complaints, and prosecution as its primary means of addressing child maltreatment (Costin, 1980).

As SPCCs appeared across the United States, a schism arose between the investigative, protective, and "child rescue" approach taken by the New York SPCC and an approach that emphasized family strengthening and abuse prevention, as represented by the Massachusetts SPCC. The debate between child rescue and preventive work to support families under stress was discernable in the origins of early social welfare institutions. The Charity Organization Societies, first established in the 1880s as organizations coordinating the work of many private charities serving

Table 3.1

Historical Milestones in the Development of
Early Home Visitation Services to Prevent Child Abuse and Neglect

1850s	Home health visiting begins in Great Britain, focused on hygiene and sanitation
1875	New York Society for Prevention of Cruelty to Children organized
1890s	"Friendly visitors" befriend poor families in urbanized settings in the United States
1900s	Massachusetts Society for the Prevention of Cruelty to Children, headed by Carstens, promotes preventive measures to address causes of abuse
1950s to present	Attachment theorists such as Mary Ainsworth and John Bowlby focus attention on the importance of parent-infant attachment
1962	C. Henry Kempe organizes conference on the "battered child syndrome"
1973	Home Start programs for families of young children launched in Great Britain
1974	Child Abuse Prevention and Treatment Act (P.L. 93-247) passes
1976	C. Henry Kempe reports on the health-visitor concept in preventing child abuse
1977 to present	Ecological model advanced by James Garbarino, Jay Belsky, and others, emphasizing contextual causes of child maltreatment
1980	Adoption Assistance and Child Welfare Act (P.L. 96-272) passes, encouraging the development of family preservation services
1980s through 1990s	Research findings highlight the importance of the first 3 years of childhood for later life opportunities
1980s to present	Outcome studies reporting the effectiveness of early home visitation programs appear with increasing frequency
1986	David Olds and colleagues publish first landmark findings of the Elmira, New York, trial of early home visitation, demonstrating child maltreatment reduction in low-income unmarried teens

Table 3.1
(Continued)

1991	U.S. National Advisory Board on Child Abuse and Neglect recommends phasing in a nationwide system of neonatal home visitation services
1991	Gail Breakey and Betsy Pratt publish description and early findings of the Hawaii Healthy Start model of early home visitation services
1992	National Committee to Prevent Child Abuse launches the Healthy Families America campaign to foster early home visitation programs across the United States, anchored in the Healthy Start model
1993	Family Preservation and Support Services program passes, amending Title IV-B of the Social Security Act, providing federal funding for family support programs, including home visitation services
1993	The Packard Foundation's *The Future of Children* publishes landmark volume on early home visitation services; other professional journals follow suit
1997	David Olds and colleagues report home visitation preventive effects into the teen years on child maltreatment and its consequences
1999	*The Future of Children* revisits evaluation studies in home visitation, highlighting the need to more carefully consider design and implementation issues in home visitation

the poor, asserted in a statement from the 1899 National Conference of Charities and Corrections:

> Your committee is emphatically of the opinion that the "ounce of prevention is better than a pound of cure," and it strongly urges upon all charitable people the absolute necessity for preserving the home whenever possible.
>
> Do not be in a hurry to send the children to an institution until you are convinced of the hopelessness of preserving the home. Remember that

when the home is broken up, even temporarily, it is no easy task to bring it
together again, and that a few dollars of private charity, a friendly visit, a
kind word, and a helping hand will lift up the courage of the deserving
poor; and this is half the battle, because discouragement begets careless-
ness. (quoted in Bremner, 1971, p. 352)

As the 20th century progressed, the withdrawal of private agencies
from child protection work and the advent of the psychoanalytic movement led to a dormancy of activity around the issue of child abuse and
neglect until its rediscovery in the 1950s and 1960s. However, the schism
between family support and child rescue remained when child maltreatment re-emerged as a high-profile public issue.

THE PARADOXICAL ADVENT
OF CHILD PROTECTIVE SERVICES

In the 1950s and early 1960s, advances made in radiological technology
aided in "bringing to light" nonaccidental broken-bone injuries in young
children, igniting broad public interest in the problem of maltreatment
(e.g., Caffey, 1946; Kempe & Silver, 1959; Kempe, Silverman, Stele,
Droegmueller, & Silver, 1962; Silverman, 1953; Wolley & Evans, 1955).
The medical profession's role in rediscovering the problem of child maltreatment through a newly coined diagnostic label, the "battered child
syndrome," helped to galvanize public attention by initially framing the
problem as pathological violence against vulnerable children. The public's awareness of such sensational incidents helped spur the rapid development of publicly funded child protective service agencies, which from
their inception were designed to find and protect such battered children
from further devastating harm. The subsequent passage of the federal
Child Abuse Prevention and Treatment Act of 1974 (P. L. 93-247 or
"CAPTA") helped institutionalize child protective services systems
across the nation, emphasizing case finding, after-the-fact investigation,
and protection through child placement in cases of serious maltreatment.
Although CAPTA included the word *prevention* in its title, such prevention was not well specified and was largely directed at the prevention not
of maltreatment's occurrence, but rather its recurrence. The emphasis of
legislative efforts at the state and federal levels, including CAPTA, was
on mandating professionals to identify those children suspected to be the
victims of abuse and neglect so that they could be protected from further

devastating treatment by abusive or neglectful parents. Despite this increased public activity to address the problem of child maltreatment, Costin, Karger, and Stoesz (1996) have emphasized that

> it would be a mistake to conclude that efforts to protect children repre-
> sented a linear and progressive improvement in the nation's ability to care
> for its young. Far from it. Rhetoric aside, federal legislation reflected an
> amateurish use of social research by human service professionals to de-
> termine optimal responses to child trauma, a willingness on the part of
> children's advocates to pander to ideological fashion, and welfare bureau-
> crats' sacrifice of the "best interests of the child" in favor of self-interest
> defined by categorical programs. As a result, the federal incursion into
> child welfare contributed to a paradox of enormous proportion: while the
> child abuse industry prospered, many children were maimed or killed after
> they had been placed in the care of the very agencies mandated to protect
> them. Having rediscovered child abuse, the nation experienced—ironi-
> cally—a crisis in child welfare. (p. 107)

The paradoxes of child protective services have, in fact, turned out to be multilayered. Mandating the reporting of suspected child maltreat-ment and the increased public awareness of the problem contributed to staggering increases in the numbers of identified child abuse and neglect cases in just a few decades. At the same time, child welfare systems faced declining public support and increasingly scarce dollars available to address the needs in such cases (Courtney, 1998). Duncan Lindsey (1994) has noted that during the time that reports to protective services systems were skyrocketing in the 1970s and 1980s,

> The mood in society and government was turning increasingly skeptical
> toward social programs. Throughout the decade of the eighties, expendi-
> tures for social services were repeatedly cut. Paradoxically, while the pub-
> lic continued to demand greater efforts be made to curb child abuse, it was
> increasingly unwilling to fund those efforts. (p. 97)

As a result, state child protection systems across the United States became overwhelmed, awash in cases without adequate resources or person-power to attend to the complex and entrenched problems many families presented. Among the many consequences of the increasingly acute fiscal squeeze placed on protective services systems in the United States were those that severely hindered their capacities to function. Pro-tective services systems faced a need to scale down on the training and degree backgrounds of workers hired to make complex and difficult decisions involved in protective services investigations (e.g., Pecora & Austin, 1983). Along with a scarcity of well-qualified protective services personnel came unwieldy caseloads, highly bureaucratized settings, and contradictory agency mandates, all of which have been credited with the high rates of worker burnout, inefficacy, and turnover found in protective services work (Guterman & Jayaratne, 1994; Jayaratne & Chess, 1984).

The tremendous strain on protective services systems across the country has encouraged an increasingly narrowed focus on screening, decision making, and monitoring activities, driving out any remaining capacity to provide direct services to families (Kamerman & Kahn, 1990). Indeed, services are no longer provided within the system but rather are contracted out to other agencies, with case management and monitoring the only vestiges of service typically in place within the system.

In the face of such enormous systemic pressures and problems, mounting media attention on such case failures as the deaths of Adam Mann, Eli Creekmore, and other children known to child protective services systems heightened public pressure to a more acute level in search of reforms and alternative approaches to the problem of child abuse and neglect. The U.S. Advisory Board on Child Abuse and Neglect, a 15-member multidisciplinary group commissioned by amendments made in 1988 to CAPTA, issued its first formal report in 1990, evaluating the nation's response to the problem of child abuse and neglect. At that time, the Advisory Board stated,

> The system the nation has devised to respond to child abuse and neglect is failing. It is not a question of acute failure of a single element of the system; there is chronic and critical multiple organ failure. In such a context, the safety of children cannot be ensured. Indeed, the system itself can at times be abusive to children.
>
> Moreover, the Board estimates that the United States spends *billions* of dollars on programs that deal with the results of the nation's failure to prevent and treat child abuse and neglect. Billions are spent on law enforcement, juvenile and criminal courts, foster care and residential facilities, and the treatment of adults who themselves were maltreated in a prior generation. Billions more are spent on efforts to prevent substance abuse, eating disorders, adolescent pregnancy, suicide, juvenile delinquency, prostitution, pornography, and violent crime—all of which have substantial roots in childhood abuse and neglect. (pp. 2-3)

The work of the Board and others made it painfully apparent that some children coming to the attention of protective services fall through the cracks, continuing to be maltreated, and even lose their lives while being "protectively served." In other instances, children are taken from their homes in seemingly indiscriminate fashion, or conversely, in an overtly discriminatory fashion. For example, placement decisions disproportionately affect families of color and impoverished families (cf. Courtney et al., 1996). Unfortunately, it remains not uncommon for some children, once placed outside the home, to experience multiple, sometimes damaging placements, living in family after family, ultimately ending up in institutional and highly costly settings as a last resort. Summarizing the dilemmas presented by the design of services entrusted with protecting children in the United States, the National Commission on Children reported in 1991,

> If the nation had deliberately designed a system that would frustrate the professionals who staff it, anger the public who finance it, and abandon the children who depend on it, it could not have done a better job than the present child welfare system. (p. 293)

A host of reform efforts have ensued since the building of child protective services in the United States. As an example, the Adoption Assistance and Child Welfare Act (P.L. 96-272) passed in 1980 required states, among other steps, to show reasonable efforts at preventing child placement, thereby spurring the development of "family preservation services" programs aimed at preventing maltreated children from being placed into foster care. As later extensions, the Family Preservation and Support Services Act of 1993 (P.L. 103-66) and subsequently the Adoption and Safe Families Act of 1997 (P.L. 105-89) for the first time earmarked federal funds for family preservation programs as well as for family support programs (under which early home visitation programs also fall), promoting the expansion of out-of-home placement prevention and child maltreatment prevention programs nationwide. Other reform efforts enacted within protective services systems have attempted to sharpen what has been asserted is the relatively blunt child protection gateway, seeking to improve child protection decision-making processes so that they more validly reflect the risks children face, with the goals of minimizing inappropriate protective interventions and maximizing efficiency (cf. Gelles, 1996; Larner, Stevenson, & Behrman, 1998; Waldfogel, 1998).

Careful examinations of such reform efforts have pointed out their sobering limitations. For example, reviewing the available array of controlled outcome studies of family preservation programs, a report from the National Research Council and Institute of Medicine noted that placement rates in families receiving services ranged from 21% to 59%, compared to placement rates ranging from 20% to 59% in control group families. Although, in some instances, family preservation services may delay placement out of the home and temporarily assist families facing an immediate crisis, the report concluded "there is little evidence to date that the services resolve the underlying family dysfunction that precipitated the crisis or improve the child's well-being or the family's functioning" (Chalk & King, 1998, p. 105; see also McCroskey & Meezan, 1998; Schuerman, Rzepnicki, & Littell, 1994).

Likewise, reviews of formalized risk assessment systems to improve child-protection decision making have demonstrated that 13% to 26% of families screened via such systems are falsely identified as likely to abuse their children again (i.e., they later did not) and that 14% to 86% are falsely identified as families *un*likely to abuse their children again (i.e., they later did; Lyons, Doueck, & Wodarski, 1996). The fundamental limitations of risk assessment screening in reducing the substantial misclassification of families in protective services investigations have been clearly pointed out (Caldwell, Bogat, & Davidson, 1988; Kaufman & Zigler, 1992):

> To illustrate, consider a sample of 1,000 parents. A 5% abuse rate implies that 50 of these parents are abusers, and 950 are not. If 95% of the abusers were correctly identified, only three parents would have escaped detection. With comparable predictive power for detecting nonabusers, 902 parents would be correctly classified and 48 parents would be falsely labeled potential abusers. Forty-seven abusive parents would have been correctly identified, and 48 nonabusive parents would have been falsely accused, resulting in half of all identified parents as being misclassified. *It is simply not statistically feasible to accurately predict a low base-rate phenomenon like child abuse* [italics added]. (Kaufman & Zigler, 1992, p. 272)

Such sobering knowledge about the limits of reforming child protection from within has prompted still more fundamental calls for change, for example, by privatizing child protection systems or transferring child maltreatment investigations and case handling to law enforcement officials (e.g., Costin et al., 1996; Lindsey, 1994). Several states including

Arkansas, Florida, and Texas have, indeed, begun to experiment with such a shift. Sweeping reforms adopted in the design and execution of child protection have not yet appeared to yield any demonstrable improvements in the rates of child maltreatment, the severity of child maltreatment, fatality rates, or other identifiable outcomes of concern for children. Indeed, in some cases, major reform efforts have been accompanied by increases in child maltreatment fatalities (Bernstein, 1999a).

These harsh realities have raised fundamental questions as to whether the system is indeed reformable. As Lisabeth Schorr (1997) has pointed out, "Child welfare reformers nervously wonder whether the system can be mended before the call to end it becomes irresistible" (p. 199). Child maltreatment scholars themselves have increasingly begun to call for fundamental rethinking (e.g., Costin et al., 1996; Krugman, 1999; Lindsey, 1994). For example, Richard Krugman, editor-in-chief of the journal *Child Abuse and Neglect,* recently stated,

> We need to be willing to experiment with other models. Not every country has the system we do. In most countries, reporting is not mandatory. . . . Experimenting with other models will require the admission that we are not protecting children, and will require a change in our present legal framework for protecting children. (1999, p. G-1)

UNRAVELING THE PARADOX—THE FUNDAMENTAL MISMATCH BETWEEN CHILD MALTREATMENT AND THE CHILD PROTECTION SOLUTION

The profound problems of child protection must be considered in light of what is presently understood as the etiology of child abuse and neglect (reviewed in Chapter 2), particularly the degree to which the solution of child protection appropriately fits the problem of child maltreatment. To understand this, it is necessary to examine some of the underlying premises on which the protective services system has been built. Although not immediately apparent, the rationale of the child protective services system in the United States rests on a legal framework derived from the English legal doctrine of *parens patriae,* which establishes the grounds on which the state can justifiably intervene in family life. *Parens patriae* presumes the primacy of family privacy but makes exceptions when parents are unable or unwilling to care for or control their children according to the requirements of society (Stein, 1993). Such historical precedents shape the purview of protective services by focusing its core concerns on

- Whether the state has legal grounds for intervening in family life in a way that takes precedence over a family's right to privacy
- Whether a protective services investigation reveals enough evidence to charge parents with maltreatment
- The extent to which children are at risk of imminent harm, requiring the consideration of an out-of-home placement or other in-home alternatives (Guterman, 1997b)

As noted by Waldfogel (1999),

> The (child protective services) system focuses on identifying and respond-
> ing to child victims and adult perpetrators. The initial contact with the
> family is reactive and investigative, concentrating on gathering infor-
> mation to confirm or disprove the allegations made by the reporter. Inves-
> tigators and families are also keenly aware that the information being
> collected during the investigation might be used as evidence in future court
> proceedings. To the extent that parents are seen as perpetrators, it is as-
> sumed that they are part of the problem, not part of the solution. It is also
> assumed that many parents will not cooperate without the use or threat-
> ened use of state authority. Thus, the model for CPS operations, particu-
> larly at the investigative stage, is adversarial: It is reactive, investigative,
> suspicious of parents, and authoritative. (p. 69)

A major focus in a protective services intervention is, thus, placed on the collection of evidence (for example, regarding observable bruises or hazardous living conditions) to justify a state's right to intervene in what are viewed normatively as "private family matters." *Parens patriae* and the child protection system founded on its premises establishes that such intervention must, therefore, be after-the-fact, given that the state has no legitimate grounds to interfere in family life if no evidence exists to justify overruling a family's right to privacy. In this way, protective services intervention has been viewed as akin to intervention in instances of criminal activity: That is, no intervention is made until an act has been committed that establishes its justification, at which point, intervention becomes authoritative, and in most cases involuntary and adversarial.

The doctrine of *parens patriae* and child protective services intervention predicated upon it form a troubling fit with what is presently understood as the etiology of physical child abuse and neglect. Evidence examined in Chapter 2 points out that, although physical abuse and neglect manifest in the parent-child domain, the most potent origins of the problem stem from ecological factors that are exogenous to the parent-child relationship and that erode parents' control and power, leading to an unfolding pattern toward abusive and/or neglectful parenting. Although some causal elements in the child maltreatment equation are located in the private interior of family life, the weight of the empirical evidence underscores the clear influence of external factors in which family life is nested, particularly those environmental conditions experienced as unresponsive and aversive, constraining in opportunities, and diminishing parents' capacities to efficaciously manage the parenting role. Whereas physical child abuse and neglect are most potently shaped by these exterior webs of influence undermining parents' sense of control and power, protective services' legal underpinnings focus it on uncovering interior family problems that justify the state's right to violate such privacy.

Protective services then interviews only *after* parents have lost control in the parenting process, and it does so in an involuntary and adversarial fashion. Yet, investigating and monitoring parents' behavior toward their children without their consent, requiring them to take steps to demonstrate their competency (for example, through required court appearances, mandated parenting classes, or treatment), and threatening the loss of their children may compound parents' perceptions of coercive and unresponsive environments, potentially deepening their feelings of inefficacy, helplessness, and powerlessness. The adversarial and stigmatizing nature of protective services intervention, although aimed at promoting children's safety, can rather jeopardize parents' feelings of support and confidence during a highly vulnerable time. To the extent that such intervention thus engenders in parents deeper feelings of powerlessness and adds additional ecological challenges, it may even heighten the risk of child maltreatment—precisely the opposite of the stated purpose of the intervention. By focusing on the aftermath of maltreatment in this fashion without attending to its sources, child protective services intervention may be viewed as coming too late and as mismatched to the nature of the problem.

In short, although protective services intervention is designed to address the problem of child abuse and neglect, such a solution is contraindicated in fundamental ways when considered in relation to the etiology of the problem. From this vantage point, it is no surprise that many have characterized the U.S. child protective services system as having failed, being in a state of collapse, and needing fundamental reform (Costin et al., 1996; Schorr, 1997; U.S. Advisory Board on Child Abuse and Neglect, 1991). Indeed, almost half of the states' child protection agencies across the U.S. have been placed under court orders due to failure to perform adequately in protecting children in their care (Child Welfare League of America, 1997).

Such developments continue to provoke much soul-searching, efforts at reform, and initiatives to examine alternatives to the prevailing protective services solution aimed at the problem of child abuse and neglect. In this dark context, early home visitation approaches to the problem of child maltreatment have re-emerged as one beacon of hope.

THE RE-EMERGENCE OF
EARLY HOME VISITATION SERVICES

Apart from the troubles of child protection, several broader historical developments have been credited for the recent re-emergence of early home visitation services specifically concerned with the problem of child abuse and neglect. These include deinstitutionalization within children's services, which recognized the detrimental effects of separating children from their parents and the benefits of supporting the parent-child attachment (e.g., Bowlby, 1951; Goldfarb, 1945; Spitz, 1945; Yarrow, 1961). Accompanying this was a growing scholarly emphasis on attachment theory and an ecological model of child development and maltreatment (Belsky, 1980; Bronfenbrenner, 1977; Garbarino, 1977), which provided the initial intellectual undergirding for early intervention services in the home.

The War on Poverty in the 1960s saw both the advent of preventive social programs in practice, seeking to avert the debilitating effects of poverty on cognitive achievement, and a heightened awareness of the need to evaluate programs for their cost and clinical effectiveness (Wasik et al., 1990). Perhaps most notable among the first-generation early prevention programs were the Early Training Project (Gray & Klaus, 1970; Gray, Ramsey, & Klaus, 1982), the High/Scope Perry Preschool Project (Weikert, Bond, & McNeil, 1978), and, on the largest and most visible scale, Project Head Start (Ziegler & Muenchow, 1992). Although these programs did not directly target the problem of child abuse and neglect, they nonetheless laid the groundwork for later child maltreatment-

oriented home visitation programs by providing high-quality data documenting the benefits of intervening early in the lives of children and their
families *before* identified problems occur. For example, targeting cognitive and social outcomes of youngsters, a randomized trial of the High
Scope/Perry Preschool Project documented transitory short-term improvements in IQ, as well as long-term improvements in academic
achievement, employment status, use of welfare, and reductions in criminal activity (Schweinhart, Barnes, & Weikart, 1993).

Support for early home visitation services in the United States was
also drawn from the longer tradition of such services in most northern
and western European countries, where they have often formed a routine
part of maternity care (Wasik et al., 1990). Denmark, for example, initiated a national program of home health visiting to reduce infant mortality in 1937, mandating the availability of such services throughout the
country in 1971. Other European countries followed suit with similar
publicly funded initiatives after World War II (Kamerman & Kahn,
1993). The first home visitation services specifically designed to prevent
child abuse and neglect were initiated in 1973 in Leicester, England, with
the launching of the Home Start model (Harrison, 1981). With referrals
from social workers or health visitors, Home Start supports were provided to families by volunteer parents; thus, the program was conceived
of as a network of "mutual care" whereby recipient families could access
another nonthreatening family, unaffiliated with the local child protection authority. The program expanded rapidly in its early years and
attracted the interest of those in other countries.

In the context of these developments, C. Henry Kempe (1976) first
proposed and later tested a health visitor program in the United States as
a preventive measure specifically for the problem of child abuse and
neglect. Kempe was well aware of promising findings reported in allied
early intervention studies and the increasing emphasis on the parent-
infant bonding process. At the same time, he recognized that the vast
majority of families at risk were accessible before maltreatment could
take place via health care settings at birth or during prenatal medical
visits. Kempe, along with Jane Gray and colleagues, first studied in a
controlled fashion early home visitation aimed at reducing future maltreatment risk. The Kempe group reported hopeful findings linked with a
possible reduction in severity of maltreatment-related injuries, although
their overall findings were not statistically significant (Gray, Cutler,
Dean, & Kempe, 1979).

The Hawaii Healthy Start Program

Influenced by the findings of Gray, Kempe, and colleagues, Calvin Sia, a pediatrician and member of Hawaii's child protective services advisory committee, invited Kempe to plan child abuse prevention activities for families in Hawaii. In 1975, Dr. Sia and the director of the Family Stress Center, Gail Breakey, obtained a grant from the National Center for Prevention and Treatment of Child Abuse and Neglect to implement a pilot home visitation program developed by Kempe and a child protective services advisory committee (Breakey & Pratt, 1991; Earle, 1995). The Hawaii Healthy Start program grew out of this original effort initiated on Oahu, and it expanded to five additional sites on neighboring islands between 1977 and 1980. In 1985, Healthy Start began as a state-funded demonstration program in Oahu serving a high-risk population. A glowing informal evaluation conducted after 3 years of services received national attention: "Not a single case of abuse among the project's 241 high risk families had been reported [to child protective services] since the demonstration began" (Breakey & Pratt, 1991, p. 16). Although in hindsight, such early exciting reports may have been too heavily relied upon, given the lack of a control group and the short follow-up period, they nonetheless helped to support a statewide expansion of Healthy Start and attracted the attention of Prevent Child Abuse America (then the National Committee to Prevent Child Abuse), suggesting a model service program around which to advance a nationwide prevention initiative (Duggan et al., 1999; see Practice Exemplar 3.1).

Apart from the Hawaii Healthy Start initiative, findings from an increasing number of randomized trials of early home visitation programs targeting maltreatment and parent-child interactions were disseminated in the 1980s (e.g., Hardy & Streett, 1989; Larson, 1980; Lealman, Haigh, Phillips, Stone, & Ord-Smith, 1983; Siegel, Bauman, Schaefer, Saunders, & Ingram, 1980; Taylor & Beauchamp, 1988). These studies, reported largely in medical journals, found a mixture of outcomes, some positive and some reporting undetectable effects of early home visitation on child maltreatment, raising some hope but a number of questions, as well, about the efficacy of early home visitation. In 1980, an American Academy of Pediatrics conference determined that evidence was as yet insufficient to recommend early home visitation services on a national basis (American Academy of Pediatrics, Council on Child and Adolescent Health, 1998).

PRACTICE EXEMPLAR 3.1

The Hawaii Healthy Start Program Model

The Hawaii Healthy Start model was explicitly developed with the aim of preventing child abuse and neglect by achieving the following interrelated goals: (a) improving family coping, (b) promoting positive parenting, (c) facilitating parent-child attachment, (d) promoting optimal child development, and (e) improving the use of community resources, particularly ongoing access to a "medical home" for the family (Breakey & Pratt, 1991; Daro, McCurdy, & Harding, 1998). The program has drawn its theoretical basis from the work of Ray Helfer (1987), Selma Fraiberg (1980), and social learning theory, emphasizing the need to "reparent the parent" to break a cycle of abuse and neglect. The program consists of universal screening for risk among families within a health care system. Once a family is screened positively for high risk, paraprofessional home visitation support is initiated within 3 months of the child's birth. Families are screened via a two-tiered process: First, hospital admission or public health clinic records are reviewed for the presence of specified risk factors. Families showing initial risk are then interviewed by family assessment workers, using the Family Stress Checklist (Murphy, Orkow, & Nicola, 1985). If families are identified as high risk on this index, they are then offered home visitation services.

Paraprofessional home visitors attempt to initiate visits prenatally or within a week of the infant's birth, and, in cases where a family's situation appears more difficult, outreach may persist for several months to secure the family's participation. At the initial phases, home visitors attempt to visit families weekly and build a relationship by offering emotional support, concrete assistance, and guidance in parent-child interaction. Home visitors and families mutually establish an individualized family-support plan identifying goals for service. Typically, home visitors engage parents in a parenting education curriculum and seek to assess families' needs that can be addressed with available community resources and supports such as Medicaid, child care, housing, financial assistance, and referrals to substance or domestic abuse agencies. In addition to helping families obtain necessary services, home visitors seek to identify a "medical home" for the infant and family and then assist the family in maintaining ongoing linkages with medical care providers. Particularly during the first year of life, the infant's health and development are carefully monitored with standardized assessment instruments such as the Denver Developmental Screening Test or the Nursing Child Assessment Satellite Training (NCAST).

As families achieve initial goals and show stability, they are graduated to a less intensive level of service, tapering over time until the child reaches 3 to 4 years old and family risk appears to be reduced (Breaky & Pratt, 1991; Center on Child Abuse Prevention Research, 1996; Daro et al., 1998; Earle, 1995). As an adjunct to home visitation services, Healthy Start also provides center-based support groups, often focusing on issues such as child development, nutrition, or parent-child interaction.

Beyond an initial uncontrolled evaluation of Healthy Start, several subsequent, more carefully controlled examinations of the model have now been reported (Center on Child Abuse Prevention Research, 1996; Duggan et al., 1999). Although the model continues to show some promise, these evaluations have reported less positive findings than the initial uncontrolled evaluation reported by the State of Hawaii, allowing researchers to examine aspects of the program that may need to be extended or modified (Daro & Harding, 1999). For example, findings from the recent randomized trial reported by Duggan et al. (1999) have prompted more careful consideration of the engagement and retention process, given that 50% of families across sites dropped out of the program within the first year. The Hawaii sites also now provide ongoing support until the child reaches 3 to 4 years of age, whereas the original prototype program served families until the child reached kindergarten (Windham, 1998). The program, as well, presently faces reconsideration of its screening process (see Chapter 6). Nonetheless, the model continues to enjoy perhaps the widest emulation of any U.S. early home visitation program specifically targeting child maltreatment, given that the infrastructure to transfer Healthy Start-like programs across a wide variety of community settings is well developed and coordinated by Prevent Child Abuse America (formerly National Committee to Prevent Child Abuse).

The Prenatal/Early Infancy Project

Paralleling these developments, David Olds and colleagues initiated the Prenatal/Early Infancy project in Elmira, New York, which turned out to be a milestone in the advancement of early home visitation services in the United States (Kitzman, Olds, et al., 1997; Olds, Henderson, & Kitzman, 1994; Olds, Henderson, Chamberlin, & Tatelbaum, 1986; Olds, Henderson, Tatelbaum, & Chamberlin, 1986; Olds, Henderson, et al., 1998; Olds et al., 1999). The initial study, conducted between 1978 and 1982, implemented a rigorously controlled randomized trial of nurse home visitation services targeted to primiparous (first-time) mothers located in a semirural, impoverished, high-risk community. The initial follow-up reported a select but broad array of positive outcomes traceable to intervention services in the domains of pregnancy (e.g., increased birth weight, decreased smoking), child development (e.g., infants' cognitive development in smoking mothers), and maternal life course (e.g., fewer subsequent pregnancies, fewer months on welfare; Olds, Henderson, Tatelbaum, et al., 1986; Olds et al., 1999). Most promising for the prevention of child maltreatment, Olds, Henderson, Chamberlin, et al. (1986) reported that during the first 2 years of life, 4% (one case) of the low-income unmarried teen mothers who received nurse home visitation were substantiated for child maltreatment compared to 19% (eight cases) among low-income unmarried teens not receiving home visitation (reported as a marginally statistically significant finding). Olds and colleagues also reported at the initial follow-up that the infants of nurse-visited women were seen in the hospital emergency room fewer times than controls and that low-income teens receiving home visitation services punished and restricted their children less frequently and provided their children a larger number of appropriate play materials. Because of the careful research design executed in the Elmira trial, the positive outcomes of the program were touted as the first hard evidence that early home visitation services, if designed and implemented appropriately within the right context, could indeed reduce child maltreatment risk before the fact. (See Practice Exemplar 3.2.)

The ongoing work by Olds and colleagues has made an important contribution to establishing the scientific credibility of the efficacy of early home visitation services and to extending the knowledge base in this area. Olds and colleagues have continued to follow up the Elmira cohort of families and children. At 4 years follow-up, the researchers observed that the effects on substantiated child maltreatment rates "washed out"

PRACTICE EXEMPLAR 3.2

**The Prenatal/Early Infancy
Nurse Home Visitation Program Model**

The Prenatal/Early Infancy program first tested in Elmira, New York, was designed to address broad areas of maternal and child development. It was specifically designed to improve the outcomes of pregnancy, the qualities of maternal caregiving, child health and development, and maternal life course development (Kitzman, Cole, & Yoos, 1997; Olds, Kitzman, Cole, & Robinson, 1997). The program is grounded in human ecology theory originally developed by Bronfenbrenner (1979), theories of human attachment, and Bandura's (1977) theory of self-efficacy. It has been refined over 20 years with detailed visit-by-visit protocols developed to guide nurse home visitors. The program focuses on low-income primiparous mothers and initiates home visits during pregnancy. Services are provided in ongoing weekly to biweekly home visits, tapering off until the child reaches 2 years of age. Mothers are given information prenatally on maternal health habits and pregnancy complications, with an emphasis on how their behavior affects their own health, their labor and delivery, and the health of their unborn child. Mothers and their support people are prepared for birth, and attention is provided to assist in the development of plans for employment, schooling, and ongoing family planning. The nurse visitors help to coordinate care with physicians, and, after birth, they teach mothers how to identify and address common childhood illnesses.

As the women establish themselves as parents, the nurse visitors help them to set achievable objectives, building their confidence so that they can effectively handle their new roles and attain their de-

and that home-visited mothers punished their children to a *greater* extent than control mothers. At the same time, they observed that home-visited children lived in homes with fewer hazards, reported fewer injuries, and made fewer visits to hospital emergency rooms (Olds et al., 1994). Although such findings somewhat dampened the enthusiasm over the sired life goals as parents. Nurses conduct assessments and deliver specific interventions to address identified issues. Nurses address developmental milestones, encourage mothers to read and respond to infants' cues, and give mothers ideas for specific activities, which may enhance the infant's development. As the infants mature, nurses help mothers attend to infants' educational needs and safety concerns, teaching mothers strategies for handling the challenges of toddlerhood. Nurses encourage the women to involve their husbands, boyfriends, mothers, or other family members in home visits, and fathers or primary support people are specifically asked to take part in several visits after birth. Ongoing communication and coordination are maintained with primary physicians, and families are referred to other health and human services in the community as needed (Kitzman et al., 1997; Olds, 1982; Olds et al., 1999; Olds, Henderson, Tatelbaum, & Chamberlin, 1988; Olds, Hill, & Rumsey, 1998).

As the outcomes in the Elmira trial were reported on a sample of largely white mothers, Olds, Kitzman, and colleagues sought to replicate the study and its findings in a primarily African American sample of women in Memphis, Tennessee. Although this study did not report protective service data and although the gains observed were on the whole less comprehensive than those attained in the Elmira study, the Memphis trial demonstrated that home-visited families had fewer and less severe child hospitalizations, improved child-rearing attitudes, and more supportive home environments for the children's development (Kitzman et al., 1997). Thus, the program has significantly demonstrated that its effects are potentially transferable to other community contexts. The program is presently being disseminated across the state of Oklahoma and in a select number of communities across the United States (Olds, Hill, et al., 1998).

initial findings, a subsequent follow-up when the children were 15 years old reported a reintroduction of discernable and significant program effects on the reduction of child abuse and neglect reports. This 15-year follow-up also discerned that home-visited, unmarried, low socioeconomic status mothers had fewer subsequent births spaced further apart, relied on public assistance for a shorter length of time, reported fewer problems with substance or alcohol abuse, and had less criminal involvement than control group mothers (Olds, Eckenrode, et al., 1997). In addition, the children of home-visited mothers showed a host of significant reductions in behavior problems thought to be consequences of child maltreatment in comparison to control group children. For example, compared to control group children, home-visited children had fewer incidents of running away, fewer arrests, fewer criminal convictions, fewer lifetime sex partners, and lessened involvement in drugs and smoking (Olds et al., 1998). Such significant findings 15 years after the initiation of perinatal home visitation services were and continue to be pivotal in propelling early home visitation services forward as a hopeful solution to the problem of child maltreatment and its consequences.

The Elmira study and the subsequent study in Memphis, Tennessee, were further complemented throughout the late 1980s by an increasing array of other well-executed scientific reports on other early home visitation services, many of which specifically targeted child maltreatment reduction (e.g., Barth, 1991; Barth, Hacking, & Ash, 1988; Caruso, 1989; Dawson et al., 1990; Hardy & Streett, 1989; Infante-Rivard et al., 1989; Infant Health and Development Program, 1990; Seitz, Rosenbaum, & Apfel, 1985; Taylor & Beauchamp, 1988). These efforts provided an ever-expanding knowledge infrastructure guiding evidence-based advancement in early home visitation services to prevent child maltreatment (see Chapters 4 and 5 of this volume; Guterman, 1997a, 1999).

Given the expanding evidence base in home visitation services and the increasingly recognized dire state of child protection in America, the U.S. Advisory Board on Child Abuse and Neglect issued a report in 1991 recommending "the replacement of the existing child protection system with a new, national, child-centered, neighborhood-based child protection strategy" (p. ix). Within this approach, the Board singled out as its most important recommendation the immediate phasing in of "universal voluntary neonatal home visitation system" of services (U.S. Advisory Board on Child Abuse and Neglect, 1991, p. xlvii). This recommendation was unanimously supported by all 15 Board members as home visitation services were viewed as one of the most hopeful new strategies to stem the tide of maltreatment. The Board emphasized that "complex problems like child maltreatment do not have simple solutions. While *not a panacea,* the Board believes that *no other single intervention* has the promise that home visitation has" (U.S. Advisory Board on Child

Abuse and Neglect, 1991, p. xvii). Such a recommendation served to undergird perhaps the largest-scale and boldest efforts to advance early home visitation services across the United States.

Initiation of Healthy Families America

The agenda of the National Committee to Prevent Child Abuse (now Prevent Child Abuse America or PCAA), established in 1972 by Donna Stone and directed in the early years by Ann Cohn, had long been to support the development of comprehensive child abuse prevention services across the United States. PCAA's early work included the convening of several research conferences aimed at identifying and promoting promising prevention strategies, and included among these were home visitor "perinatal support programs" (Cohn, 1982). On the heels of the U.S. Advisory Board's recommendation, the PCAA launched a national initiative to promote the development of early home visitation programs in communities across the country.

In the Hawaii Healthy Start program, the PCAA found a fitting model from which to advance the development of such programs in communities across the United States. The Healthy Start model had been the most comprehensively disseminated program at a statewide level (PCAA, undated), proving it to be an approach that could "go to scale," expanding from a program to a statewide system of services. Furthermore, the Healthy Start model matched the PCAA's view that child abuse stems from a complex and diverse set of causes, and thus the ideal programmatic approach would be one that served to build on and coordinate existing community supports and services, individualizing services in ways that matched families' unique needs. In this way, the Healthy Start model was viewed as a linchpin program around which other community-based family supports could be orchestrated at the case level (Daro & Harding, 1999; Daro & Winje, 1998; Mitchel & Cohn Donnelly, 1993). As stated by Daro and Winje (1998), the initiative sought to "create and sustain a community-based system of support for all new parents such that they [would] have the resources they need to care for their children" (p. 1). Furthermore, the early positive, although informally executed evaluation reports of the Hawaii Healthy Start program made the model an attractive one to adopt for a national dissemination strategy.

After receiving large-scale funding from the Ronald McDonald Children's Charities, the PCAA launched its initiative in January 1992. The initiative advanced rapidly in its initial years. In its first-year progress report, the Healthy Families America initiative reported 46 states were planning or developing new services (Healthy Families America, 1993). Daro and Winje (1998) reported that about a dozen new sites per year were identifiable in 1991 and 1992; by 1995 and 1996, there were over 70 new sites a year. In 1999, 330 programs linked with the Healthy Families America initiative were in operation, representing an almost 20-fold increase in the number of programs over the 7-year period from 1992 to 1999 (Daro & Winje, 1998; Prevent Child Abuse America, 1999). Such rapid advancement in the number of Healthy Families America sites shows the great interest that home visitation approaches have generated among funders and legislators willing to support pilot and statewide efforts. Indeed, Daro and Winje (1998) identified at least 14 states that have initiated broad legislative efforts to expand the availability of such services throughout their respective states.

The Healthy Families America initiative clearly succeeded in generating early momentum toward the U.S. Advisory Board's ultimate goal of developing a nationwide system of neonatal home visitation services. Annual national surveys conducted by PCAA have shown that, in just the last few years, an increasing proportion of families with very young children have reported receiving home visitation services (Daro, 1999). As depicted in Figure 3.1, about 1 in 3 families surveyed in 1999 had received such services, up from about 1 in 14 surveyed in 1992.

The recent rapid expansion of early home visitation services has posed a dilemma in sustaining the movement's momentum (Daro & Winje, 1998). A variety of early home visitation programs targeting child maltreatment prevention are now being tested on a large-scale basis in multiple sites across the United States, so that the experience of such programs can now be more carefully weighed and considered. For example, in a synthesis of multiple available Healthy Families America program evaluations across a wide variety of contexts, Daro and Harding (1999) offer a more nuanced and cautious assessment of the impact of this model of home visitation on family outcomes, highlighting that services appear to be most noticeably linked with promoting appropriate parent-child interactions and parenting capacity. At the same time, they note that Healthy Families America sites have not been able to clearly demonstrate benefits due to home visitation in families' social supports, child developmental outcomes, and official reports of child maltreatment. Furthermore, available evaluation data from programs under the Healthy Families America umbrella have raised important questions

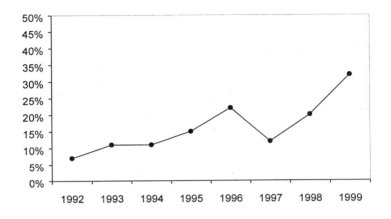

Figure 3.1. Percentage of U.S. Families With Children Under 1 Year Old Reporting Receipt of Home Visitation Services
SOURCE: Data from Daro (1999).

about participant engagement and retention through the course of services (e.g., Duggan et al., 1999).

These more nuanced and fine-grained trends reflect the most recent generation of well-controlled outcome evaluations appearing in the literature. A special issue of *The Future of Children* in 1999, for example, reports findings from a selection of the most widely disseminated and well-funded early home visitation programs in the United States. Included among these is an evaluation of the Parents as Teachers program, which aims to prepare children to succeed in school and to enhance parenting competence (Wagner & Clayton, 1999). Also included in this issue was a summary evaluation of the Comprehensive Child Development Program, reporting few positive effects as a result of this broad-based case management and home visitation program targeting enhanced physical, social, emotional, and intellectual development of children in low income families (St. Pierre & Layzer, 1999). Also notable in this more recent generation of evaluations of home visitation services are findings reported on the Infant Heath and Development Program, a home-visiting educational intervention aimed at reducing developmental delays in low-birth-weight premature infants (e.g., Bradley et al.,

1994; Brooks-Gunn, Klebanov, & Liaw, 1995; McCarton et al., 1997; McCormick, McCarton, Brooks-Gunn, Belt, & Gross, 1998). Although these programs were not explicitly designed to prevent child maltreatment (unlike the Healthy Families America initiative), the generally mixed findings reported on improvements in the quality of parenting across these studies continue to provoke significant questions for the field about optimal intervention design, the fit between program services and family needs, and the quality of program implementation in practice (e.g., Gomby et al., 1999), placing the future of home visitation services at a crossroads.

Chapter 4

INSIDE EARLY HOME VISITATION
Core Elements of Service

Angela is a 19-year-old African American woman who is 7 months pregnant and lives with her boyfriend in public housing. During a prenatal visit to the local public health clinic, a worker tells her about a program of services that will provide a visitor to her home who can assist with parenting matters and with accessing needed supports for her and the baby. Angela asks if the home visitor can assist her in getting food stamps and Medicaid for the baby. The clinic worker tells her that she can help with these as well as other concerns, such as learning about breast-feeding, helping her think about child care options, or even helping her with housing. After learning about the program, Angela agrees to enroll and completes the necessary paperwork. A home visitor makes her first home visit shortly before Angela's due date. The home visitor notes that Angela is living in a tidy four-room sparsely furnished apartment with six other adults and two children. After they sit down in the kitchen, Angela begins to tell her home visitor that she'd like to move out soon, not only because of the crowded living conditions but because she is aware of drug dealing in the building. She relays a story concerning an argument her boyfriend was involved in with one of the dealers in the building. After the second meeting, the home visitor and Angela agree to focus on improving Angela's housing situation, assist her in enrolling her child in Medicaid, and work with her to help her understand the transitions she will experience during the upcoming birth of her first child and shortly after.

Early home visitation programs include a diversity of models, approaches, and service activities. However, all share the simple yet unique notion that providing services to families in their homes holds many significant advantages over providing services in professional settings. What are the unique advantages of early home visitation? Are these home visitation strategies that can be pinpointed as those responsible for meaningfully reducing child maltreatment risk? Are there other identifiable strategies which help explain why some home visitation programs have failed to report noticeable risk reduction? The wide variety of reported home visitation approaches for families at risk of child maltreatment shows common core elements, and, at the same time, a number of critical junctures where programs often diverge. Such diversity can bewilder those searching for ideal home visitation program and practice strategies. However, variations found across carefully studied programs provide the opportunity to compare differing strategies with their reported outcomes, thereby helping to distinguish empirically supported best practices in the field of home visitation. The present chapter examines the rationale for early home visitation services, the common elements of home visitation services as they are currently designed across program types, and elements that vary across programs. As to these variations across programs, this chapter will weight the empirical base to identify evidence-based best practice principles—that is, those home visitation strategies receiving the most favorable empirical support in reducing child maltreatment risk.

HOME VISITATION AS A
PRIMARY VENUE FOR SERVICE DELIVERY

Rather than asking families to come to a site where professional helpers are centrally located—often in staff teams and supported with technologies, information, and the accoutrements of the professional office—

home visitors reach out and enter the homes of families, both literally and figuratively. Home visitation services, by their design, thus embody an ecological approach to the problem of child maltreatment by acknowledging the importance of delivering services within, rather than divorced from, the ecological contexts in which parenting and family life transpire.

Why provide services in families' homes? Simultaneously, there are obvious advantages and unusual dilemmas presented by a home visitation service model. Children do not grow up in professional offices, and parents do very little of their parenting in the formalized settings within which professionals work. It is, therefore, eminently sensible to serve families in the settings where children develop and parents rear their children. Particularly given that services are aimed at improving the parenting process, home visitation services are able to access and therefore work most directly with the "stuff" of parenting.

Providing services in the home can help to reduce many of the commonly identified barriers that often accompany agency-based service provision, such as geographic distance, difficulties with transportation, money, time, and physical impairments that may hinder travel to an office setting (Wasik et al., 1990). Furthermore, when services are provided in their home, a family's fears about the unknown, differences across professional and cultural boundaries, and a reluctance to engage with traditional social or health care services may more easily recede into the background. Families receive services in their own context, among people and scenes familiar to them.

Workers providing professional services in the office have often struggled to overcome barriers to engage and service families of a variety of backgrounds, particularly families of color. In addition, studies have reported especially high rates of underuse by high-risk families (e.g., Griffin, Cicchetti, & Leaf, 1993; Sussman, Robins, & Earls, 1987). Preventive parenting-education programs provided in professional centers have reported failure to engage families beyond a first session at rates ranging from 28% to 40%, even when programs use intensive recruitment and engagement procedures (Barth, Ash, & Hacking, 1986; Birkel & Reppucci, 1983; Dumka, Garza, Roosa, & Stoerzinger, 1997; Firestone & Witt, 1982). Similarly, professional center-based parenting-education programs have reported attrition rates ranging from 28% to 51% through 2 to 4 months of services (Danoff, Kemper, & Sherry, 1994; Firestone & Witt, 1982; Resnick, 1985; Wolfe, Edwards, Manion, & Koverola, 1988).

By contrast, although it has been asserted that home visitation programs show "relatively low rates of engagement . . . [and] high attrition rates" (Gomby et al., 1999, p. 17), in fact, these programs report comparatively higher rates of engagement and retention than center-based programs. For example, Table 4.1 shows the reported engagement and retention rates, as well as the magnitude of observed intervention effects on child maltreatment (intervention effect sizes are discussed below) in the existing body of early home visitation outcome studies.[1] As is evident in Table 4.1, the existing early home visitation program studies have reported a median rate of accepting services through initial interviews of 77% (with a range of 71% to 92%). Programs reporting outcomes at 3 to 6 months have reported a median attrition rate of 13% at 6 months (ranging from 0% to 26%), and a median attrition rate of 15% at 12 months (with a range of 8% to 51%).

A range of home visitation studies have reported especially high rates of engagement and comparatively favorable child maltreatment-related outcomes with African American and Latino families (Dawson et al., 1990; Kitzman et al., 1997; Marcenko & Spence, 1994; Olds, 1996; Rau, Anisfeld, & Guterman, 1999; Wagner & Clayton, 1999). Such findings suggest that the vehicle of home visitation may be particularly well suited to families from ethnic groups that traditionally underuse formalized but voluntary support services, and who later face heightened chances of contending with traditional involuntary child welfare services (cf. Courtney et al., 1996).

In the home, workers can learn firsthand about family stressors and supports, patterns of relating, surrounding community resources, and even conditions of the physical environment. Whereas workers in office settings can ask parents to inform them about their struggles as parents or about home health hazards (such as lead paint or unsecured cleaning supplies), home visitors can *see* and work with such challenges immediately, as well as with indigenous supports and resources available to assist families. Clinicians emphasizing skill development have frequently highlighted the importance of training new skills *in vivo,* within the environment in which they will most often be used, so as to promote lasting skill integration and maintenance. In this way, the home can be viewed as a unique "learning laboratory" for promoting changes in parenting processes that may more likely generalize over time (e.g., Hodges & Blythe, 1992; Moreland, Schwebel, Beck, & Wells, 1982; Schaefer & Briesmeister, 1989). In short, service delivery in the home provides the immediacy and directness that work in the office lacks, as well as access to

Table 4.1

Early Home Visitation Outcome Studies, Their Reported Engagement and
Retention Rates, and Effect Sizes on Child Maltreatment Outcomes

Study Author(s) (Year)	Engagement Rate[a]	Retention Rate	Effect Size: Child Protective Services Reports[b]	Effect Size: Child Maltreatment Proxies[c]
Barkauskas (1983)		85% at 6 months[d]		0.000
Black et al. (1994)	78%[e]	72% at 18 months[e]		+0.279
Brayden et al. (1993)		88% at 24 months[d]	−4.6%	
Caruso (1989)			+7.2%	
Center on Child Abuse Prevention Research (1996)	71%[d]	83% at 6 months[e]	+1.8%	+0.006
Dawson et al. (1989, 1990)	92%[e]	73% at 12 months[d]		+0.202
Duggan et al. (1999)	76%[e]	49% at 12 months[e]	+1.0%	+0.017
Field et al. (1982)		93% at 4 months[d] 85% at 12 months[d]		+0.076
Gray et al. (1979)				
Hardy & Streett (1989)		92% at 23 months[d]	+8.3%	
IHDP (1990); Bradley et al. (1994); McCormick et al. (1998); Brooks-Gunn et al. (1995)	76%[e]	93% at 36 months[e]		+0.119
Infante-Rivard et al. (1989)	72%[e]	84% at 9 months[e]		+0.224
Kitzman et al. (1997)	88%[e]	90% at 6 months[e] 92% at 12 months[e]		+0.076

(Continued)

Table 4.1
(Continued)

Study Author(s) (Year)	Engagement Rate[a]	Retention Rate	Effect Size: Child Protective Services Reports[b]	Effect Size: Child Maltreatment Proxies[c]
Larson (1980)	78%[e]	78% at 18 months[e]		+0.207
Lealman et al. (1983)		81% at 18 months[e]	+0.4%	
Marcenko et al. (1996); Marcenko & Spence (1994)	92%[e]	90% at 12 months[d]		0.000
Olds, Henderson, Chamberlin, et al. (1986)	80%[e]	79% to 85% at 24 months[e]	+5.0%	+0.052
Olds, Henderson, Chamberlin, et al. (1986): poor unmarried teens			+15.0%	+0.338
Osofsky et al. (1988)		80% at 20 months[e]		0.000
Siegel et al. (1980)	76%[e]	74% at 4 months[e]	–3.9%	+0.007
St. Pierre & Layzer (1999)		58% at 36 months[d]		0.000
Taylor & Beauchamp (1988)	76%[e]	100% at 3 months[d]		+0.475
Wagner & Clayton (1999): Salinas		57% at 36 months[d]	–0.086	
Wagner & Clayton (1999): teens		43% at 24 months[d]		+0.060

Note: Whenever possible, engagement and retention data are reported on home-visited families only. However, most studies combined engagement and retention rates of home-visited plus control group families. Thus, they are denoted as follows: [d] data reported on home visited families only and [e] data reported on home-visited and control group families combined.

a. Engagement rate defined as percentage of families participating in a first interview after having been offered enrollment.

b. Effect sizes for child protective services reports defined as the percentage of families in the control group reported to protective services minus the percentage of families in the home-visited group reported to protective services.

c. Effect sizes for child maltreatment proxies are calculated using conventional effect size formulae as reported in Wolf (1986). Further details of effect size calculations can be found in Guterman (1999). Effect sizes are reported as Pearson's r correlation coefficients.

understanding and working directly within the world in which parents and children live and grow.

THE CHALLENGES OF
EARLY HOME VISITATION SERVICES

While providing a number of distinct advantages to the delivery of services, home visitation services also persistently face a number of challenges and limitations. Some of these limitations have been identified in explaining the mixture of reported outcomes associated with home visitation services, some positive, some neutral, and some even negative (e.g., Gomby et al., 1999; Guterman, 1997a; Olds & Kitzman, 1993).

From findings reported in Table 4.1, Figure 4.1 plots the observed impact of the array of home visitation programs studied under controlled conditions. The degree of a program's impact was determined by calculating an effect size for each study on child maltreatment-related parenting measures, summarized in Table 4.1.[2] Each single point in Figure 4.1 represents the magnitude of the observed impact of home visitation services on child maltreatment-related parenting for a single study. As Figure 4.1 shows, the degree of impact of home visitation services on child maltreatment-related parenting varies considerably across a wide variety of studied programs and served families. As is evident in this figure, a substantial number of programs (n = 7) have reported no discernable impact of home visitation services on child maltreatment-related parenting (and, indeed, one study reported a slightly negative impact). At the same time, a majority of programs studied have reported positive although generally small to modest reductions in child maltreatment-related risk. This variety of reported outcomes makes clear that the delivery of home visitation services per se will not assure a reduction in child maltreatment risk. The distribution of outcomes found across studies, thus, points out that although home visitation services hold clear potential to reduce child maltreatment risk before the fact, programs face important challenges in delivering on their promise. Given that differing programs have reported substantially differing outcomes, it is essential to examine specific program strategies and practices when considering how best to achieve positive change. A number of critical programmatic variations are scrutinized below as to their capacity to effect change within the vehicle of home visitation services.

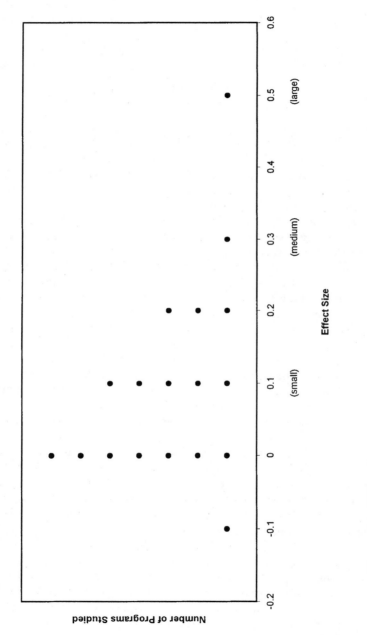

Figure 4.1. Effect Sizes of Home Visitation Programs on Child Maltreatment-Related Parenting

Home visitation services as a whole present a set of unique "on the ground" challenges requiring concerted attention if they are to yield a meaningful preventive impact. For example, by the nature of their role, home visitors leave behind the professional office and, with it, much of the formalized professional supports and structures built into health and human services settings—quick access to supervisors, offices, information, and technologies that might serve to hone interactions with family members, the authority associated with professional organizations, and the presence of supportive and skilled colleagues. In the home, workers are faced with family life "in action," striving to be of assistance as it unfolds. Because of the turf difference, home visitors must often put in place alternative structures that take the place of those within which they may be accustomed to providing services. Even such basic issues as visit scheduling, where and whom to meet during visits, and the conditions for such visits often become important matters for consideration in the course of work between home visitors and families.

PRACTICE PRINCIPLE 4.1: To effectively service families in their homes, workers must structure their work to bound and clarify their focus with families.

Home visitors must pay careful attention to clarifying their roles with the family, distinguishing their assistance from the assistance that others may provide in the home (Wasik et al., 1990). For example, special consideration must be given to the scheduling and timing of home visits, given that home life has its own rhythms and may unfold more spontaneously than life in professional work settings. Unlike professionals conducting visits in an office setting, home visitors must consider not only the schedule of the mother and infant when setting a time but also the scheduling needs of other members of the household or the family's social web. Home visits hold relatively greater opportunities for unexpected interruptions by the entrance of other household members, or pressing events that may occur during the worker's visit. Given this, home visitors must be prepared to manage such unplanned events in the course of their work.

Similarly, a variety of unique safety considerations may arise in the course of home visiting. Although families may feel more comfortable at home, home visitors may experience concerns about their own safety as they travel to unfamiliar settings, whether these be rural locations or urban neighborhoods. Thus, greater consideration and advanced planning are often required in preparation for home visitation, regarding issues such as whether to bring an escort or a cellular phone and which route may be the safest in traveling to the client's home.

Beyond the many day-to-day case-level considerations such as these, home visitation services as a field has evolved a core set of practice domains around which structured service protocols have been applied, providing focus to the work of home visitors. Here, again, programs vary substantially; yet, many programs expressly targeting child-maltreatment risk reduction overlap in their core service elements. These commonly include (a) parenting education, (b) activities to address health-related concerns, and (c) specific linkage activities for mobilizing community supports.

PARENTING CURRICULA IN THE HOME

Parent education activities are, in many ways, the backbone of home visitation services targeting child maltreatment, given that one of the central aims is to improve the parenting behaviors of those receiving services. Indeed, delivering direct parenting information and teaching parenting skills have been viewed as *sine qua non* activities for home visitation (Guterman, 1997a), especially in the face of eroding social institutions that may have once provided such guidance:

> For a first-time mother chances are good she will be very much on her own. The revolution in health care may have resulted in her being discharged from the hospital within 12 hours of delivery. Her relatives are not likely to live nearby. Because she was working and not home much, she does not know her neighbors. If she happens to be one of the growing numbers of poor in America, chances are high that she is returning to a home where she and her new baby are at-risk for a long list of threats to their safety and well-being. And, while the roles are slowly changing for the better, the father of the child, if he is present, is little more prepared or encouraged now than he has ever been for the responsibility he carries (in poor communities, there are often disincentives at work—such as a punitive welfare system). The isolation and vulnerability of new parents has become the norm. The support system has all but disappeared, and with it the myth of instinctive parenting. (Pew Charitable Trusts, 1996, p. 1)

Many educational curricula on parenting have been developed in response to broader social changes, covering a wide variety of topics.

Early home visitation programs that target child maltreatment prevention often draw from a selection of these curricula, adapting them for delivery in the home. Among the more commonly used curricula are Barnard's (1979, 1990) Nursing Child Assessment Training (NCAST), the Born to Learn curriculum of the Parents as Teachers program (Winter, 1999), Bavolek and Bavolek's (1988) Nurturing Parenting Program, the Minnesota Early Learning Design (MELD) (A. Ellwood, 1988), and the Resource Mother's Program (INMED, 1999). Each curriculum holds somewhat different emphases and outcome targets, but all seek to enhance competencies in the parenting role, particularly with respect to parent-child interactions. Educational curricula on parenting most frequently provide learning activities involving common early childhood concerns, including

- Feeding, nutrition, and weaning
- Attachment behaviors and nurturance, such as reading and responding to infant cues (e.g., crying), soothing, making eye contact, providing tactile response, and communicating verbally and nonverbally
- Safety of the home environment and infant first aid
- Babies' biological cycles of sleep, feeding, and elimination
- Normative development and milestones
- Developmentally appropriate play
- Managing such difficult challenges as sleep deprivation, physical recuperation after birth and exhaustion, and/or fussy or colicky babies
- Early discipline and limit setting

Many parenting curricula use specific skills-development exercises, whereas others employ parenting handbooks or audiovisual materials to guide the learning process. The Nurturing Parenting Programs (Bavolek, 1998), described in Practice Exemplar 4.1, are one example of a well-specified parenting curriculum expressly designed to reduce the risk of child maltreatment.

The array of available parenting curricula reflects a diversity of approaches and the interdisciplinary nature of the parenting education field. Each curriculum emphasizes somewhat differing aspects of competency development. Although the developing knowledge base on the efficacy of parenting education programs is positive (e.g., Dickie & Gerber, 1980; Dickinson & Cudaback, 1992; Field et al., 1998; Pfannenstiel & Honig, 1995), most outcome studies have examined

PRACTICE EXEMPLAR 4.1
The Nurturing Parenting Programs

The Nurturing Parenting programs developed by Stephen Bavolek and colleagues at Family Development Resources provide a well-developed set of parent education protocols for a variety of families at different stages of child development. Among the available parenting education protocols, Nurturing Parenting programs include modules for expecting families and for families with children from birth to age 5. Educational activities target the reduction of child maltreatment risk, promotion of supportive and healthy family interactions, improvement of empathy among family members, and promotion of self-esteem in family members.

The Nurturing Parenting programs have detailed session-by-session guidelines and engage parents in activities through workbooks, videotapes, and art activities. Parents are taught specific skills and knowledge concerning parenting in early childhood, such as developmental milestones, diapering, bathing, and infant massage. More generic relationship skills are also addressed in areas such as empathy, power assertion, discipline, and limit setting. Program activities are designed to help parents exercise appropriate family communication and expressiveness, build family cohesion, increase sensitivity to developmental needs, use alternatives to yelling and hitting, and learn ways to have fun as a family. Specific programs have been culturally tailored for both African American families and Latino families within a Spanish language context. Sensitive to many of the co-occurring risk conditions accompanying child maltreatment risk, specialized Nurturing Parenting programs have been developed for teen parents; for adults with learning, cognitive, or emotional difficulties; and for families in substance or alcohol abuse treatment and recovery.

Studies of the Nurturing Parenting programs have been conducted in a variety of agency contexts and have consistently reported positive gains from pretest to posttest on parenting scales, including the Bavolek's Adult-Adolescent Parenting Inventory, as well as child gains in a number of behavioral domains (Bavolek, 1998). As in the broader field of parenting education, however, further outcome study of the Nurturing Parenting programs using comparison or randomized control group designs is necessary to more clearly establish their efficacy.

parenting education modules lodged within larger programs that provide other conjoint services, varying as to their overall programmatic goals and service structure (e.g., home-based versus center-based). Thus, little is yet known about the "stand alone" efficacy of parenting curricula, making it all the more critical to consider carefully the fit between a specific parenting curriculum and a program's goals and service population (e.g., Berlin, O'Neal, & Brooks-Gunn, 1998).

The structure and prescriptiveness often found in parenting curricula have not been free from controversy, with questions raised as to the respect they accord to families' own functional yet individual or culturally based parenting styles. Normative child-rearing patterns can vary widely across and within the contexts of culture and class—for example, in ways of responding to a crying infant, feeding patterns, discipline practices, supervision, and attention to health concerns (e.g., Cazenave & Straus, 1979; Korbin, 1994). Further complicating the tasks of parenting curricula, risk and protective factors shaping child maltreatment potential, as well as the manifestations of child maltreatment itself, vary substantially across cultural contexts (e.g., Garbarino & Ebata, 1983; Leung & Carter, 1983). As such, home visitors and the parenting curricula employed in home visits must sensitively attend to normative differences in child-rearing patterns, acknowledging that such work is not only conducted inside the homes of families but also inside the cultural ecologies in which families are embedded. Home visitors must, thus, take pains to avoid promoting a view or set of parenting behaviors that are not compatible with families' own functional and culturally acceptable means of parenting.

Many home visiting programs, particularly those that employ paraprofessionals, have traditionally contended with the complexity of culturally linked variations in child-rearing practices by striving to match families with home visitors of the same ethnic background and community. This strategy aims to minimize misjudgment and the imposition of culturally inappropriate practices on families by placing the home visitor in the role of translator between the family and the program's overall aims. At the same time, the content of most parenting curricula used in home visitation programs has seldom been adapted to or derived from nondominant cultural contexts. This present reality raises significant questions about the culturally appropriate implementation of parenting curricula, given that most families receiving such services derive from nondominant cultural and class contexts. How do home visitors adapt such curricula in ways that prevent imposing white middle-class parenting beliefs on families from other backgrounds? How do home visitors educate families in ways that are congruent with messages families receive within their own cultural and class contexts? Although little attention has yet been paid to this issue, preliminary evidence suggests that cultural factors can clearly complicate service delivery. As one example of this, the following was reported by the Home Visitation 2000 study, which implemented Olds's nurse-based Prenatal/Early Infancy protocol, comparing nurses with paraprofessionals chosen from the same community as the families they served:

> Some paraprofessionals commented that the content of many of these teaching tools felt stilted and artificial and questioned whether they were in fact relevant or merely reflected middle class parenting styles. . . . The curriculum consisted of involving mothers in actively reading their babies' cues and recognizing what their children were communicating. Approximately one month into the curriculum, however, supervisors discovered that half of the paraprofessionals had not been using these materials. When asked why, the visitors stated that they had not interacted with their own babies in the structured manner suggested . . . and their children were functioning quite normally. In other words, the curriculum felt foreign and unnecessary. (Hiatt, Sampson, & Baird, 1997, p. 86)

In an effort to deploy parenting curricula that are appropriately fitted to the needs of families within their cultural contexts, a limited number of parenting curricula have been specifically adapted for major subcultural groups in the United States, for example, for Latino parents (AVANCE, Nurturing Parenting, MELD), for African American families (Nurturing Parenting), and for Hmong families (MELD). However, as the adaptation of parenting curricula across cultural contexts remains a relatively recent development, little is yet known about their cultural validity, their adaptability to intracultural variation, or their overall effectiveness.

Specialized parenting curricula have also recently been tailored to address the unique needs of parents at risk of delivering low-birth-weight babies (Resource Mothers) or parents needing specific support in developing sensitivity and responsiveness to the infant (the Partners in Parenting Education program; Butterfield, 1996). Given the increasing diversity and specialization of parenting curricula, what must be emphasized at present is the importance of adopting well-structured curricula with clear objectives and protocols, so that programs can weigh and then adapt them to fit identified family needs within a specific community niche.

PRACTICE PRINCIPLE 4.2: Early home visitation programs should adapt and/or adopt parenting educational curricula with clear objectives, structured protocols that directly address those objectives and do so in ways that are compatible with and respectful of families' own cultural and individual contexts.

The AVANCE program for Mexican American families, described in Practice Exemplar 4.2, is an example of a program that draws from established parenting theory and educational principles and has fitted specific program activities to respond to the needs of the local population served within its own cultural context.

HEALTH-RELATED ACTIVITIES IN THE HOME

A continuous focus of home visitation activities since their inception in the late 1800s has been the physical health of the mother and the infant. Activities aimed at promoting the physical health of the infant often work in tandem with those specifically aimed at preventing child maltreatment. Such activities attend to, among other concerns, the prevention of accidents and injuries in the home, improvement of overall home safety, and reduction in parents' use of psychoactive substances—all areas that are, at times, intertwined with parenting deemed as neglectful or abusive. Meta-analytic reviews have observed that the most robust and clearly demonstrable outcomes of home visitation services as a field have been those related to injury and accident prevention as well as other related medical outcomes (Guterman, 1997a; Hodnett & Roberts, 1999).

PRACTICE PRINCIPLE 4.3: Evidence suggests that home visitation programs have shown their most clearly demonstrable gains in the area of health outcomes associated with child maltreatment risk.

Programs that have included direct attention to maternal and infant health-related concerns during home visits have targeted an array of common issues around which home visitors focus their work with families. These have included

- Diet and exercise for mothers and infants
- Pregnancy and birth-related health complications

PRACTICE EXEMPLAR 4.2
The AVANCE Program

Established in 1973, the AVANCE program in San Antonio, Texas, provides family supportive services for low income Mexican American families with very young children. The program provides parent education and additional supportive services such as case management, family literacy education, child care, transportation, and advocacy, serving families both in the home and in an agency setting. The program is specifically designed to address the needs of Latino families and draws its theoretical guidance from the work of Uri Bronfenbrenner, Jean Piaget, and Burton White. A 1-year structured parenting curriculum is followed by a second year that aims to promote families' economic advancement. The weekly classes provided in a group format focus on child development and growth and include toy-making activities and speakers from the local community. Group toy-making activities provide venues for parents to share common experiences with one another. Once made, the toys give parents means to provide their children cognitive stimulation and promote their gross motor skills development. Program staff teach classes in a bilingual format and promote parents' own advancement in the English language. The program also devotes attention to common problems associated with recent immigration and draws on participants' religious traditions and celebrations. The program draws on *comadres, AVANCE* graduates who volunteer with program families to provide parenting guidance, and to reduce their isolation from other parents with young children. Also, parents volunteer to provide day care as part of a required child-care practicum, and program graduates make up the large majority of current staff at AVANCE (Rodriguez & Cortez, 1988; Walker, Rodriguez, Johnson, & Cortez, 1995).

Included as a part of AVANCE is a parent education program for fathers that emphasizes the relationship between fathering and marriage, as well as topics such as violence, stress management, and the attachment between the male parent and the child during formative years. An initial evaluation of the program that included comparison/control groups has reported comparative gains in mother-infant interaction patterns, improved overall quality of the home environment, and increases in mothers' educational status. Differences were not found on mothers' depressive symptomatology (Perez de Colon, 1999; Walker et al., 1995).

- Smoking and intake of alcohol and other drugs that affect pregnancy and parenting
- Common illnesses in early childhood and infant first aid
- Accident and poisoning prevention in the home
- Family planning and birth control
- Screening for and information about environmental toxins, for example, lead testing
- The need for well-baby care, and immunizations

In addressing these areas, home visitation programs frequently strive to coordinate supports with medical care providers in clinics and hospitals. This partnership strategy helps maintain ongoing guidance and monitoring of treatment and prevention with regard to the health-related domains of parenting. Home visitation programs deploying medical professionals, such as those that use nurses as home visitors, are especially well positioned to dispense medical information and guidance directly in the home. Nurse visitors may, for example, immediately respond to and advise families during home visits on such issues as postpartum health complications, infant first aid, or illnesses encountered in infancy. (For an example of one program's work in this area, see Practice Exemplar 4.3.)

LINKING FAMILIES
WITH COMMUNITY SUPPORTS

Home visitors are often viewed as key bridges serving to link families with needed resources and supports in the care of their children. Home visitors by themselves cannot possibly address the many concerns and challenges that families may present during the early childhood years, particularly in high-risk situations. Although home visitors may assess, for example, that families need housing, medical assistance, child care, or mental health services, it is simply not possible for home visitors to play all the varied and specialized roles that directly address such needs. Recognizing the diverse and sometimes multifaceted needs of families, home visitors commonly provide case management support, whereby they help access and coordinate ties with important community-based supports for families. Workers may conduct case management activities in diverse ways, and they typically tailor such activities on a case-by-case basis. In some circumstances, home visitors may merely provide

PRACTICE EXEMPLAR 4.3

Addressing Health Concerns
in the Prenatal/Early Infancy Program

The Prenatal/Early Infancy Program reported by David Olds
and colleagues has served as an exemplary model of early home
visitation services and includes a well-developed consideration of
health-related issues for new mothers and their infants. Beginning
before the 24th week of pregnancy, nurse visitors discuss with
women factors that influence fetal and infant development, encouraging healthy prenatal habits that promote the development of their
children. Before the third trimester of pregnancy, mothers are
taught about the physiology of pregnancy, the stages of labor and
delivery, and the ways their behavior is related to these. Topics addressed during home visits include diet and exercise, monitoring
of weight gain, eliminating the use of psychoactive substances,
and identifying signs of pregnancy complications. As women enter
their third trimester, nurse visitors begin to prepare the mother and
her support person for labor and delivery, helping them understand
the benefits of early and extended contact with the newborn. Home
visitors make sure that a pediatrician has been selected and that
supplies are gathered for the baby's arrival. As the due date nears,
nurse visitors review the common tasks necessary for physical care
of the newborn (Olds, 1982; Olds, Henderson, Chamberlin, et al.,
1986).

After birth, nurse visitors focus on assisting parents to learn
about physical care of the infant, attending to such topics as bathing, feeding, treating diaper rash, and caring for the umbilical cord.
Additional attention is given to common health problems in in-

referral information to families and later monitor a family's ongoing use
of a local service. In other circumstances, visitors may provide active
case-level advocacy, working directly with agencies when families face
difficulties accessing services themselves. As families each present a
unique set of needs, visitors must assess and prioritize each family's individual needs while maintaining a clear pulse on available local resources. For these reasons, home visitation programs often seek to hire

fancy, home and car safety, and the need for routine immunization. Mothers wishing to breast-feed their infants are also provided lactation guidance. The program has developed a detailed curriculum to address each of these topics, and nurses adapt and adjust the curriculum as needed to each family's presenting needs. In addition, nurses work closely with clinic personnel to assure timely and appropriate oversight of health concerns and serve as translators of physicians' recommendations to families.

In addition to documenting some immediate and long-term preventive effects with regard to child maltreatment in the Elmira, New York, randomized trial, as reviewed in Chapter 3 (Olds, Henderson, Tatelbaum, et al., 1986; Olds, Eckenrode, et al., 1997), the program has reported an impressive and broad array of short- and long-term improvements in health-related outcomes in families receiving home visitation services both in the Elmira, New York, and the Memphis, Tennessee, randomized trials (e.g., Kitzman et al., 1997; Olds, Henderson, Chamberlin, et al., 1986). Among these are fewer subsequent pregnancies that are spaced further apart, fewer health care encounters for which injuries or ingestions were the problem, fewer accidents and poisonings, more extensive use of nutritional supplements, greater dietary improvements, decreased cigarette smoking, and improved birth weight and length of gestation for infants of young adolescent and smoking mothers (Olds, Henderson, Chamberlin, et al., 1986; Olds et al., 1988; Olds et al., 1999). In the randomized trial conducted in Elmira, the program also reported fewer emergency room visits through the first 4 years of life, as well as fewer behavior-related impairments related to alcohol or substance use (Olds et al., 1994; Olds, Eckenrode, et al., 1997).

workers who already have intimate familiarity with a local community's network of resources and supports serving families with young children.

Programs have noted that home visitors often work with families to help manage their informal helping networks, as well. Although this is not technically a form of case management services, home visitors must also consider how best to guide families to tap their own indigenous social networks to promote family well-being. Some programs have attempted to assist families in problem-solving skills or have provided direct counseling to help them manage difficult interactions with network members (e.g., Black et al., 1994; Dawson, Van Doorninck, & Robinson, 1989; Larson, 1980). Other programs have sought to involve fathers and other extended family members in home visitation services (Olds et al., 1988; Olds, Henderson, Tatelbaum, et al., 1986) or to refer families to a project social worker or educator to address psychosocial concerns (Hardy & Streett, 1989). Still other programs have sought to address and improve informal supports by engaging families in support groups (e.g., Center on Child Abuse Prevention Research, 1996; Dawson et al., 1989; McCormick, et al., 1998).

Unfortunately, findings on the capacity of home visitation programs to improve and enhance mothers' informal supports have, on the whole, raised more questions than answers, with somewhat troubling outcomes reported (see Chapter 7). However, just as home visitors play a linchpin role with formal supports, they also hold the potential to help families improve their informal supports, which play a crucial role in shaping child maltreatment risk. As this remains an emerging issue throughout the field of home visitation, Chapter 7 will provide focused attention to forging advances in this area.

THE EFFECTIVE HOME VISITOR

Effective home visiting programs rest on services delivered by skilled home visitors. Home visitation programs have employed service professionals with a wide variety of qualities and educational backgrounds. Programs have drawn on such varied personnel as nurses, paraprofessionals, psychologists, social workers, pediatricians, nutritionists, early childhood education specialists, and trained volunteers (e.g., Black et al., 1994; Brayden et al., 1993; Gray et al., 1979; Hiatt, Michalek, Younge, Miyoshi, & Fryer, 2000; Larson, 1980; Olds, Henderson, Chamberlin, et al., 1986; Osofsky, Culp, & Ware, 1988). Many programs have opted for one primary direct service deliverer, whereas others have deployed teams of professionals to provide services directly to families. This wide variation in personnel approaches to home visitation reflects an unresolved set of questions in the field concerning the requisite knowledge, professional competencies, and skills necessary for home visitors to deliver effective services to families. Should home visitors' primary focus be placed on establishing solid relationships with families through which they can receive ongoing support during the difficult early years of parenting? Should home visitors be trained and recognized as those competent to provide health care advice and direction? Should home visitors primarily be skilled in providing technical guidance to parents about psychosocial development of infants? Should parents receiving support perceive the home visitor as someone like themselves and with whom they may more clearly identify or as someone with professional authority whom they can trust to help them chart a path over unfamiliar terrain in the early days of parenting? Clearly, each of these elements is relevant. Yet, because of the broad charge of the home visitor and perhaps due to the fact that services are provided away from any organizational niche dominated by a single profession (e.g., a hospital, or mental health, or social services organization), no clear path has yet been struck that clearly prescribes the optimal personnel arrangement for home visiting.

At this point in the field's development, this state of ambiguity has spawned an ongoing controversy surrounding the question of who should directly provide home visitation services to families. This controversy has, to date, become somewhat polarized around whether professionally trained and degree-holding nurses can provide optimal services, or rather trained paraprofessionals. No doubt, the nurses versus paraprofessionals debate has been fueled by the divergent strategies taken by the two most highly visible program models specifically targeting child maltreatment risk reduction in the United States: the Hawaii Healthy Start model, which deploys trained paraprofessionals in the home; and the Prenatal/Early Infancy Program of David Olds and colleagues, which deploys nurse practitioners in the home.

Deploying nurses as home visitors emphasizes the need for specific, professionally recognized health care skills in addition to such nonspecific factors as the capacity to form meaningful bonds with families receiving services. Also, using nurses highlights the benefits of using professionals trained to recognize the importance of following clearly specified health and behavioral regimens, as well as the benefits of employing authoritatively recognized professionals in the helping role. Using trained paraprofessionals emphasizes a somewhat "softer" approach to home visitation. This latter approach tends to place greater emphasis on the importance of the relationship of the worker to the family and on shared life experiences and backgrounds between worker and family, particularly within a broader ethnic and community context. Programs using trained paraprofessionals most often explicitly draw work-

ers from the same communities—both geographically and ethnically—
as families receiving services. Those programs using paraprofessionals
emphasize workers' personal experiential understanding of the families' life experiences within their sociocultural contexts as even more
requisite than the technical skills held by degree-holding nurses. At the
same time, paraprofessional-based programs typically provide intensive
training that aims to equip home visitors with needed on-the-job skills in
assessment, parent education, and case management, which are at the
core of work in home visitation.

A recent randomized trial conducted by David Olds and colleagues in
Denver, Colorado, has attempted to shed light on the relative efficacy of
paraprofessionals versus nurses as home visitors. Although the reported
findings in this study appear to suggest that nursing professionals may
hold some slight advantage in a limited number of areas (e.g., Korfmacher et al., 1999), such findings are difficult to interpret for the
broader field of early home visitation services for several reasons. The
Olds program was originally designed to be implemented by nurse home
visitors (e.g., Olds & Kitzman, 1993), and thus the program protocols
used in the Denver trial may have, *a priori,* formed a better fit with the
use of nurses over paraprofessionals. Thus, questions are raised about
whether the study provides a completely unbiased test, solely examining
the preferred background and training characteristics of service deliverers. Indeed, some of the research design elements as executed may have
promoted a lack of equivalence in groups. For example, substantial age
differences were found between the paraprofessional and nurse groups
(Hiatt et al., 1997). Furthermore, paraprofessionals in this study reported
discomfort with delivering the program protocol originally designed for
nurses, even making unplanned changes that resulted in significantly different emphases on home visit topics across paraprofessional and nurse
groupings (Korfmacher, 1999). Unfortunately, the paraprofessional
group in the Denver trial experienced inordinate and unplanned staff
turnover (50% in the first 2 years), raising additional questions about the
degree to which a greater disruption of relationships played a part in outcomes achieved in the paraprofessional group (Hiatt et al., 1997). With
such a substantial lack of equivalence across groups, differences found
are difficult to attribute solely to the professional status of the service
deliverers.

Raising questions about the degree to which insights from this study
are applicable to other settings, paraprofessionals used in the Denver
trial had less on-the-job training and preparedness than paraprofes-

sionals used in other programs. As noted about the Denver Trial, "in order to highlight the contrast between paraprofessional and nurse home visitors . . . [we] refrained from hiring applicants who possessed bachelors' level education" (Hiatt et al., 1997, p. 80). The paraprofessionals in the Denver trial also held no academic credentials in relevant fields such as nursing, education, psychology, or social work. These background characteristics are in contrast to those reported in studies of large-scale paraprofessional home visitation initiatives such as the Parents as Teachers program (Wagner & Clayton, 1999), representing over 2,000 sites (Winter, 1999), or Healthy Families America, representing over 330 programs using paraprofessional home visitors (Daro & Harding, 1999). For example, a recent national study of home visitors within the Healthy Families America initiative reported that 81% held bachelor's degrees or some college experience, and 10% had postgraduate training. Furthermore, the study reported that 85% had prior work experience in home visitation programs, most in the field of early childhood and child abuse and neglect and that 75% of the home visitors held specialized educational training in child development, social work, nursing, or education (Daro & Winje, 1998).

Looking at evidence beyond the Denver trial conducted by Olds and colleagues, other well-controlled studies indicate that both nurses (e.g., Black et al., 1994; Kitzman et al., 1997; Olds, Henderson, Chamberlin, et al., 1986) and paraprofessionals (e.g., Dawson et al., 1990; Hardy & Streett, 1989) can and do provide services that reduce child maltreatment risk. Even graduate students of psychology have been found to deliver services that promote positive change in parenting processes (Field, Widmayer, Greenberg, & Stoller, 1982; Larson, 1980).

PRACTICE PRINCIPLE 4.4: Programs that deploy nurses as home visitors can produce positive program effects related to child maltreatment reduction, as can those deploying trained and supervised paraprofessionals and graduates in the study of psychology. The existing empirical evidence does not clearly identify whether one of these personnel models provides advantage over another in specifically reducing child maltreatment risk.

Although it is not clear what, if any, single professional background will emerge as the credential of choice for home visitors, evidence does not appear, interestingly enough, to support personnel models using multidisciplinary teams of professionals. For instance, several approaches that have been tested have included teams with pediatricians, psychologists, nurses, social workers, and paraprofessionals. Ironically, despite the likely increased expertise and costs associated with such teams, the available studies reporting these more elaborate personnel arrangements have not been able to report observable positive outcomes related to abuse and neglect (Brayden et al., 1993; Gray et al., 1979; Marcenko & Spence, 1994; Marcenko, Spence, & Samost, 1996).

PRACTICE PRINCIPLE 4.5: Programs do not appear to increase their advantage by deploying multidisciplinary teams, either with regard to outcomes related to child maltreatment or with regard to cost efficiency.

Despite the lack of clarity about optimal personnel arrangements for home visitation staff, what appears to be at stake in considering whom to deploy as home visitors is a set of underlying critical factors shaping programs' success:

1. *The link between program and family goals and the capacities of home visitors to effect those goals.* Differing programs have used different personnel configurations as they are deemed appropriate for overall programmatic goals (Wasik & Roberts, 1994). Those programs using nurses have often explicitly included as goals the improvement of maternal and child health status, in addition to child maltreatment-risk reduction, whereas those programs that have used early childhood educators often specifically target cognitive gains for the children served. Those programs also targeting community development and capacity enhancement as a programmatic aim often hire and intensively train paraprofessionals, which secondarily serves to equip members in the local community with augmented professional experience.

2. *Home visitors' legitimacy, credibility, and acceptance.* It has been asserted that paraprofessionals face greater legitimacy challenges when they seek to enlist the cooperation of and to collaborate with other professionals who may be involved in the lives of families on their caseload (Hiatt et al., 1997). Equal or more important, it has been suggested that nurse home visitors may be more easily accepted into the home than paraprofessionals as families are more likely to perceive them as addressing physical needs as an extension of health care provided in the course of prenatal, birth, and well-baby health care (Olds et al., 1999). Conversely, it has been asserted that, in instances where the parapro-

fessional holds similar community and life experiences to the mother receiving support, greater opportunities exist for identification with the home visitor and, therefore, for more solid engagement and persuasive role modeling to take place (Wasik, 1993).

3. *The ability to engage and maintain an effective working relationship between home visitor and the family.* To serve as effective change agents within the lives of families, home visitors must first form a strong and trusting relationship with their families (Kitzman et al., 1997; Korfmacher, 1998; Wasik et al., 1990). Several authors have suggested that one of the advantages of hiring paraprofessionals from the same ethnic and/or geographic community as families receiving services is that workers and families share overlapping life experiences, which serves to lessen the social distance to be overcome in the engagement process, thereby easing the delivery of important developmental knowledge and parenting skills through the worker-family relationship (Olds, Kitzman, et al., 1997; Powell, 1993; Wasik, 1993).

Empirical evidence does not suggest that home visitors of different training backgrounds hold any noticeable comparative advantage or disadvantage in engaging or retaining families in services. Findings in Table 4.1, for example, show that home visitation programs employing nurses as home visitors have reported a median engagement rate of 78% (ranging from 72% to 88%; Black et al., 1994; Infante-Rivard et al., 1989; Kitzman et al., 1997; Olds, Henderson, Chamberlin, et al., 1986; Taylor & Beauchamp, 1988). Programs employing paraprofessionals as home visitors have similarly reported a median engagement rate of 76% (ranging from 71% to 92%; Center on Child Abuse Prevention Research, 1996; Dawson et al., 1989, 1990; Duggan et al., 1999; Infant Health and Development Program, 1990; Marcenko et al., 1996; Siegel, Bauman, Schaefer, Saunders, & Ingram, 1980). Also, nurse-based home visitation programs have reported retaining a median 83% of families in services lasting 3 to 24 months (ranging from 72% to 100%; Barkauskas, 1983; Black et al., 1994; Infante-Rivard et al., 1989; Kitzman et al., 1997; Olds, Henderson, Chamberlin, et al., 1986; Taylor & Beauchamp, 1988). Paraprofessional-based programs have similarly retained a median 81% of families in services lasting 4 to 36 months (ranging from 49% to 93%; Center on Child Abuse Prevention Research, 1996; Dawson et al, 1989, 1990; Duggan et al., 1999; Hardy & Streett, 1989; Infant Health and Development Program, 1990; Marcenko & Spence, 1994; Marcenko et al., 1996; Osofsky et al., 1988; Siegel et al., 1980; Wagner & Clayton,

1999). Given these findings, both nurses and paraprofessionals appear similarly successful in soliciting families' participation despite their differences in background and training.

   4. *The capacity and skills to attend to more specialized service challenges.* Perhaps one of the most fundamental considerations involved in the decision regarding whom to deploy as home visitors concerns the workers' capacity to handle more complicated or specialized concerns, such as diagnosing and treating less common illnesses of early childhood, giving advice on immunization scheduling, or addressing problems linked with the use of medications or abuse of substances. Such consideration has been one of the most persuasive arguments for deploying credentialed nurses rather than paraprofessionals, as the latter may require intensive on-the-job training in specialized skills that the former may already hold and be legally recognized to implement. The many and complicated risks associated with child maltreatment could pose challenges for even the best trained professionals with the highest degrees, for example, in assisting a mother to address a substance abuse problem as it affects her parenting, in attending to a pattern of problematic parent-to-child relationships that may originate several generations back, or in overcoming obstacles to accessing the essential material resources to provide basic needs for a family. As such, regardless of the training background of the home visitor, effective home visitation services rest on careful coordination and collaboration with a network of helpers.

   5. *The program's relationship to the larger community, and whether it is viewed as a community-based initiative engaging and involving community members in the operations of the program.* It has been noted that programs using paraprofessionals often serve as sources of employment and career advancement for home visitors, serving a secondary purpose of enhancing the economic and skill base of others in the community beyond targeted service recipients (Bell, Burnstein, & Orr, 1987; Rau et al., 1999).

   6. *The costs associated with differing options.* The decision to deploy paraprofessional home visitors has often been determined by their apparent cost savings over degree-holding professionals such as nurses, given comparatively higher salaries that must be paid to the latter. For example, in the Denver trial conducted by David Olds and colleagues, the average total costs for nurse home visitors was $7,681 per family and for paraprofessional home visitors, $5,178 per family (Korfmacher et al., 1999).

It has been emphasized, however, that although paraprofessionals may command lower salaries overall than professionals, they also may require more time-intensive models of supervision than professionals. Such additional requirements may somewhat diminish the anticipated cost savings of using paraprofessionals rather than nurses or other professional service providers (Harkavy & Bond, 1992; Hiatt et al., 1997; Powell, 1993; Wasik, 1993).

Although the specific degree and/or training of choice for home visitors is as yet unclear, it is largely agreed in the field, with preliminary supporting empirical evidence (Korfmacher, Kitzman, & Olds, 1998), that workers must, at a minimum, have the interpersonal capacities to promote effective relationships with families (Daro et al., 1998; Kitzman et al., 1997; Olds, Kitzman, et al., 1997; Wasik et al., 1990). It is equally clear that workers' educational background, skills, and training are all likely important in the degree of fit they form with programmatic goals and needs of families receiving services. Such considerations heighten the importance of embedding home visitation service delivery within supportive and learning organizational contexts from which home visitors can perform, problem-solve, and progressively expand their competencies to manage the difficulties of working with families struggling with multiple challenges. Supervisory and training supports appear particularly critical in this respect, helping to build on and supplement workers' own qualities and skills they bring to the role of home visitor (see Wasik, 1993).

PROGRAM DOSAGE

Another complicated but critical consideration in home visitation practice concerns the chosen dosage for program services: that is, the level of intensity of services, their length, and the timing of their initiation. Studies reporting positive outcomes on child-maltreatment risk reduction have ranged in length from 3 weeks postpartum (Taylor & Beauchamp, 1988) to 3 or 4 years of family contact (Center on Child Abuse Prevention Research, 1996). Although many longer term interventions (2 years postpartum or more) have reported positive child maltreatment-related outcomes (e.g., Bradley et al., 1994; Breakey & Pratt, 1991; Caruso, 1989; Center on Child Abuse Prevention Research, 1996; Hardy & Streett, 1989; Olds et al., 1994; Olds, Henderson,

Chamberlin, et al., 1986), others have not (Brayden et al., 1993; Osofsky et al., 1988; St. Pierre & Layzer, 1999; Wagner & Clayton, 1999). In each of the longer term programs showing little discernable impact on child maltreatment-related outcomes, home visits were delivered with relatively low frequency, on average once per month or less (except in the first month of the program reported by Osofsky et al., 1988). In comparison, programs delivering biweekly or weekly visits have typically reported positive outcomes (e.g., Black et al., 1994; Caruso, 1989; Dawson et al., 1990; Hardy & Streett, 1989). In line with this trend, findings reported by Powell and Grantham-McGregor (1989) on urban infants and toddlers in Jamaica indicated that families visited biweekly showed significant improvements in child developmental outcomes when compared with those visited monthly or those in control groups. Families that were visited monthly showed no significant differences from a control group.

Programs providing more frequent home visits have also tended to report lower overall attrition rates, suggesting that greater frequency of contact may facilitate more solid home visitor-to-family bonds and deeper family participation in services (cf. Barkauskas, 1983; Brayden et al., 1993; Field et al., 1982; Infant Health and Development Program, 1990; Kitzman et al., 1997; Larson, 1980; with the exception of Hardy & Streett, 1989). Taken together, such findings underscore the relative importance of service *intensity* over service duration (e.g., Daro & McCurdy, 1994; Guterman, 1997a; Olds & Kitzman, 1993; Ramey & Ramey, 1998), suggesting that programs may fare best when services are delivered with at least a moderate degree of intensity in visits (i.e., biweekly or weekly).

It is important to emphasize that because of the real-world exigencies associated with providing services in the homes of high-risk families, programs rarely succeed in delivering the originally planned intensity of home visits to families (e.g., Gomby et al., 1999; Korfmacher et al., 1998). As such, programs that consider the planned intensity of services over time must also take into account that real-world obstacles will likely operate to diminish the actual intensity of services offered.

PRACTICE PRINCIPLE 4.6: Programs that deliver, in practice, at least moderately intensive services—biweekly or more frequent—are linked with more favorable family participation and child maltreatment-related outcomes than those providing less intensive services. This trend holds for the frequency of services actually delivered, not for the frequency planned to be delivered.

It is important to note that some programs with relatively short duration have reported positive outcomes, underscoring that the dosage variable is a complex one (cf. Field et al., 1982; Schinke, Schilling, Barth, Gilchrist, & Maxwell, 1986; Taylor & Beauchamp, 1988). Findings reported in these studies raise the important issue of how "successful outcomes" are defined, and especially when outcomes are assessed in relation to the duration of services. For example, some short-term programs have reported positive outcomes at 3 months (Taylor & Beauchamp, 1988), whereas others have faced greater difficulty in reporting positive outcomes at later follow-up points (cf. Barth, 1991; Barth et al., 1988; Infante-Rivard et al., 1989). Similarly, Field et al.'s (1982) program lasting 6 months reported positive outcomes in parent-infant interactions at 4 months of services, which later washed out at 8 months and beyond.

The 3-year Infant Health and Development Program, in some contrast, reported no observable differences in the quality of parenting and home environment 1 year into service delivery but a noticeable intervention impact at 3 years (Bradley et al., 1994). Taken as a whole, these findings suggest that specific outcomes should be assessed at a point contiguous to the period in which services targeting such outcomes are delivered. As well, these findings and those of the Olds program reporting washout and reintroduction of child maltreatment findings at 4 and 15 years follow-up (see Chapter 3) raise the complicated issue of the appearance and washout of program effects over time. Most fundamentally, they raise important questions about the maintenance of early home visitation's preventive effects on child maltreatment over time.

PRACTICE PRINCIPLE 4.7: Both short- and long-term programs can achieve positive gains, and the observable gains appear to be linked with the time horizon by which successful outcomes are defined and assessed.

It is important to note here that longer term programs have tended to report persistent problems of increasing family attrition rates as the service duration extends (e.g., Duggan et al., 1999; Gomby et al., 1999; St. Pierre & Layzer, 1999; Wagner & Clayton, 1999). For example, the Hawaii Healthy Start program has reported a declining family participation rate over time from the point of engagement, yielding a 51% dropout at 1 year of services (Duggan et al., 1999). Given persistently deteriorating rates of family participation over time, longer term programs face the prospect of diminishing returns as their service horizon lengthens. In light of the relatively high rates of program engagement found at enrollment for home- rather than center-based services, and given that service intensity rather than program duration is most clearly linked to positive outcomes, home visitation services may fare best when they are intensive and of limited duration. Such a strategy allows for concentrating services and resources early, when families are most likely to be involved and receptive to services, rather than spreading them out over more lengthy time horizons with diminishing returns.

PRACTICE PRINCIPLE 4.8: More intensive models of limited duration appear to hold greater promise for positive outcomes, where families are more likely to be engaged and involved in services, in comparison to approaches with less intensive services and longer service horizons.

Related to this issue, the timing of service initiation has also been deemed a key variable predicting program effects, given that early parenting has been thought to pass through a sensitive period of vulnerability and opportunity prior to settling into more established patterns (George & Main, 1979; Kennell, Voos, & Klaus, 1976; Meisels, Dichtelmiller, & Liaw, 1993). Larson's (1980) study of services initiated at varying points during the perinatal transition period suggests that initiating services prenatally may provide some advantage in promoting positive outcomes. In his study, Group A mother-infant pairs, who received support starting prenatally and continuing intensively through the first weeks after birth, showed significantly better outcomes on an array of parenting indicators than Group B pairs, whose support began in the child's sixth week of life. Furthermore, the Larson study found that mother-infant pairs in Group B, although they received home-based support from 6 weeks to 15 months postpartum, showed almost no differences in outcome from a control group receiving no supports.

Although no other single study has directly replicated the findings reported by Larson (1980), findings reported across studies lend some further support to this trend. For example, a broad array of studies initiating services after birth have reported little to no positive impact on child maltreatment-related outcomes (e.g., St. Pierre & Layzer, 1999; Siegel et al., 1980; Wagner & Clayton, 1999), and several studies reporting the most robust and durable outcomes are those that initiated services prior to birth (e.g., Caruso, 1989; Dawson et al., 1989, 1990; Olds, Eckenrode, et al., 1997; Olds, Henderson, Chamberlin, et al., 1986). Furthermore, as findings in Table 4.1 indicate, programs initiating services prenatally have tended to report somewhat higher enrollment rates, with a median of 84% (ranging from 72% to 92%; e.g., Black et al., 1994; Brayden et al., 1993; Dawson et al., 1990; Infante-Rivard et al., 1989; Kitzman et al., 1997; Marcenko & Spence, 1994; Olds, Henderson, Tatelbaum, et al., 1986), in comparison to services initiated at birth, with a median of 76% (ranging from 71% to 76%; Center on Child Abuse Prevention, 1996; Duggan et al., 1999; McCormick et al., 1998; Siegel et al., 1980; Taylor & Beauchamp, 1988). Furthermore, some programs with the highest retention rates have initiated services prenatally (Kitzman et al., 1997; Marcenko et al., 1996), whereas some programs initiating services after birth have documented among the lowest retention rates in the field (e.g., Duggan et al., 1999; St. Pierre & Layzer, 1999; Wagner & Clayton, 1999). These trends, however, are not entirely uniform, and select studies initiating services after birth have also reported positive gains and still high retention rates (e.g., Hardy & Streett, 1989; Taylor & Beauchamp, 1988).

Nonintervention studies indicating the influence of prenatal parental depression and substance or alcohol abuse in shaping future attachment patterns and child developmental outcomes further underscore the importance of striving to serve families prenatally when feasible and when such risks appear present (Field et al., 1998; Zuckerman & Brown, 1993; see also Chapter 6).

PRACTICE PRINCIPLE 4.9: Prenatally initiated services are associated with more favorable engagement rates and reported outcomes. Furthermore, services initiated prenatally hold the opportunity to address significant problems that shape the *in utero* environment and that later heighten risk for both maltreatment and for a host of poor developmental outcomes.

Although the available evidence points to the advantages of initiating services prenatally, some of the comparatively positive findings reported (with the exception of Larson, 1980) may have as much to do with participant characteristics as with service characteristics. Namely, it is clearly possible that those mothers who were enrolled prenatally did so because they sought prenatal care, possibly suggesting a higher degree of motivation and willingness to engage in supportive services as compared to those enrolled postnatally. This opens an additional set of key questions and considerations, addressed in the next chapter, surrounding who receives and benefits from early home visitation services.

NOTES

1. Studies chosen for inclusion in Table 4.1 follow criteria used in previous meta-analyses of early home visitation services on child maltreatment outcomes as reported by Guterman (1997a, 1999) and are supplemented by additional studies uncovered since then (including Bradley et al., 1994; St. Pierre & Layzer, 1999; Wagner & Clayton, 1999). Criteria for inclusion include use of comparison/control groups, measurement of child maltreatment through protective services data or parenting proxies related to maltreatment, and the initiation of intervention services prior to any identified maltreatment.

2. The study effect sizes plotted in Figure 4.1 are derived from a meta-analysis of early home visitation studies reported in Guterman (1999) and extended by studies noted in Note 1. Meta-analysis is a quantitative technique that allows the calculation of a study effect size, a standardized metric of the magnitude of the observed intervention impact reported by each study. Meta-analysis facilitates the aggregation and comparison of findings across studies and programs, although the process has several caveats and limitations, as discussed relevant to home visitation in Guterman (1999). Each point in Figure 4.1 represents the effect size of a single study (reported weighted mean intervention effect) on child maltreatment-related proxy measures, rounded to the nearest tenth, according to conventional meta-analytic procedures reviewed in Guterman (1999). Measures included in reported effect sizes are those of parent-child interaction, qualities of the home environment, parenting attitudes, and child abuse potential assessed at a minimum after 4 months of age of the target child. By convention, a mean effect size (r) of .10 represents a small effect, .3 a medium effect, and .5 a large effect (Cohen, 1977). Effect sizes on child protective services reports, although not included in Figure 4.1, are found in Table 4.1 and show a similar distribution. See Figures 5.1 and 5.2 in Chapter 5, and Guterman (1999) for further attention to these reported effects throughout the field.

Chapter 5

MAKING THE CONNECTION WITH FAMILIES

Who Receives and Benefits From Home Visitation Services?

Among the most fundamental considerations for early home visitation services are those that concern the interrelated yet distinct questions of who receives services and who benefits from services. The first question concerns how home visitation programs determine whom to target and serve, as well as whom not to serve. Thus, it forms the starting point for configuring the content and focus of services to meet the needs of those families, once identified. The second question entails whether home visitation efforts will, in fact, take hold and promote risk reduction. Thus, it concerns families' own motivation to participate in home visitation services. Although families ultimately determine their own participation in home visitation services given their voluntary nature, programs must still consider such fundamental issues as how to maximize participation and minimize attrition so that families may reap intended program benefits.

AUTHOR'S NOTE: Figures 5.1 and 5.2 and selected text in this chapter have been reprinted from N. B. Guterman, "Enrollment Strategies in Early Home Visitation to Prevent Physical Child Abuse and Neglect and the 'Universal Versus Targeted' Debate: A Meta-Analysis of Population-Based and Screening-Based Programs," *Child Abuse and Neglect, 23,* 863-890. Copyright 1999. Reprinted with permission from Elsevier Science.

The first part of this chapter considers the problem of identifying families for program enrollment and focuses on the issue of screening and the appropriate targeting of services. The second part of this chapter considers the interrelated problems that programs face as they reach out to enroll, engage, and promote families' meaningful participation in ways that ultimately lead to preventive benefits.

WHO RECEIVES SERVICES?
IDENTIFYING FAMILIES AND THE
"UNIVERSAL VERSUS TARGETED" DEBATE

Early home visitation practices are most immediately shaped by the presenting needs of families enrolled for services. Given this, the question of program enrollment in a most fundamental way drives the design of home visitation services by determining the character of families who will be served by a program. Only after enrollment parameters identify a population to be served does a program consider the best fit between needs and services. Given the prefatory nature of the question of whom to serve, on what basis should programs decide to segment the population for services? Within community settings, how can programs most appropriately identify families who should receive early home visitation services?

The question of whom to serve in early home visitation holds broad clinical and cost implications and has thus emerged as a public policy issue framed in the form of "universal versus targeted" early home visitation services (Krugman, 1993). At the policy level, the term *targeting* of services has connoted using risk criteria for enrollment in order to focus efforts on those families deemed most in need of services. In contrast, the term *universal* early home visitation services has connoted offering services widely to all families, without employing identifiable eligibility criteria. In the universal versus targeted debate, those who support universal services address the strategic question of whom to serve simply by aiming to reach and serve *all* families giving birth within any given community niche.

Underlying the policy debate are long-standing values differences in U.S. political culture about the "deservingness" of troubled families to receive publicly supported services and the state's responsibilities vis-à-vis parents' own private responsibilities in the rearing of children. Most overtly raised in the debate, however, are concerns over the cost-effectiveness of early home visitation services and the strategic deployment of scarce resources to those deemed in need. Some, for example, have asserted that targeting services may serve to deploy scarce resources in an optimally cost-effective way by reserving resources for those most in need (Daro & McCurdy, 1994; Wekerle & Wolfe, 1993). From this viewpoint, it has been argued that because only a small proportion of families will, in fact, ever maltreat their children, reserving scarce resources for only those families most at risk should allow for the provision of more intensive and concentrated efforts to those most in need. It has been argued that targeting of early home visitation services thus prevents the "watering down" of limited resources entailed in providing universal services to far larger groups of recipients, regardless of risk (e.g., Daro & McCurdy, 1994).

In counterpoint, it has been argued that screening only high-risk families into services categorizes families into those deemed not at risk of maltreatment and those carrying the socially stigmatizing label of "high-risk parents" or "potential child abusers." It is also argued that risk assessment systems will inevitably misclassify a significant number of families in a stigmatizing way. Advocates of universal approaches warn that targeting services not only encourages families' own self-consciousness regarding their high-risk label but also facilitates public blaming and stigmatizing of families receiving services, much as "welfare mothers" were stigmatized in the formerly titled Aid to Families With Dependent Children (AFDC) program in the United States. Indeed, the recent dismantling of such categorical programs as AFDC has suggested to those arguing for a universal approach that when services are provided only to at-risk populations, the long-term political sustainability of such programs is undermined, as they set aside scarce public money for highly unpopular "special" groups. Thus, the argument against a targeted approach emphasizes that targeting will facilitate a withdrawal of public support and resources in retrogressive political and fiscal climates. Largely for these reasons, the U.S. Advisory Board on Child Abuse and Neglect adopted a recommendation in 1990 that the federal government initiate the development of a universal approach rather than a targeted one with respect to early home visitation services. Summarizing the Board's position, Krugman (1993) noted,

> A universal approach avoids stigmatization. There was feeling by some Board members that, unless home visiting was perceived by the public as "mainstream, necessary and for everyone," it would fail. In fact, several

hundred home visitor programs to prevent child abuse were federally
funded in the late 1970s. Nearly all died after the 1981-82 budget reductions. Many Board members perceived this history as evidence that, unlike
Head Start, programs for those at risk of physical abuse were not considered mainstream and, therefore, were not worthy of funding. Further, the
Board expected that a universal program could still target some subgroups
for special focus and more intensive service. (p. 187)

Despite the Board's policy recommendation in 1990, disagreements
remain on universal versus targeting policy for early home visitation
services, and these disputes have been reflected at the service level in a
complex way. Actual enrollment strategies in programs have rarely represented purely universal or targeted approaches. Some early home
visitation programs have not included any active risk-screening efforts
or criteria, yet most have enrolled participants within community niches
or agency contexts where the population is characterized by demographically based risks, such as low socioeconomic status or high rates of single or teen parenthood (Caruso, 1989; Dawson et al., 1989, 1990; Field
et al., 1982; Hardy & Streett, 1989). In a sense, such programs, while seg-
menting services based on their location in high-risk settings, also hold
universal properties because they reach out to serve entire subpopulations. Other programs have included some deliberate eligibility requirements but only according to demographically based parameters, such as
teen parenthood or primiparity status rather than according to an individual psychosocial risk profile (Infante-Rivard et al., 1989; Larson, 1980;
Olds, Henderson, Chamberlin, et al., 1986; Wagner & Clayton, 1999).
This strategy can be viewed as aiming to serve entire populations or
subpopulations of families, as it does not employ active screening criteria at the individual level.

In contrast to these population-based strategies, other programs have
actively screened families living in a variety of community niches (both
high-risk and not) by employing individual risk-assessment tools, such
as checklists, that combine demographic markers with the presence or
absence of individual psychosocial problems deemed to heighten risk,
such as substance abuse, mental illness, history of incarceration, or
unwanted pregnancy (e.g., Black et al., 1994; Lealman et al., 1983;
Marcenko & Spence, 1994; Marcenko et al., 1996). Even more intensively, some programs have actively screened subjects according to specific high-risk psychosocial profiles, using detailed individual psychosocial inventories (e.g., Brayden et al., 1993; Center on Child Abuse

Prevention Research, 1996; Duggan et al., 1999; Gray et al., 1979). Programs using these latter two strategies, in contrast to those that enroll on the basis of population-based factors alone, actively screen larger populations for specific cases, most clearly targeting on the basis of individual factors deemed to heighten risk.

Although each of these four strategies carries some face valid rationale for enrollment, it is essential to consider what programmatic effects such strategies may have and, in particular, what role they may play in promoting positive outcomes in families once enrolled. A recent meta-analytic study of the existing body of early home visitation studies compared the latter two screening-based enrollment strategies to the former two population-based strategies on their reported outcomes. The findings from this study indicate that whereas both types of programs show similar rates of family engagement and retention, programs employing population-based enrollment, on the whole, report more robust outcomes in child maltreatment risk reduction (see Figures 5. 1 and 5.2; Guterman, 1999). Indeed, child maltreatment-related outcomes reported by screening-based programs were, in the aggregate, almost negligible, whereas population-based programs reported clinically meaningful reductions in child maltreatment reports and associated improvements in parenting behavior. As such, it would appear that program enrollment strategies have consequences not only for who will be served by home visitation but also for the degree to which programs are able to promote gains in families once enrolled.

PRACTICE PRINCIPLE 5.1: Programs that employ population- or demographically based criteria for enrollment appear to hold an advantage in child maltreatment-related risk reduction over programs that actively screen for psychosocial risk at the individual level.

Why should the enrollment practices adopted by early home visitation programs have an impact on outcomes when enrollment procedures are not in and of themselves change strategies? Should not the promotion of positive outcomes be attributable to the nature of the supportive services rather than the way families are identified to receive services? What might be the connection between enrollment practices and the capacity of programs to create positive change? There are several interrelated reasons why population-based enrollment strategies are linked with clinically effective services whereas individual screening-based strategies are not.

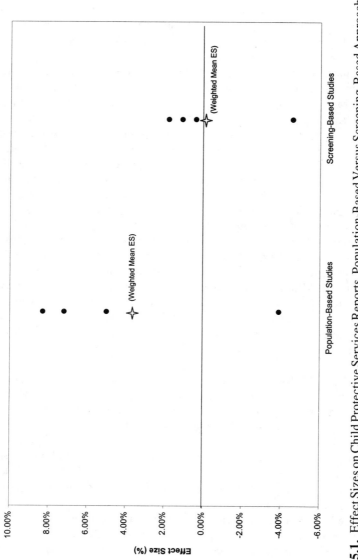

Figure 5.1. Effect Sizes on Child Protective Services Reports, Population-Based Versus Screening-Based Approaches

SOURCE: Reprinted from *Child Abuse and Neglect*, 23, N. B. Guterman, "Enrollment Strategies in Early Home Visitation to Prevent Physical Child Abuse and Neglect and the 'Universal Versus Targeted' Debate: A Meta-Analysis of Population-Based and Screening-Based Programs," pp. 863-890. Copyright 1999, with permission from Elsevier Science.

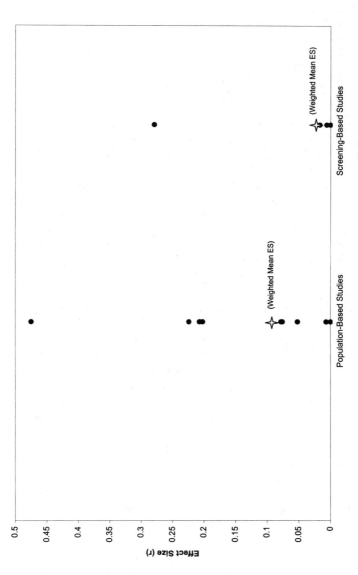

Figure 5.2. Effect Sizes on Maltreatment Proxies, Population-Based Versus Screening-Based Approaches

SOURCE: Reprinted From *Child Abuse And Neglect*, 23, N. B. Guterman, "Enrollment Strategies in Early Home Visitation to Prevent Physical Child Abuse and Neglect and the 'Universal Versus Targeted' Debate: A Meta-Analysis of Population-Based and Screening-Based Programs," pp. 863-890. Copyright 1999, with permission from Elsevier Science.

SCREENING PROBLEMS AND THE
MATCH BETWEEN HOME VISITATION
AND ENROLLED FAMILIES' NEEDS

Although risk screening at the individual level may be the preferred method to identify families for early intervention services targeting other problems such as developmental or cognitive delays (e.g., Meisels & Wasik, 1990), screening to identify specific families for early child maltreatment prevention services presents a number of problems. Although empirical knowledge has increasingly identified risk factors correlated with child maltreatment, psychosocial risk screens for the problem of child maltreatment hold questionable predictive accuracy in identifying future maltreatment (Browne & Saqi, 1988; Caldwell et al., 1988; Korfmacher, 2000; Leventhal, 1988; Lyons et al., 1996; McCurdy, 1995; Rodwell & Chambers, 1989) and, therefore, may screen in families with low propensity to maltreat and for which services will not lead to further risk reduction. For example, child maltreatment risk screens applied in child protection settings have persistently reported high false-positive rates (incorrectly identifying future nonmaltreating families as high risk) and false-negative rates (incorrectly identifying future maltreating families as not high risk; Lyons et al., 1996). Risk-assessment instrumentation specifically applied during the perinatal phase has also reported high rates of inaccuracy, variously reporting false-positive rates ranging from 48% to 89.4% and false-negative rates of 1% to 3% (Altemeier et al., 1979; Lealman et al., 1983; Murphy, Orkow, & Nicola, 1985). The unusually high false-positive rates reported in perinatal risk screens are particularly troublesome for early home visitation services because high proportions of families screened positive for services will, in fact, never maltreat their children. Simply put, screening-based programs face difficulty in demonstrating they are preventing maltreatment when the majority of families identified as high risk will never maltreat their children, with or without services.

Furthermore, several studies have reported that the predictive accuracy of maltreatment risk screens appears to decline over time (Altemeier et al., 1984; Daro et al., 1998), whereas the predictive accuracy of demographic factors in relation to maltreatment may actually increase over time (Daro et al., 1998). Such findings suggest that psychosocial risk screens conducted at a single point near birth may tap family variables related to maltreatment that are less stable and change over time (for example, life stressors, social supports, or attitudes toward the

infant), in comparison to demographic realities such as family impoverishment and single or young parenthood status. It is also important to
emphasize that the available risk-profiling screens employed in early
home visitation services have largely been designed to predict physical
child abuse rather than physical child neglect (cf. Altemeier et al., 1984;
Murphy et al., 1985), despite the fact that child neglect is a more prevalent problem and one more closely associated with demographic realities
such as economic impoverishment (Children's Bureau, 1998; Sedlak &
Broadhurst, 1996). Thus, home visitation programs screening for psychosocial risk, in contrast to those that report no active screening (or
those that base eligibility on demographic risks), may face greater difficulty in demonstrating positive change overall, given that they may pro-
portionately serve greater numbers of families with less stable and, in
some cases, descending risk, over time.

As pointed out in Chapter 3, the problem of predictive validity for risk
screens is a persistent one, given that child maltreatment is a low base-
rate phenomenon, occurring with relative infrequency in the broader
population at large. Attempts to accurately predict a low base-rate problem like child maltreatment inevitably lead to misclassifying high proportions of parents as potential child abusers. Such parents, therefore,
will be improperly enrolled in screening-based home visitation programs, given that many would never maltreat their children in the first
place (cf. Caldwell et al., 1988; Kaufman & Zigler, 1992).

Perhaps the most fundamental difficulty with psychosocial screening
is that it may inadvertently serve to exacerbate a mismatch between programmatic services and the presenting needs of families enrolled for
service. Early home visitation services on the whole target problematic
parenting and the need to mobilize necessary supports on behalf of families. At the same time, early home visitation programs have rarely reported implementing specific service protocols addressing a number of
the problems that commonly appear on risk screens serving as positive
identifiers for enrollment into home visitation services. For example,
screening programs often identify substance abuse as a risk factor for
program enrollment (e.g., Black et al., 1994; Center on Child Abuse Prevention Research, 1996; Duggan et al., 1999; Marcenko & Spence, 1994;
Marcenko et al., 1996). At the same time, programs rarely report program protocols or intervention strategies that explicitly address the inter-
linked problems of substance or alcohol abuse and child maltreatment
(including Black et al., 1994, which intervened exclusively with substance-abusing mothers). Similarly, domestic violence between partners

has been reported as a frequently co-morbid condition in child mal-treatment cases (McKay, 1994; Milner & Gold, 1986), and indeed, a number of screening-based approaches identify domestic violence as a risk factor for program enrollment (Center on Child Abuse Preven-tion Research, 1996; Duggan et al., 1999; Marcenko & Spence, 1994). Again, however, home visitation programs rarely report specialized service protocols to address the co-occurring risks of domestic violence and child maltreatment. Home visitation programs most often address such problems through referral activities and coordination with other service providers. However, it remains questionable whether referral and coordination with other community agencies can adequately address such problems so intimately intertwined with parenting difficulties and maltreatment risk.

The use of psychosocial screening to identify a target pool of service recipients in a cost-effective way may, thus, ironically yield a pool of enrolled families that home visitation services are not yet adequately equipped to handle. Several key areas of service need that have not yet been well addressed in the existing home visitation program protocols are considered in the next three chapters. For example, Chapter 6 consid-ers means of expanding home visitation services in ways that attend to substance abuse concerns, given persistent findings linking child mal-treatment risk with substance abuse. Chapters 7 and 8 consider means of augmenting early home visitation services to more fully and systemati-cally address social ecological influences, such as domestic violence, social isolation, and parental disempowerment as they potently shape maltreatment risk.

In sum, individualized psychosocial risk screening in home visitation programs that target child maltreatment raises concerns and does not appear warranted for several key reasons:

- Psychosocial risk screens show persistently poor accuracy in identifying families at risk for future child maltreatment.
- Programs using psychosocial risk screens show comparatively poorer out-comes than those not using such screens.
- Psychosocial risk screens may exacerbate a mismatch between the needs of families enrolled for services and the present service capacities of early home visitation programs.
- Psychosocial risk screening may engender heightened stigma in families labeled "high risk" and enrolled for services.
- Psychosocial risk screening activities involve additional monetary costs.

In the face of cost constraints, programs must still strive to segment larger populations for services efficiently and effectively. Given this, employing demographically based eligibility criteria such as single- or teen-parent status may most appropriately optimize programs' capacity to promote change. As the majority of programs reporting the most positive outcomes have employed only demographically based enrollment criteria or have targeted services to high-risk community niches, the following alternative practice principle appears presently warranted:

PRACTICE PRINCIPLE 5.2: Programs may best define service populations by opting for demographically based criteria for enrollment, particularly those that may indicate heightened responsiveness of services to families' needs.

In this regard, it is important to highlight that some demographic characteristics appear linked with heightened responsiveness to services. For example, almost all programs that have served teen parents or that have examined subgroup findings on teen parents have reported significant and/or comparatively greater program effects on child-maltreatment risk reduction for this subpopulation (Caruso, 1989; Dawson et al., 1989, 1990; Field et al., 1982; Olds, Henderson, Chamberlin, et al., 1986; with the exception of Osofsky et al., 1988). At the same time, it should be noted that whereas some studies also note higher participation rates by younger parents (e.g., Herzog, Cherniss, & Menzel, 1986; Olds & Kitzman, 1993), other studies have reported less favorable participation by younger mothers (e.g., Josten, Mullett, Savik, Campbell, & Vincent, 1995; Wagner & Clayton, 1999). Such findings underscore that programs must carefully consider service contents and the fit they form with the unique needs of groups targeted for services.

Similarly, the majority of programs that have served only or predominantly primiparous (first-time) parents have, on the whole, also noted comparatively larger programmatic effects than those serving multiparous parents (e.g., Dawson et al., 1989, 1990; Kitzman et al., 1997; Olds, Henderson, Chamberlin, et al., 1986; Taylor & Beauchamp, 1988; with the exception of Barkauskas, 1983). It remains unclear whether primiparity status itself or some other variable (such as younger age) accounts for this comparatively favorable trend in the empirical findings. Olds et al. (1999) have suggested that, given their lack of experience as parents, primiparous mothers may hold a heightened sense of vulnerability and, therefore, greater receptivity and responsiveness to services.

Furthermore, intervening with a first child may hold the potential to alter parenting practices with subsequent children. Also, evidence from Olds, Henderson, Chamberlin, et al. (1986) indicates that such services can positively influence family planning for subsequent child-bearing, holding additional benefits for later family well-being. The comparatively greater service gains observed in teen and primiparous parents, along with the evidence pointing out the benefits of initiating services prenatally (reviewed in Chapter 4), suggests that in multiple ways, the earlier the intervention, the better. That is, it appears favorable not only to intervene earlier in the life of the mother and earlier in the life of the child but also to target services early in the family's life cycle.

PRACTICE PRINCIPLE 5.3: Demographically targeting and serving less experienced and younger parents may promote more favorable outcomes than intervening with more experienced and older parents.

At present, in the face of scarce resources, programs may best succeed by using no active screens when they are lodged in community niches holding high proportions of subpopulations (such as teen or primiparous parents) most likely to benefit from services or when enrolling families only on the basis of such demographic factors. Once families are enrolled, service content and intensity may then be calibrated to fit their individual presenting risk profiles and needs (Krugman, 1993; Wekerle & Wolfe, 1993).

What emerges from this broad set of findings linking family characteristics with outcomes is that decision making about how best to identify families for services must be seamlessly integrated with the decision making guiding the fit of services to families' needs, once enrolled. The findings on screening-based programs and the overall small effect sizes found across the field of early home visitation services suggest that the field can further progress in its integration between enrollment strategies and service strategies, targeting subpopulations for enrollment that will benefit from services and then targeting services to the specific needs of the subpopulations identified. This emphasizes the comparative and critical importance of thorough clinical assessment over risk assessment to promote an optimal fit between service provision and family needs.

PRACTICE PRINCIPLE 5.4: Early home visitation services must strive to conduct thorough clinical assessments, not for enrollment decision-making purposes but rather for tailoring service goals and activities to meet the unique needs of individual families enrolled for services. Such assessments should systematically include consideration of major etiological influences in maltreatment risk, including substance abuse, domestic violence, mothers' own history of personal victimization, and mental illnesses such as parental depression.

WHO BENEFITS FROM SERVICES? FAMILIES' PARTICIPATION IN HOME VISITATION

The match between services and the presenting needs of families clearly plays an influential role in families' own degree of participation in early home visitation services. To the degree that families perceive services as irrelevant or unresponsive to their needs, they are likely to be less motivated to participate in home visitation services. Without a family's active engagement and participation in services, intervention content, no matter how well conceptualized, is not likely to take hold and benefit families in the ways intended (Korfmacher, Kitzman, & Olds, 1998; Liaw, Meisels, & Brooks-Gunn, 1995; Ramey & Ramey, 1992).

Family participation has traditionally been conceived as consisting of two components, namely, their *engagement* and *retention* through the life of the program. In fact, home visitation services must address family involvement through a series of phases, striving to fit services to the needs of families from a point prior to the initial contact with families all the way through to the conclusion of services. Scholars in the field have only recently begun to move beyond simply assessing global engagement and retention rates to considering a series of stages and degrees of participation in home visitation services (Berlin, O'Neal, & Brooks-Gunn, 1998; Korfmacher et al., 1998; Ramey & Ramey, 1992).

Programs must address an evolving set of concerns related to family needs at a variety of points in time through their service duration, considering the best fit between services and family needs throughout this series of phases. These phases and service tasks associated with family participation in early home visitation services include:

- Identifying an eligible target group (as discussed earlier)
- Receiving referrals, recruiting, and reaching out to families
- Securing a family's agreement to participate in services

- Engaging a family in identifying service goals and reaching an agreed-on service plan
- Maintaining a family's cooperation in ongoing services that address goals
- Promoting a family's substantive and self-motivated participation in services

Families may be engaged or retained in services, but if home visitation services do not successfully pass through all of these phased tasks, families are unlikely to reap the hoped-for benefits. Looked at differently, families may engage or disengage with home visitation services at a variety of points along this continuum. For example, they may choose to engage or disengage during initial recruitment and outreach efforts, at the point of formal enrollment, and/or when service goals are identified and subsequently addressed. Furthermore, once engaged, each family may differ in its degree of receptivity to and participation in home visitation service activities aimed at achieving service goals. Whereas some families may be consistently available for scheduled home visits and actively implement steps to achieve named goals, other families may cancel appointments or show minimal interest in following through with named goals, such as parenting skill learning or linkage with local supports.

Despite the critical importance of this process for promoting positive outcomes, only relatively rudimentary empirical information is presently available to shed light on families' engagement and participation in early home visitation services. As noted in Chapter 4, many early home visitation programs have reported comparatively favorable overall rates of initial engagement in services when compared to center-based prevention programs (Prevent Child Abuse America, 1995), often enrolling 75% or more of the families approached for services. At the same time, select programs have reported lower enrollment rates (e.g., Center on Child Abuse Prevention Research, 1996; Infante-Rivard et al., 1989). Perhaps of greater concern for home visitation services is that families rarely participate in the number of home visits originally intended over the life of a program, and several programs have recently reported concerning rates of family attrition over time (Duggan et al., 1999; Gomby et al., 1999; Korfmacher et al., 1998; Olds et al., 1999; St. Pierre & Layzer, 1999; Wagner & Clayton, 1999). Several recent evaluations of the Healthy Start model, for example, have reported that about half of enrolled families have not remained in services after 1 year (Duggan et al., 1999), although evaluations of the same program model in other community niches have reported retention rates of more than 90% at 1 year (Rau et al., 1999). Processes that are linked with meaningful engagement and participation in services have not been systematically explored in the empirical literature, and in this regard, findings from an ongoing multisite study on engagement and retention conducted by Prevent Child Abuse America should make a special contribution to understanding these issues.

Evidence reviewed in Chapter 4 has pointed out that programs initiating services prenatally tend to report more favorable engagement rates with families and that services provided on a more frequent basis appear to be linked with improved retention rates over time. However, aside from these trends, the empirical base does not yet provide clear guideposts as programs consider how best to promote family participation throughout the phases of home visitation services. Conflicting findings have been reported linking engagement rates to risk status and maternal age, with some studies reporting that younger mothers at higher risk are more difficult to engage, whereas other studies have reported younger and higher risk mothers engaging at higher rates (Birkel & Repucci, 1983; Daro & Harding, 1999; Firestone & Witt, 1982; Josten et al., 1995; Olds & Kitzman, 1993; Osofsky et al., 1988; Wagner & Clayton, 1999). Outside the home visitation field, studies have tended to find more severe risk status associated with higher attrition rates (e.g., Cohen & Hesselbart, 1993; Kazdin & Mazurick, 1994; Wahler & Dumas, 1989; Webster-Stratton, 1990).

Clearly important to consider are specific barriers or inhibitors to participation in services, as well as facilitators or enabling factors influencing family involvement (cf. Andersen, 1995). Specific to home visitation services, these may include:

- Parents' perceived needs and the degree to which home visitation services are viewed as meaningfully addressing those needs
- Perceived stigma of home visitation services, and, more generally, the degree of positive and/or negative valence attributed to home visitation services
- Concrete obstacles, such as time conflicts with employment, job training, family activities, or even an infant's nap schedule
- The presence of other significant stressors that may distract parents from or compel parents to participate in home visitation services, or that may impair coping and help-seeking skills

- The nature of previous experiences with similar helpers such as visiting nurses, social workers, or other volunteers that color parents' beliefs in the efficacy and helpfulness of home visitation services
- Parents' values with regard to family privacy, which may inhibit their willingness to allow a formal helper into the home
- The degree to which program services are viewed by the family as compatible with their own personal and cultural values
- The specific influences of social network members such as fathers or grandmothers in encouraging or discouraging parents' involvement in services (see Birkel & Repucci, 1983; Daro & Harding, 1999; Fontana, Fleischman, McCarton, Meltzer, & Ruff, 1988; Gomby et al., 1999; Larner, Halpern, & Harkavy, 1992; Marcenko & Spence, 1994; McKay, McCadam, & Gonzales, 1996; McKay, Stoewe, McCadam, & Gonzales, 1998; Santisteban et al., 1996; Spoth, Redmond, Hockaday, & Shin, 1996)

Although not yet applied to early home visitation services, specific engagement strategies that problem-solve with families around barriers to service participation have been shown to substantially improve high-risk urban families' degree of service engagement on behalf of their children (McKay et al., 1996). Such findings demonstrate the potential for home visitation services to enhance family participation in services by extending traditional front-end engagement activities with intensive problem-solving and outreach procedures. Working with families to identify and enact strategies to overcome such barriers holds the potential to improve ongoing service participation and, ultimately, to maximize programs' intended benefits. In sum, although further information is necessary to identify specific strategies that programs can adopt to enhance family engagement and participation in services, the following does appear warranted:

PRACTICE PRINCIPLE 5.5: Home visitors should address specific barriers to ongoing service participation as well as those elements that may serve to facilitate and enhance a family's motivation for ongoing service.

Several indicators suggest that parents' own perceived need for services, rather than objective indicators of risk, may be a critical factor predicting their engagement and participation in home visitation services (e.g., Larner et al., 1992; Olds & Kitzman, 1993). Parents' sense of their vulnerability in relation to their children, coupled with beliefs that a program holds the potential to assist them in addressing their concerns, may form the essential mix in heightening parents' ongoing receptivity to home visitation services. Olds and Kitzman (1993), for example, assert that

> some families served in home visiting experiments eventually grow to believe that they simply do not need the service that is being offered; from their perspective, the reason for their being served is not clear. Unless the child has experienced some developmental challenge, such as prematurity, or the family has some concrete need, such as to obtain housing or to resolve problems associated with welfare benefits, the motivation for being visited is not as strong. The promotion of their child's health or development, from the parents' perspective, is often an abstract goal, especially when their child looks and acts like other children in their family and neighborhood. . . . The challenge in these programs is for the visitors to build upon parents' pressing and immediate concerns and to forge a long-range commitment to their own growth and development and to the improved care of their child. (p. 87)

Further study is needed to identify factors that shape parents' perceived needs as they evolve in relation to home visitation services. However, engagement intervention studies outside the home visitation field have shown that when workers try to form alliances with both parents and key social network members, and when they reframe parents' concerns in light of what services have to offer, such activities can substantially enhance family participation in formalized services (e.g., Santisteban et al., 1996; Szapocznik & Kurtines, 1989; Szapocznik, Perez-Vidal, Hervis, Brickman, & Kurtines, 1990). Such findings underscore that programs clearly face opportunities to influence family participation by helping parents understand how home visitation services can respond to their needs over time. Although home visitation programs may have limited immediate influence over more objective risk factors shaping family participation, such as educational status, parental age, or single parenthood, they may nonetheless be able to help families recognize and prioritize specific needs and then tailor services in ways that respond to those identified needs (cf. Larner et al., 1992). To maximize their benefits, home visitation services must not only create a programmatic fit between service activities and characteristics of families targeted for enrollment but also serve families in ways that are attuned to their individual needs, encouraging their participation in the home visitation service agenda.

In this regard, it is clear that home visitation services must make more progress in attending with greater fidelity to several of the most pressing etiological factors identified in child maltreatment risk. To what degree do early home visitation services address family struggles to cope, survive, and grow in the face of such challenges as ongoing family substance abuse, undermining social networks, or constrained and disempowering social ecological contexts? To the degree that such services can sensitively and meaningfully assist families in these persistently identified challenges contributing to child maltreatment risk (as pointed out in Chapter 2), they will be more likely to respond to factors presaging later maltreatment, while simultaneously tapping prime motivators for ongoing participation in such services. As the next three chapters will point out, however, early home visitation as a field has, as yet, not adequately addressed these specific domains. By better matching home visitation services to families' ongoing struggles and the known etiological processes that promote child maltreatment risk, early home visitation programs should be able to show improved capacities to engage and maximize family participation in services and to demonstrate greater impact on maltreatment-related outcomes. In particular, Chapters 6, 7, and 8 consider the pathways in which early home visitation services may efficaciously aid families contending with parental substance abuse, help to improve families' informal social networks, and empower parents to more effectively manage social ecological challenges in ways that reduce child maltreatment risk.

Chapter 6

COMBATING DUAL ABUSE

Addressing Substance Abuse in
Home Visitation to Prevent Child Maltreatment

LaTanya was a high school graduate who, at age 28, gave birth to her first and only child, Jeremiah. LaTanya's case file suggests that she was physically abused and neglected as a child, but she was never placed in foster care. She had a criminal record for prostitution and drug possession, and she admitted to the heavy use of drugs, including cocaine, amphetamines, and alcohol.

When Jeremiah was born, medical personnel noted traces of cocaine in his body. . . . The day following Jeremiah's birth, medical personnel made a report to the local child welfare agency. Jeremiah's case file indicates that child welfare workers attempted to follow up on the report but were unable to locate him and his mother; his case was closed without an investigation.

One month later, the child welfare agency received a phone call from one of LaTanya's relatives, who said that Jeremiah was being physically abused by his mother. [A child welfare worker] interviewed LaTanya and examined Jeremiah. Jeremiah's temperament was described as "very easy" and "cherubic." . . . The worker was aware that Jeremiah was born exposed to drugs and had been reported previously, but she did not see any evidence on this occasion to suggest that intervention with the family was needed. A month later, the child welfare agency again received a report concerning Jeremiah . . . for "caretaker absence or incapacity."

Finally, just 2 weeks later, when Jeremiah was 2½ months old, a fourth report for child maltreatment was logged with the agency. This time, the man with whom LaTanya and Jeremiah were living—a friend of the family—called the police, telling them that LaTanya had left the house the day before and had not yet returned; he was no longer willing to care for the child. Jeremiah was placed in an emergency foster home where he lived for a month; he was later moved to his uncle's home, where he stayed for the next 7 months. . . . He was returned to his mother. . . . Within a few months, however, LaTanya had abandoned Jeremiah, and he was again placed in foster care. (Duerr-Berrick et al., 1998, p. 42)

Although early home visitation programs are designed to address a variety of factors that heighten the risk of child maltreatment, preciously little attention has been paid throughout the field to the unique challenges presented by families struggling with ongoing substance abuse (Guterman, 1997a). Given that large proportions of maltreated children identified by protective services come from homes involving parental substance abuse and that very young children appear to face especially heightened risk, home visitation programs may demonstrably enhance their capacity to reduce maltreatment by advancing attention to this area. Although a wide spectrum of substance use patterns exists (U.S. Department of Health and Human Services, 1999), this chapter is specifically concerned with substance or alcohol abuses and addictions, where harm or impairments directly result from the substance use or where the use of substances has advanced to such a degree that the person is unable to control their use, showing physiological, psychological, and behavioral dependence (Substance Abuse and Mental Health Services Administration, 1994; U.S. Department of Health and Human Services, 1999). As we shall see, early home visitation programs face the largely uncharted but daunting terrain of developing effective strategies to assist families contending with dual risk of child and substance abuse.

THE INTERTWINED PROBLEMS
OF SUBSTANCE AND CHILD ABUSE

About 8.3 million U.S. children presently live with one or more substance-abusing parents, almost a million of them are under 2 years of age (Huang, Cerbone, & Gfroerer, 1998). Of all births in the United States each year, it has been estimated that about 221,000 of the infants (5.5%) are born prenatally exposed to illicit drugs and that 140,000 pregnant women (3.5% of all pregnant women) drink heavily, exposing their children to risk of fetal alcohol effects *in utero* (Centers for Disease Control and Prevention, 1997; National Institute on Drug Abuse, 1994). Substance abuse comes in many forms, not only the illicit abuse of substances such as heroin, cocaine, marijuana, or methamphetamine but also the abuse of legal drugs such as alcohol or prescription medications (Kelley, 1998).

It has been emphasized for several decades that inordinate numbers of children reported to protective services systems for physical abuse and neglect come from homes where one or more parents are contending with substance abuse problems (e.g., Black & Mayer, 1980; Fanshel, 1975; Magura & Laudet, 1996; Murphy et al., 1991). Representatives of child protective services systems across the United States have, over the last several years, increasingly identified substance abuse as one of the top two problems exhibited by families reported for maltreatment, from 76% in 1994 to 85% in 1998 (Wang & Harding, 1999).

Studies of child welfare caseloads have variously found the proportion of physical child abuse and neglect cases involving substance abuse ranging from 13% to over 70% (Magura & Laudet, 1996). Surmounting some of the biases inherent in retrospective studies of already identified maltreatment cases, Chaffin et al. (1996) prospectively examined the predictive link between substance abuse and physical abuse and neglect in a nationally representative sample. In line with earlier studies, Chaffin and colleagues found substance abuse to be a strong predictor for the onset of physical abuse and neglect, tripling the risk for later maltreatment. Such findings clarify that substance abuse not only co-occurs with child abuse but also substantially heightens the risk that parents will maltreat their children (cf. U.S. Department of Health and Human Services, 1999). These findings critically point out the clear potential for early intervention that meaningfully addresses substance abuse to directly reduce maltreatment risk, as well.

Younger children appear to be especially affected by parental substance abuse (Jaudes, Ekwo, & Van Voorhis, 1995). About half the substantiated cases of child maltreatment where substance or alcohol abuse was identified involved children 4 years old and under (National Center on Child Abuse and Neglect, 1993). Furthermore, one state-level study indicated that more than 40% of all child abuse reports involved substance-exposed infants (Goerge & Harden, 1993). Such statistics likely reflect, in part, state policies that tend to encourage reporting of maltreatment when the presence of maternal substance or alcohol abuse is detected at birth (Albert, Klein, Noble, Zahand, & Holtby, 2000). However, it is also clear that exposure to alcohol or other substances prenatally, and ongoing parental substance or alcohol abuse in the early years of life, can cause clear and sometimes profound detriment to the developing child.

THE ROLE OF SUBSTANCE ABUSE
IN HEIGHTENING MALTREATMENT RISK

The presence of substance abuse in a family heightens maltreatment risk in the specific impact the substance abuse has on the developing infant and parent-infant attachment, and through the many additional challenges often accompanying substance-abusing patterns of behavior. Studies of substance-abusing women have discerned an array of frequently co-occurring problems that increase the likelihood that abuse or neglect will result. For example, studies have found that women with substance abuse problems frequently also contend with depression or other psychiatric disorders, childhood histories of physical or sexual abuse, domestic violence, and/or sexual relationships with partners at high risk of transmitting HIV (Bayatpour, Wells, & Holford, 1992; Bennett & Kemper, 1994; Chavkin, Paone, Friedman, & Wilets, 1993; U.S. Department of Health and Human Services, 1999). For women facing such additional concerns, substance use may, in part, be a form of self-medication, an attempt to cope with the pain wrought by multiple overwhelming struggles. Although using a psychoactive substance may temporarily anesthetize the pain accompanying such problems, the substance use itself poses unique challenges for women facing the realities of pregnancy and later parenting of an infant.

Exposure to alcohol or drugs *in utero* may cause profound and long-term detriment to the child. Psychoactive substances cross the placenta and the blood-brain barrier, entering the developing fetus's metabolism (Zuckerman & Brown, 1993). Studies have found that ingestion of cocaine, opiates, or alcohol during pregnancy is associated with an extensive array of problems. These have included medical complications during labor, fetal alcohol syndrome, sudden infant death syndrome (SIDS), abnormal structural organization of the developing brain, smaller head circumferences, lower birth weights, withdrawal symptoms, poor motor coordination, hyperactivity, irritability, inconsolability, sleeping and feeding difficulties, and other developmental delays (e.g., Deren, 1986; Grief & Drechsler, 1993; Kandall, Gaines, Habel, Davidson, & Jessop, 1993; Phillips, Sharma, Premachandra, Vaughn, & Reyes-Lee, 1996; U.S. Department of Health and Human Services, 1999; Zeitlin, 1994; Zuckerman, 1994; Zuckerman & Brown, 1993). Findings increasingly point to the importance of the postnatal environment—and most especially the quality of the caregiving interactions and the contexts in which they are embedded—in exacerbating or mitigating the behavioral outcomes of substance exposure in utero (e.g., Chasnoff et al., 1998; Espy, Riese, & Francis, 1997; Zuckerman & Brown, 1993). As noted by Zuckerman (1994),

Consider, for example, a child born to a cocaine-using mother who did not eat well during her pregnancy and received minimal prenatal care. Following a three-day hospitalization, the infant has difficulty remaining alert and is minimally responsive. The child's passivity engenders maternal feelings of inadequacy that may deepen already existing depressive symptoms and promote continued reliance on cocaine to alleviate these painful feelings. During the first year, the mother's attempts to get her infant's attention lead to overstimulation, general irritability, and at times, inconsolable crying. The mother's feeling of inadequacy and depression increases, and she continues to use drugs and alcohol to self-medicate these painful feelings. In the second year of life, as the child strives for independence, struggles develop between the mother and her toddler. The mother sets unusual or inconsistent limits, and most interactions with her child are negative and involve commands, especially on the days following a drug or alcohol binge. At two years of age, the child is hyperactive and impulsive, with delayed language development. What is the cause of these developmental and behavioral problems? Are they secondary to poor prenatal nutrition, to prenatal cocaine exposure, or to both? Or, are they the result of mother's depression? The transactional model of child development provides the best explanation as it considers all of these factors and their interactions with one another. (p. 50)

As Zuckerman and a number of other scholars emphasize, the unfolding set of interrelationships between the ongoing substance abuse, the mother's coping patterns, environmental challenges, and the infant's own behavioral patterns results in a potentially profound impact on the developing parent-infant attachment (Davis, 1994). Studies have consistently shown impaired attachment patterns in substance-abusing mothers and their infants, including decreased maternal responsivity and disturbances in infants' attachment behaviors, such as crying, smiling, consolability, and irritability (Gottwald & Thurman, 1994; Householder, Hatcher, Burns, & Chasnoff, 1982; Kelly, 1999; Singer et al., 1997). Such detriment has been found to continue as children develop autonomy and require greater guidance and direction. Studies have shown that substance-abusing parents often employ ineffective and inconsistent discipline, sometimes acting inattentively or overreacting with harsh or coercive discipline (Kumpfer & Bayes, 1995; Tarter, Blackson, Martin, Loeber, & Moss, 1993).

Perplexingly, little is known about the role of fathers' substance or alcohol abuse and child maltreatment in early childhood. Substance abuse patterns in fathers have been clearly linked with heightened child maltreatment risk (e.g., Ammerman, Kolko, Kirisci, Blackson, & Dawes, 1999; Moss, Mezzich, Yao, Gavaler, & Martin, 1995), and one study using protective services data reported that 59% of the maltreatment cases that involved substance abuse identified fathers as substance abusers (Murphy et al., 1991). Fathers' or male partners' substance and/ or alcohol abuse is likely to influence child maltreatment risk through multiple pathways. These may include the impact on family financial stability, the impairment of functioning in the parental dyad, the heightening of domestic violence risk, the influence on a mother's own substance use and patterns of parenting behavior, or fathers' direct efforts at providing child care (see Chapter 7 for further discussion of fathers' role in maltreatment risk). Despite the paucity of information on fathers' role in dual substance and child maltreatment risk, it remains clear that from pregnancy throughout childhood, the substance abuse patterns of both mothers and fathers (or male partners) play a substantial role in the risks for physical child abuse and neglect.

ATTENDING TO SUBSTANCE ABUSE CHALLENGES IN EARLY HOME VISITATION

Paralleling a broader lack of integration between child welfare services and substance abuse services, early home visitation programs have yet to attend adequately to the substantial role that substance abuse plays in maltreatment risk. For example, early home visitation services have rarely reported tailored or integrative service protocols for home visitors working with families also contending with substance abuse. Providing parenting guidance and referrals to formalized supports without also fully accounting for the role substance abuse or addiction plays in the parenting process raises serious dilemmas in supporting families and reducing their child maltreatment risk. During the prenatal phase, how can home visitors assist substance-abusing mothers to minimize substance or alcohol ingestion in ways that prevent potentially profound detriment to the developing fetus? After the child is born, how can home visitors assist mothers to consider breast-feeding the infant if they are ingesting substances that may be passed to the infant during nursing? How can visitors help families consider attachment behaviors or child care arrangements in instances where the mother or father are under the influence of alcohol or other psychoactive drugs? Indeed, how can the home visitor help substance-abusing or addicted parents assure an infant's safety when under the influence?

At present, home visitation programs have most typically attended to the role of substance abuse by incorporating it as a variable in some screening and risk assessment protocols (e.g., Black et al., 1994; Duggan et al., 1999; Marcenko et al., 1996) and by referring clients to community substance abuse services when they acknowledge that a substance problem exists (e.g., Breakey & Pratt, 1991; Marcenko & Spence, 1994).

Perhaps the most well-documented attention to problems associated with substance and alcohol abuse is found in the Prenatal/Early Infancy Program (PEIP) reported by David Olds and colleagues (O'Brian & Baca, 1997; Olds, 1982). Although not directly tailored to address the ongoing and long-term problems of substance abuse or addiction, this program nonetheless provides attention to reducing the use of alcohol, cigarettes, or drugs during pregnancy. In the PEIP, nurse home visitors emphasize to mothers during pregnancy that their behavior affects their own health as well as the health of the fetus, and they provide praise for gains made without conveying negative messages if progress is not made. Such an approach is aimed at heightening the incentive for reducing substance use in pregnancy and afterward (Olds, 1982). Although the attention to substance use problems lies mostly during the prenatal phase in the PEIP, Olds and colleagues have reported some reduction in cigarette smoking after the cessation of home visiting services and, over the long term, some reduction in behavioral impairments due to substance abuse in the Elmira, New York, randomized trial (Olds, Eckenrode, et al., 1997; Olds, Henderson, et al., 1998). Intriguingly, Olds, Henderson, et al. (1998) also reported in the same sample that children of unmarried and single mothers who received home visitation services smoked fewer cigarettes and consumed less alcohol at 15 years of age. Such trends, however, were not found for the entire sample of women receiving home visiting services. Furthermore, no reports are available about improvements in substance use patterns from the replication of the PEIP in Memphis, Tennessee.

Although not specifically geared to the reduction of substance use, the home visitation program reported by Black et al. (1994), which served only women self-reporting prenatal cocaine or heroin use, showed a marginally significant reduction in substance use and significant improvements in emotional responsiveness and increased opportunities for stimulation with the infant. The findings reported by Olds and colleagues and Black and colleagues form the extent of the empirical base on home visitation services' impact on substance abuse-related problems. Although these findings are scant, they provide early evidence of the potential for home visitation to serve as a meaningful vehicle to address dual substance use and child maltreatment risk in families where substance abuse is at issue. At the same time, however, substance abuse problems and addictions are most often chronic conditions subject to likely relapse, with recovery a long-term project. Given this, home visitation programs still face a need to augment their intervention strategies to effectively address the ongoing and intertwining problems of substance and child abuse risk. As yet, no carefully controlled outcome study has reported on such an integrative and longer term model of home visitation services.

EMERGING DIRECTIONS IN ADDRESSING THE ROLE OF SUBSTANCE ABUSE WITHIN HOME VISITATION SERVICES

Evidence suggests that pregnancy and the prospect of becoming a parent may be prime motivators for women seeking help for substance abuse problems. If they are aware of the potential effects of substances on the developing fetus and infant, women may have an opportunity to rethink their use or abuse of substances and attempt to turn over a new leaf. Indeed, evidence suggests that the effect of substance abuse on children is a key motivator for women who enter and progress in substance abuse treatment, and this is especially clearly documented in instances where women fear losing custody of their children because of their substance use (Gerstein, Johnson, Larison, Harwood, & Fountain, 1997; Laken, McComish, & Ager, 1997; Pursely-Crotteau & Stern, 1996; Substance Abuse and Mental Health Services Administration, 1996; U.S. Department of Health and Human Services, 1999). Thus, early home visitation services, despite their present underdeveloped state in addressing substance abuse concerns, may be uniquely positioned to affect parenting and substance abuse patterns synergistically.

How might early home visitation programs augment their services to effectively serve families contending with substance abuse issues? Although home visitation programs already frequently provide referral and case management to address substance or alcohol abuse problems, this strategy is a limited one. By attending to substance or alcohol abuse concerns directly within the context of home visits, workers have an opportunity to help parents see the links between use of alcohol or other drugs and their own health, the health of their infant, and their parenting role. By emphasizing that reduction in parental substance use will improve their infants' health and well-being, home visitors may increase parents' motivation to make changes in both parenting and substance use realms. Because of their purview, home visitors can also assist parents to circumscribe their substance or alcohol use and to consider its impact on their children, reducing the risk of detrimental consequences. Integrative strategies that can be incorporated within home visitation may include

- Systematic clinical assessment of family needs related to substance use and parenting issues, beyond mere risk screening for eligibility purposes
- Supportive activities during home visits to encourage the reduction of substance use and its harmful effects on the developing child

- Assertive management and monitoring of formal and informal supports as they are specifically related to substance abuse problems
- Linking of families with mutual support networks to reduce stigma, to promote the development of an alternative and long-term support network to assist in managing substance use problems, and to address possible future relapses

Clinical assessment of substance use patterns. Many early home visitation programs employ risk-screening protocols that specifically probe for substance abuse problems. However, as noted in the previous chapter, such information is collected for the purposes of enrollment decision making and does not typically provide the necessary depth to determine the extent of the substance abuse, its manifestations, the family's motivation to reduce or abstain from substance use, and conditions that may worsen or mitigate substance use. As substance abuse behavior patterns are often hidden, home visitors must take care, with a minimum of bias, to garner information that can discern substance use patterns, informing the planning of home visitation services. Studies have often found inadequate attention to substance abuse assessment training, and workers often overlook the presence of such problems when addressing child maltreatment concerns more broadly (Gregoire, 1994; Kagel, 1987; Tracy, 1994). Yet, home visitors and other service providers unaware of or lacking comprehensive clinical information about substance or alcohol abuse patterns are hampered in their abilities to promote positive parent-child attachment and interactions, to assist families to manage stressors, and to promote a positive adjustment to the role of parenting a new child.

As the vast majority of settings providing referrals for home visitation services are not substance abuse treatment settings, extant knowledge about substance-using behavior patterns may not be readily available to workers. Hospitals referring families may provide some helpful drug-screening data using medical instrumentation, for example, via urine drug screening. Urine drug screening, however, is limited in its capacity to detect substance exposure beyond a few days, precluding critical information about long-term substance use patterns. Also, such drug screening may be applied in a race- or class-biased fashion (e.g., Byrd, Neistadt, Howard, Brownstein-Evans, & Weitzman, 1999).

Thus, it is important for home visitors to routinely and directly ask families about substance use patterns to become better informed about the extent and the impact that the substance use has on the family and those around them and to learn whether the problem and need for change are acknowledged. Information from family members can then be compared as congruent or discrepant from any existing records, such as drug screens in the medical file.

PRACTICE PRINCIPLE 6.1: Home visitors should routinely and sensitively assess the presence and role of substance and/or alcohol use and abuse patterns early in their work with families.

Timing and the approach that home visitors adopt with families in directly assessing substance use patterns are critical. Assessment interviewing concerning substance use patterns must be managed in a highly sensitive way. Substance-abusing pregnant women or new parents face a palpable social stigma, not only from society at large but from other health care and social services providers, who may judge their substance-using behavior critically, especially in light of the perceived effects on childbearing and rearing (Finkelstein, 1994; Trinh, 1998). Substance abusers also may hold realistic fears that divulging accurate information about a substance use problem may jeopardize child custody or even provoke criminal prosecution (Wallace, 1991). In addition, substance-abusing behavior is often accompanied by intense personal shame and cognitive processes such as denial and minimization, and, as such, requires home visitors to employ sensitive and strategic probing about substance use patterns (Finkelstein, 1994). Home visitors should convey an accepting and optimistic tone, broaching substance use concerns when families appear to have some trust and alliance with the visitor.

Well-established clinical guidelines in substance abuse assessment interviewing are available and can be readily adapted for home visitation services (e.g., Barber, 1995; Griffin, 1991; Rollnick & Morgan, 1996; Straussner, 1993; Washton, 1996). The domains of concern summarized in Table 6.1 appear particularly critical in assessing for substance abuse in the context of early maltreatment prevention.

In the assessment process, home visitors may draw from an array of simple standardized self-report measures that have shown acceptable validity and reliability in identifying the presence and severity of substance or alcohol abuse. These include the Drug Abuse Screening Test (DAST), the CAGE questionnaire, the Addiction Severity Index (ASI), the Comprehensive Addiction Severity Index for Adolescents (CASI-A), or the Chemical Use Abuse and Dependency Scale (McGovern & Morrison, 1992). However, when planning integrative home visitation

Table 6.1

Domains of Substance Abuse Assessment in Early Home Visitation

---

- The **presence, extent,** and **nature** of any substance abuse, including frequency, amount, type, and methods of use

- The **setting** and **circumstances** of use, including who else participates in drug use, the location of use (at home, at bars, with sex partners, etc.), the means of procurement of drugs, and any potential precipitants or "triggers" for use (e.g., loneliness, fights with a loved one)

- The **impact** on or **harm** (potential or actual) to others, most especially the infant or fetus. Questions here include:
  1. Is the infant or fetus directly or indirectly ingesting any substances, or is this a future possibility (e.g., *in utero,* from smoke, breast milk, or deliberately as a sedative)?
  2. Have relationships been unstable, violent, or involving risky or unwanted sexual behaviors that may be connected with substance use?
  3. Have there been legal offenses, previous child custody issues, or financial or employment difficulties that may be connected with substance use?
  4. Are there medical consequences connected with substance use, such as sexually transmitted diseases, hepatitis, tuberculosis, pregnancy, or birth complications?

- The **history** of any substance use, including use by other family members or significant others, including:
  1. When was the onset of substance use, and under what circumstances?
  2. Is there a history of trauma or losses that may have preceded substance use?
  3. What family members or loved ones have been involved in using substances?

- The **view** of substance use, degree of **acknowledgment** of a problem, and the need for and beliefs about the capability for change

- Previous coping efforts as they exacerbate or mitigate substance use patterns, including previous help seeking for any problem, involvement in self-help groups, or prior treatment

- The **presence of co-occurring problems** that exacerbate, interact with, or complicate substance use problems, such as psychiatric disorders, domestic violence, depression, or loneliness.

---

strategies, these can only supplement a more detailed picture that must be acquired by direct interviewing concerning harm, circumstances, and motivation.

Integrative home-visit activities to reduce both substance and child abuse risk. Because women's receptivity to assistance with substance

abuse concerns may heighten when they learn they are pregnant and consider the prospect of raising children, home visitation services have the
opportunity to integrate attention given to parenting skills with discussion of substance use patterns. Psychoeducational strategies that
supportively and sensitively point out the links between parents' substance-using behavior and the associated outcomes for the child can
serve as a potential motivator for reducing substance use during pregnancy (Olds et al., 1999). For example, within the context of creating a
healthful and safe environment for the child, parents can be educated
about the risks of common chemicals in their environment, from household products, lead paint, or cigarette smoke to alcohol and other psychoactive substances (cf. Howard & Lawrence, 1998). Home visitors may
point out ways parents can act to reduce their children's exposure to such
toxins, thereby improving home safety and their children's health and
well-being. Once parents take action to reduce substance use, positive
support from the home visitor can expand parents' motivation for further
reduction in substance use.

Such a harm reduction approach, which emphasizes parental capacity
and choice, positive outcomes, and parental behaviors that minimize the
harmful effects of substance abuse on children, is not free from controversy, and many continue to promote abstinence approaches that advocate stopping all substance use, even as a condition of service (Marlatt,
1998). However, given that substance abuse problems are most commonly characterized by long-term progressive behavior patterns, it is
clear that home visitation programs must persistently strive, often
throughout the duration of services, to minimize the impact of substance
use on the developing parent-child relationship. Home visitation services may supportively assist substance-abusing parents to advance from
a state of ongoing and uncontrolled abuse or dependency through phases
of acknowledging that the behavior is harmful, through attempts to
reduce such behavior over time, and even through contending with
expectable periods of relapse (Prochaska & DiClemente, 1983).

PRACTICE PRINCIPLE 6.2: In instances where substance and/or alcohol abuse have been identified as concerns, home visitors should work
with families over the long term to directly reduce the risks and harm the
substance abuse has on the developing child and the family.

In instances where substance abuse is present, home visitation services must work to reduce specific risks or harm to the infant, and such

efforts may involve a variety of strategies, including encouraging abstinence or minimizing substance use. Home visitors working with mothers
who report an inability to control their intake of alcohol or other substances should, at a minimum, try to develop a backup safety plan for the
infant in instances when the mother's judgment may be impaired while
under the influence. Home visitors may assist parents in thinking
through options for child care in instances when their capacity is com-
promised. Also, parenting skills training in the home may become more
intensive and complicated. For example, when training to accurately
read and respond to an infant's cues, home visitors may need to delicately
point out parents' differing responses when under the influence. More
careful planning may be needed to assist mothers to respond to the
infant's needs proactively, for example, in diaper changing or "baby
proofing" the home for safety purposes. If the infant displays irritability
or conversely excessive passivity due to neurodevelopmental problems
associated with exposure to psychoactive substances, the home visitor
must more assertively work with the mother to help her cope with and
positively frame such behaviors, with the goal of facilitating the developing parent-infant attachment.

Although no available empirical evidence directly sheds light on
assisting substance-abusing fathers or male partners through the venue
of early home visitation, it is clear that home visitors must carefully
assess their role in child care and in the family more broadly. Does the
father play an active role in caregiving? If so, considerations of safety
and parent training may need to involve work with him. What role and
relationship does the father or male partner have to the mother and other
family members? Home visitors may consider ways to increase mutual
supportiveness and ways to decrease tension and/or collusion in substance use. Does his substance use contribute to an unstable presence in
the home, financial difficulties, or domestic violence risk? The presence
of a substance- or alcohol-abusing father or male partner raises many
critical questions regarding how best to fit services to families' needs.
Clearly, further study is essential to develop and test strategies that can
effectively address the role of substance-abusing fathers or male partners
in reducing early child-maltreatment risk.

Workers may also face their own personal challenges in working with
substance-abusing parents. For example, home visitors may face difficulties in maintaining a positive, accepting, and warm approach, given
the social stigma attached to parental substance abuse, particularly in
instances where a parent's behavior appears to place the infant in harm's

way. Thus, home visitors must persistently gauge their own responsiveness to parents as well as the families' engagement in services. Because families voluntarily accept supports, less external authority may be in place than within the traditional protective services domain to press parents to make direct progress on their own substance abuse challenges.

Despite a paucity of well-controlled outcome studies examining home visitation models directly tailored to the dual risks of child maltreatment and substance abuse, a number of such programs are presently in operation across the United States. Best Beginnings Plus in New York City, described in Practice Exemplar 6.1, is one such exemplary model.

Intensive and ongoing management of formal supports and services. Although early home visitation programs routinely provide case management activities for enrolled families, such activities become more complicated and critical in instances where substance abuse is present. Because of the strong social stigma attached to substance abuse in mothers (or mothers-to-be), inordinate and multiple barriers hinder women from receiving appropriate services that may assist them in contending with their substance abuse problems. For example, Sherman et al. (1998) cites facts from the case of *Johnson v. Florida* (in which Jennifer Johnson was prosecuted for her drug addiction during pregnancy), indicating that although the state reported 3,500 known substance-abusing pregnant women (with an additional 10,425 pregnant and addicted women likely to be unreported), the treatment slots available statewide for such women totaled 135.

In addition, residential treatment services rarely allow children to be admitted, and outpatient programs do not typically provide necessary child care (Sherman et al., 1998). Such services also typically provide poor coordination with obstetrical and other necessary health care services (Jansson et al., 1996). As a result, in instances where specialized professional treatment is necessary, intensive case coordination across agencies is often necessary. Home visitors must delicately broach the topic of specialized substance abuse treatment, not only because some mothers have not yet fully determined their need for help but also because many mothers fear being reported to protective services and potentially losing their children to foster care. Mothers may also fear potential prosecution and imprisonment. Furthermore, the societal stigma attached to substance abuse reinforces mothers' self-blame and guilt and thus may inhibit their efforts to seek assistance for themselves.

PRACTICE EXEMPLAR 6.1

Best Beginnings Plus

Best Beginnings Plus is a voluntary early home visitation program specifically tailored to address the needs of families contending with substance abuse (Anisfeld & Guillen, 1999). The program is lodged within a larger home visitation program (Best Beginnings) in New York City, serving an urban, largely immigrant population from the Dominican Republic. The Best Beginnings Plus program is an enrichment and adaptation of the Healthy Start program from Hawaii. It enrolls families where mothers or fathers are self-identified as having substance or alcohol use problems. The program uses intensively trained paraprofessionals with low caseloads, making visits to families more frequent and flexible than in the Healthy Start model. For example, Best Beginnings Plus families receive an average of 10 prenatal visits and then 34 visits during the first year after birth (Anisfeld, Guterman, & Estrada-Nadal, 2000). Paraprofessional home visitors are supervised by a social worker with extensive experience in substance abuse work. The program approach rests on a harm-reduction model of service (Marlatt, 1998) and draws on work by Prochaska, DiClemente, and colleagues for specific intervention strategies aimed at addressing the major stages and processes involved in changing substance abusers' behavior (Prochaska & DiClement, 1983; Prochaska, Johnson, & Lee, 1998). The overall aims of Best Beginnings Plus are to reduce stressors that may hinder the child's development, to minimize the risk of child maltreatment and the potential harms of drug use on the individual and family.

Home visitors reach out persistently to engage families during the prenatal phase or at birth and focus on identifying the woman's needs without initially focusing on drug use. Home visitors begin to raise awareness of drug use by providing information about use and by linking behavior with health and safety risks, striving to maintain a nonjudgmental viewpoint. Workers facilitate substance users' contemplation of changing their behaviors by helping parents understand the reasons for changing and by strengthening their belief that they can make healthy changes. During the early months, home visitors intensively focus efforts on enhancing parent-child interaction and discuss managing substance use in the context of the parent role. For example, the mother and the visitor establish a safety plan as a backup in the event that the mother's behavior becomes substantially impaired by substance use. The home visitor also seeks to actively engage other primary caregivers in the plan and to engage and work with the mother's network members to minimize the effects of substance use while the mother is in the parenting role.

If and when the parent acknowledges a need to change her substance use patterns, the home visitor helps her explore the available alternatives in the community, including outpatient substance abuse clinics, support groups, or residential treatment. Home visitors are also trained to assist parents if and when they relapse into substance use after a period of abstinence (Anisfeld & Guillen, 1999).

The program is presently in the midst of a randomized trial to determine its efficacy, and definitive outcome findings are not yet available. However, preliminary outcome data available at 6 months on the relatively small sample at present ($N = 24$) suggest some meaningful benefit for substance-abusing families receiving Best Beginnings Plus (BB+) services (see Table 6.2). For example, compared to randomly assigned control group families, families receiving Best Beginnings Plus services show more functional scores on

- Parent-infant communication and interaction
- Maternal sensitivity to cues
- Maternal involvement with the infant
- Mother's emotional and verbal responsiveness to the infant
- Provision of appropriate play materials
- Mother's provision of opportunities for variety in daily stimulation
- Lower maternal depression
- Overall supportiveness of the home environment for the infant.
- Infant's cognitive and motor development at 6 months (see Table 6.2)

Clearly, more complete analyses, once the sample grows larger and reaches later follow-up points, will determine to what degree these early trends are statistically significant and clinically meaningful.

Table 6.2

Preliminary 6-Month Outcomes of
Substance-Abusing Families Receiving Best
Beginnings-Plus Services Versus Randomly Assigned Control Families
($N = 24$)

Outcomes at 6 Months	Home Visit Group Mean (SD)	Control Group Mean (SD)
Qualities of Home Environment: HOME Scale[a]		
HOME Scale: Total	31.4 (7.7)	28.3 (5.5)
Emotional and verbal responsiveness	8.8 (2.5)	7.3 (2.3)
Avoidance of restriction and punishment	6.1 (0.3)	6.5 (0.6)
Organization of the environment	4.0 (1.3)	3.8 (1.3)
Provision of appropriate play material	5.5 (2.1)	5.0 (1.3)
Maternal involvement with child	3.8 (1.7)	3.0 (1.4)
Opportunity for variety in daily stimulation	3.2 (1.4)	2.7 (1.4)
Maternal-Infant Responsiveness: NCAST[b]		
NCAST Teaching Scale: Total	32.0 (5.1)	30.4 (5.1)
Sensitivity to cues	8.8 (2.2)	7.9 (1.0)
Response to distress	9.6 (2.3)	9.2 (2.3)
Social-emotional growth fostering	5.4 (1.3)	5.5 (0.8)
Cognitive growth fostering	8.2 (2.7)	7.8 (2.5)
Clarity of cues	6.7 (1.8)	7.1 (2.1)
Maternal-infant interaction scale	41.4 (7.9)	40.9 (6.5)
Maternal Depression: CES-D[c]	11.9 (7.4)	15.3 (9.2)
Infant Cognitive and Motor Development: Bayley[d]		
Mental Development Index	115.9 (14.6)	105.2 (24.8)
Psychomotor Development Index	115.5 (11.3)	99.2 (20.2)

Note: Given small *N*s and the ongoing nature of this study, inferential statistics were not applied in the above analyses. Study methods and design characteristics are detailed in Rau et al. (1999).
a. HOME: Home Observation for Measurement of the Environment Scale (Caldwell & Bradley, 1984)
b. NCAST: Nursing Child Assessment Satellite Training Scale (Barnard, 1986).
c. CES-D: Center for Epidemiologic Studies-Depression Scale (National Institute of Mental Health, 1977).
d. Bayley: Bayley Scales of Infant Development (Bayley, 1993).

PRACTICE PRINCIPLE 6.3: Because of the numerous barriers to services faced by substance-abusing mothers, home visitors must intensively and persistently orchestrate formal supports to maintain essential
health, economic, and social supports.

Because of the often broad influence of substance abuse and its frequent co-occurring conditions, home visitors are also often faced with a myriad of case management issues beyond the need to identify specialized substance abuse treatment services for families. These often include attending to additional medical needs of parents and infants that may accompany parents' substance-abusing behavior, vocational and educational needs, and requirements for public assistance and Medicaid linkage. A number of states now include drug testing to gain ongoing eligibility for public assistance funds, such as those available through the Temporary Assistance to Needy Families (TANF) program (Reiniger, personal communication, June 17, 1999). Thus, home visitors can quickly become caught in a thicket of bureaucratic and eligibility requirements as they attempt to line up essential supports for the infant and family. They must be nimble at negotiating an increasingly punitive public assistance system in order to maintain a family's linkages with formalized helping systems.

Management of informal support systems. Although home visitation services typically provide some attention to informal relationships, specific efforts to work with substance-abusing parents' informal social support systems must be highly intensive, deliberate, and sensitive to the unique challenges substance abuse behavior presents for parents' relationships with key others in their social environment. Substance-abusing women often report feeling socially isolated (e.g., Davis, 1994; Kouzekanani & Neeley, 1996), and existing social networks can play a key role in reinforcing substance use patterns and encouraging relapse (Fraser & Hawkins, 1984; Goehl, Nunes, Quitkin, & Hilton, 1993; Sorenson & Gibson, 1983). On the other hand, positive social network ties of substance abusers have been consistently associated with positive behavioral change and maintenance of sobriety (e.g., Cronkite & Moos, 1980; Gordon & Zrull, 1991; Tucker, 1982). Significant others, loved ones, and friends may join together to share drugs or alcohol, for example, in bars or "shooting galleries." Conversely, influential network members may join together, even deliberately, to inhibit the ongoing use of substances and to provide alternative means of coping with circumstances that may trigger substance use (e.g., Galanter, 1999). Home visitors, therefore, must thoroughly assess substance-abusing parents' social networks and work with parents to help shape their networks in ways that provide the maximum support for healthy behaviors and that minimize the likelihood of engaging in risky and harmful behavior for themselves and their children.

PRACTICE PRINCIPLE 6.4: Home visitors must deliberately work with parents to enrich and sculpt supportive informal networks and to minimize negative influences in existing support network ties in order to reduce both substance and child abuse risk.

In cases where parents are struggling with substance dependency, home visitors can seek to link parents with appropriate alternative self-help support systems such as Alcoholics Anonymous (AA) or Narcotics Anonymous (NA), options that offer built-in and long-term supports, well-developed belief frameworks to help the parents place their behavior in perspective, companionship, and alternative activities that may inhibit ongoing substance abuse behavior.

Surviving and growing into the role of parent is a daily challenge, one that is embedded in and influenced by a field of relationships that convey meaning, connectedness, and material resources. As such, although home visitation services are themselves a form of social support, they must in the most deliberate way seek to mobilize supportive interactions on behalf of families to reduce child maltreatment risk, both for substance-abusing and non-substance-involved families, across the board. Given their importance, the next chapter considers ways early home visitation services can more systematically address social network influences to reduce child maltreatment risk over the long term.

Chapter 7

TAPPING SOCIAL NETWORKS IN HOME VISITATION TO PREVENT MALTREATMENT

Rita is a 26-year-old undocumented immigrant from Mexico. After living in the United States for 2 years with her boyfriend, she found out that she was pregnant. When her boyfriend learned of her pregnancy, he encouraged her to have an abortion. However, she refused, stating that she wanted to mother the baby. As a result, Rita and her boyfriend broke up, and Rita was forced to move in with her brother, his wife, and their daughter. During her second-trimester prenatal visit to the local public health clinic, Rita was offered home visitation services. At the time, the assessment worker learned that Rita had no phone at her current residence and that she would like assistance in finding her own apartment before the baby was born. Rita reported to the worker that she had experienced bouts of depression over the previous 5 years, and she stated that she had little contact with her mother, who was still in Mexico. She also said that she did not go out much and had few friends, describing the neighborhood as "unsafe." Rita noted that her English was improving but that she was afraid that her undocumented status would be revealed and that she would be sent back to Mexico.

The home visitor made a number of attempts to arrange home visits, but, in part because Rita did not have a phone, she had some difficulty contacting her before she gave birth. When Rita gave birth, the home visitor went to see Rita at the hospital and provided her with information about housing possibilities, breast-feeding, and nutrition. The home visitor scheduled an initial postpartum home visit, but Rita was not home at the appointed time. Rita's sister-in-law told the home visitor that she was now staying with her sister, outside the program's catchment area. After leaving messages and making numerous unsuccessful attempts to contact Rita at her sister's home, the worker had to close the case.

Prior to the initiation of formalized supports such as home visitation, families are embedded within their own social fabrics, which potently shape parenting behaviors and child maltreatment risk. One of the most complicated and crucial issues facing home visitation programs concerns how best to consider and address the indigenous social networks of families targeted for services.

Consonant with the theoretical lens presented in Chapter 2, studies have found that maltreating parenting is intimately intertwined with problems in the way families are connected with others in webs of social and community relationships, although the exact nature of such problematic ties appears to be highly complex. Empirical findings have persistently underscored the need to intervene directly with the social networks of at-risk families and, indeed, one of the frequently stated rationales for home visitation services is to provide helpful social support in ways that reduce maltreatment risks. For example, one of the explicitly stated goals of the Hawaii Healthy Start program, like other programs, is "to expand the family's personal and community support system" (Hawaii Family Stress Center, 1994, p. 16). Similarly, home visitation services have been identified as one of the most promising strategies for "enhancing social support" for the direct purposes of reducing maltreatment risk (Thompson, 1995, p. 123). It is, thus, troubling that the available empirical findings on home visitation programs' capacities to improve families' indigenous social supports are at best mixed, with most studies showing no apparent impact on this crucial factor. Given that social support is a critical variable in the child maltreatment equation, this chapter examines ways that early home visitation programs can enhance or reconfigure their services so that families may develop more supportive webs of relationships as they face their child-rearing responsibilities. This chapter first looks at what is meant by the term *social support* in the context of early prevention of child maltreatment. This chapter then examines the role that home visitation services might take in the future to more effectively address social network deficits, which have been described as one of two "necessary conditions" for the perpetration of child maltreatment (Garbarino, 1977).

THE ROLE OF SOCIAL NETWORKS
IN THE ETIOLOGY OF CHILD MALTREATMENT

Our understanding of the role of social networks in the etiology of child maltreatment has, in part, been clouded by the theoretical complexity of the social network and social support concepts. These two terms, often used interchangeably, refer to the nature of the social connections individuals hold with others in the world around them. Here, it is important to point out that the terms social network and social support typically, but not always, refer to connections with informal (rather than formal) helpers such as family, significant others, kin, neighbors, friends, or sometimes, they include religiously affiliated ties. The latter term, *social support,* often specifically connotes positive, supportive relationships, which compose one side of social network relationships. Clearly, relationships with others can also be unsupportive, coercive, or negative in a variety of ways (e.g., Schilling, 1987; Vinokur, Price, & Caplan, 1996). Thus, the term social network will be used here to connote any kind of tie, positive or negative, and social support will be used specifically to refer to positive relationships.

Social networks can be characterized in a variety of ways and along a variety of dimensions, according to how they are organized, how they function in relation to individuals, and how they are perceived and responded to by individuals. Researchers have identified such important structural social network factors as the number, frequency, and intensity of network ties, as well as their stability, density, and homogeneity (e.g., DePanfilis, 1996; Thompson, 1995). From a functional and more dynamic perspective, researchers have pointed out the importance of how network ties are used, the reciprocity between the individual and a network member, the perceived availability of and satisfaction with network ties, and the types of support provided to the individual (e.g., Barrera, 1981; Gottlieb, 1983; Sarason, Levine, Basham, & Sarason, 1983; Schilling, 1987; Vaux, 1988).[1]

Given the complicated nature of social networks, it is no surprise that studies linking social network factors with child maltreatment risk have often been questioned or critiqued in the ways they assess important social network properties (e.g., Coohey, 1996; DePanfilis, 1996; Moncher, 1995; Seagull, 1987; Thompson, 1995). Nonetheless, broad patterns provide preliminary directions for understanding some of the important aspects of social networks as they shape maltreatment risk. These include parents' isolation from network members and community supports, which constricts the availability of important support ingredients necessary for effective parenting, and the influential role of key significant others, particularly fathers, in shaping the parenting process.

It has often been asserted that abusive and/or neglectful families are socially isolated (Salzinger, Kaplan, & Artemyeff, 1983). Social isolation entails a "lack of integration into social networks, the diminution of contacts and communication with others, and a condition of being cut off from intimate ties for extended periods" (Rook, 1984, p. 252). Chapter 2 has earlier noted that studies spanning three decades of work have, indeed, persistently identified indicators of social isolation as being associated with maltreatment risk (e.g., Adamakos et al., 1986; Altemeier et al., 1979, 1984; Chan, 1994; Coohey, 1996; Elmer, 1967; Garbarino & Sherman, 1980; Gaudin & Pollane, 1983; Gaudin et al., 1993; Kirkham et al., 1986; Lauer et al., 1974; Newberger et al., 1977; Salzinger, Kaplan, & Artemyeff, 1983; Smith, Hanson, & Noble, 1974; Starr, 1982; Straus & Kantor, 1987; Straus & Smith, 1990; Young, 1964). For example, studies have found the following dimensions of social isolation to be specifically linked with maltreatment risk:

- Decreased interactions with others outside the home or decreased opportunities to receive their support (Bishop & Leadbeater, 1999; Chan, 1994; Corse et al., 1990; Crittenden, 1985; Moncher, 1995; Polansky, Gaudin, Ammons, & Davis, 1985; Salzinger, Kaplan, & Artemyeff, 1983)

- Decreased availability and use of child care (e.g., Garbarino & Sherman, 1980; Kotch & Thomas, 1986; Kotelchuck, 1982; Oates et al., 1985)

- Decreased opportunities for respite from parenting and for activities outside the home (Disbrow, Coerr, & Caufield, 1977; Oates et al., 1985)

- Parental perceptions of loneliness and isolation (Polansky et al., 1985; Smith et al., 1974)
- Reduced interactions with kin and/or fewer adults in the household (e.g., Albarracin, Repetto, & Albarracin, 1997; Coohey, 1996; Faller, 1981; Justice et al., 1985; Kinard, 1995; Perry, Wells, & Doran, 1983; Seagull, 1987)

and as a corollary to this,

- Single parenthood (e.g., Gelles, 1989; Smith et al., 1974; Wolfe, 1985)

Based on several of these factors, most particularly that of single parenthood, it can be inferred that studies identifying social network problems as a risk factor in child maltreatment have seldom sought to independently tease out the role of economic impoverishment in both social network problems and maltreatment risk status (and, indeed, have sometimes defined low social support as *including* economic impoverishment—e.g., Crittenden, 1985; Dukewich et al., 1996).[2] Thus, it is not yet fully clear to what extent economic impoverishment serves as an overarching cause of social network problems as they are related to maltreatment risk (Kinard, 1995; Seagull, 1987) and how social network problems, independent of economic impoverishment, may act to heighten maltreatment risk. Nonetheless, of those few studies that have controlled for economic impoverishment, social network and neighborhood problems still play an independent and influential role (e.g., Chan, 1994; Garbarino & Kostelny, 1992; Hashima & Amato, 1994).

Several reasons have been advanced as to why positive and supportive social networks aid parents in ways that minimize the risk they will maltreat their children (DePanfilis, 1996; Guterman, 1990; Thompson, 1995). In social support theory, supportive ties have been thought to assist parents via two pathways: a "main effects" or "stress prevention" pathway, in which parents' self-esteem and internal capacities to competently manage difficult situations are enhanced, and a "buffering" pathway, which provides direct aid to parents as they seek to surmount immediately stressful situations (Cohen & Wills, 1985; House et al., 1988; Thompson, 1995). Researchers examining the role of social support in child maltreatment risk have pointed out that socially supportive networks can serve as primary vehicles for delivering the following important ingredients for the parenting process (DePanfilis, 1996; Korbin, 1994; Thompson, 1995):

- Tangible or material aid such as money, child care, transportation, housing, or clothing
- Emotional support, such as validation, opportunities to vent, acceptance, love, and nurturance
- Instrumental information that can be applied in effectively carrying out the role of parenthood, such as knowledge informing appropriate developmental expectations, information that facilitates parenting techniques and skill development (e.g., about breast-feeding, toilet training, helping an infant settle into sleep patterns), or information on accessing necessary and helpful resources (e.g., doctors, infant products, child care)
- Feedback information about parental performance, which can serve to validate parents' efforts, communicate social and culturally acceptable norms of behavior, and/or monitor and correct inappropriate behaviors
- Companionship, which balances and provides some respite from the parenting role, such as leisure and recreational activities, sexual fulfillment, and involvement in voluntary or community activities
- Sense of empowerment, in which parents can develop greater feelings of efficacy as parents, affirm their connectedness with others in the challenges of parenting, and confirm that they, too, can contribute in ways having a positive influence in their families and surrounding world (see Chapter 9)

Parents with less supportive networks, which fail to deliver such ingredients, face parenting with comparatively fewer material and psychological resources, less information about appropriate parenting behavior, fewer outlets, and diminished opportunities to develop essential parenting competencies.

Large or dense social networks characterized by frequent interactions do not in themselves necessarily promote positive parenting (e.g., Crittenden, 1985). Rather what appears critical in considering the role of social networks in preventing child maltreatment is the way these ingredients are transmitted to families, how families perceive the support available and received, and how they tap their networks toward these ends. For example, several studies have pointed out that parents' maltreatment risk is determined not merely by the frequency and intensity of contacts with network members but more importantly with whom they hold primary relationships, whether these relationships are perceived as supportive or conflictual, and to what degree such relationships hold a degree of reciprocity (e.g., Beeman, 1997; Coohey, 1996; Corse et al., 1990; Crittenden, 1985; DePanfilis, 1996; Garbarino & Sherman, 1980; Moncher, 1995). Beyond mere social isolation, then, families challenged with parenting young children are involved in an unfolding interactional process with a variety of others, in a network that may have helpful and meaningful elements or, conversely, difficult and undermining elements with respect to successful parenting.

THE STRENGTH OF STRONG AND WEAK TIES IN CHILD MALTREATMENT RISK

Work by Granovetter (1973) has pointed out the importance of considering the "strength of weak ties"—that is, interactions with non-primary network members that nonetheless shape opportunities, experiences, and behaviors such as parenting. Increasing attention has, indeed, been given to the important role of less primary ties, such as those with neighbors or other community members (e.g., Barry, 1994; Melton & Barry, 1994), as well as to relationships with broader exosystemic institutions and processes that help "set the stage" for family life to occur (Garbarino, 1980). For example, although macrosystemic factors such as economic impoverishment have often been viewed as prime "stage setting" factors for the occurrence of child maltreatment (e.g., Pelton, 1994), evidence suggests that neighborhood factors may mediate the pressures of economic distress on parenting processes and child outcomes (e.g., Brooks-Gunn, Duncan, Klebanov, & Sealand, 1993).

Several reasons have been advanced to explain why and how community and neighborhood influences, although most often "weaker ties" than immediate family relationships, nonetheless may interpose between economic impoverishment and maltreatment risk. Evidence suggests that economic impoverishment is associated with "social impoverishment." That is, impoverished families are more likely to be living in neighborhoods that are characterized by more stressful and less positive interactions and that provide comparatively diminished access to community resources important in the rearing of children (such as day care centers, family activities, and clubs; e.g., see Garbarino & Sherman, 1980).

Related to this, a preliminary link has been found between child maltreatment risk and the extent to which neighborhoods are characterized by social organization or disorganization, the degree to which formal and informal institutions and relations contribute to the aims of the local residents, delivering needed resources for daily living and socialization of children (Coulton et al., 1995). It has been shown that outcomes frequently occurring with high child maltreatment rates, such as high crime rates and high infant mortality rates, tend to be higher in communities characterized by greater social disorganization and lessened "social capital." Low social capital settings are those that provide relatively fewer social benefits to residents due to a paucity of opportunities to participate in civic life or in networks of relationships characterized by mutual trust and reciprocity (Bordieu, 1985; Coleman, 1990; Kawachi, Kennedy, Lochner, & Prothrow-Stith, 1997; Kawachi, Kennedy, & Wilkenson, 1999; Portes, 1998; Putnam, 1993). It has been posited that in the context of such community settings, families can withdraw from community interactions in a mutually deteriorating process, undermining local norms and their enforcement, reducing mutually available resources and supports, and therefore diminishing the overall effectiveness of community institutions and controls governing social and family life (Portes, 1998; Sampson, 1991). Work by Robert Sampson and colleagues, for example, has shown that community-level "collective efficacy" (i.e., the willingness of local residents to act for the common good within socially cohesive contexts holding prosocial norms) has been linked with the level of violence in a neighborhood. Work by Furstenberg (1993) has more directly documented that parenting success has been linked with how well neighbors know one another, feel common values, and know of neighborhood organizations in which they can participate. Such work points out that socially cohesive, mutually trusting, and helping neighborhoods can have a beneficial influence on the parent-child microsystem.

It is, however, important to point out that influences between families and their surrounding communities are highly complex, not yet well understood, and likely bi-directional. That is, although community factors may likely shape parenting behaviors, our understanding is limited by the majority of existing studies, which are largely correlational and not multileveled. Data are most frequently examined in aggregate at a single point in time, so that developmental processes between individual families and larger neighborhood effects are highly difficult to track. It has been posited, for example, that findings correlating neighborhood processes and child maltreatment may be in part due to individual rather than community influences. Namely, as noted by Coulton, Korbin, and Su (1999), it may be that high-risk parents "select or are forced to choose" high-risk neighborhoods (p. 1020). Also, a bi-directional pattern between neighborhood processes and individual responses may be present in the findings linking neighborhood factors with child maltreatment, and when these are taken into account, the unique potency of neighborhood forces to independently predict child maltreatment may become less robust (Coulton et al., 1999).

Parents' unfolding pattern of interactions with strong ties also most clearly plays an essential role in nurturing or undermining the quality of caregiving during the transition to parenthood and in the first years of a child's life (e.g., Bogat, Caldwell, Guzman, Galasso, & Davidson, 1998; Crnic, Greenberg, Robinson, & Ragozin, 1984; Crockenberg, 1987). Indeed, such strong ties as grandmothers or fathers often serve directly as sources of caregiving for children (Colletta, Hadler, & Gregg, 1981), although early home visitation services have rarely considered intervention approaches that effectively engage such significant figures as fathers or grandmothers as primary service recipients.

Drawing from attachment theory, scholars have especially noted that primary relationships with one's own parents help determine how one will interact with others later in life, including relationships with social network members and with one's own children (Steele & Steele, 1994). The nature of attachments in parents' own upbringing has, of course, long been identified as one of the most consistent factors in their potential to maltreat their children (e.g., Caliso & Milner, 1994; Milner, Robertson, & Rogers, 1990; Widom, 1989). What is suggested by these findings is a developmental and interactive process across the life span whereby individuals may have learned coercive, rejecting, disengaging, or neglectful "internal working models" of primary relationships, along with attendant social behaviors. They may then generalize these patterns of interactions to a variety of others as they grow up. George and Main's (1979) important study, for example, demonstrated that children abused by their parents later generalized both higher aggressive and self-isolating behaviors toward other children. As individuals develop into adults and make the transition to parenthood, such earlier life experiences may continue to influence relationships with others, especially such primary relationships as those with spouses, partners, or grandparents (Chen, Telleen, & Chen, 1995; Levitt, Weber, & Clark, 1986; Olds, Kitzman, et al., 1997; Sherman & Donovan, 1991).

Such relational patterns do show some plasticity and can be altered by later life experiences. For example, among parents who were maltreated in childhood, those who later successfully develop supportive primary network ties tend to show lower propensities to maltreat their own children (Egeland et al., 1988; Litty, Kowalski, & Minor, 1996; Milner et al.,

1990). As such, it appears that social supports influence and are influenced by parents' own developing social capacities and competencies in a transactional manner (Bishop & Leadbeater, 1999; Guterman, 1990; Schilling, 1987; Thompson, 1995). Some of the same competencies that parents employ to engage social networks may overlap with those that influence the quality of their parenting.

FATHERS AND MALTREATMENT RISK

Although little attention has been directly focused on fathers in early child maltreatment prevention efforts, it has been increasingly recognized that fathers are integral players in the early days of parenting, especially in relation to a family's overall child maltreatment risk status. In addition to the traditional view that economic benefits may accompany a father's presence in families with young children, fathers also play an important role in mothers' adaptation to the role of motherhood and directly in the child-rearing process itself. Although fathers may more commonly play a secondary role in direct provision of child care, recent studies have refuted preconceived notions that fathers—particularly those in young low-income families of color—are uninvolved in parenting (e.g., Danziger & Radin, 1990; Field, 1998; Hossain, Field, Pickens, Malphurs, & Del Valle, 1997; Parks & Arndt, 1990; Vandell, Hyde, Plant, & Essex, 1997), underscoring a pressing need to carefully weigh their role when serving families with young children. Fathers' involvement in child rearing has been shown to predict qualities of the home environment (Cutrona, Hessling, Bacon, & Russell, 1998) and child developmental outcomes (Feldman, Greenbaum, Mayes, & Erlich, 1997; Hodges, Landis, Day, & Oderberg, 1991), including risk for child neglect (Dubowitz, 1999). Fathers themselves may form independent attachments with their infants, promoting their security, and infants' security of attachments with mothers and fathers appear to be mutually influenced and interdependent (Field, 1998; Fox, Calkins, & Bell, 1991; Hossain, Field, Gonzalez, & Malphurs, 1994).

The quality of mothering provided to an infant is clearly linked with supports she receives from her partner, and the quality of the relationship between partners plays a substantial role in how both parents nurture and respond to an infant's needs (Brunelli, Wasserman, Rauh, & Alvarado, 1995; Donovon & Leavitt, 1989; Parks, Lenz, & Jenkins, 1992; Samuels, Stockdale, & Crase, 1994). At the same time, as partners adjust to parenting a new infant in the home, they each face increased demands and stresses that challenge their relationship. Fathers may worry about the role they will play in parenting, about increasing family burdens, and about changes linked to the infant's presence. Mothers may themselves worry about the evolving role their partners will play, and the relationship between mothers and their partners may pass through a substantial transition, raising the potential for increased conflict and declining satisfaction in the relationship (cf. Nitz, Ketterlinus, & Brandt, 1995; Osofsky, 1985).

Mounting evidence underscores that troubled relationships with partners appear notably linked with maltreatment risk, and that coercive interactions with significant others appear linked with heightened coercive behaviors toward children (e.g., Corse et al., 1990; Dumas, 1986; Kirkham et al., 1986; Straus & Kantor, 1987). Coohey (1996), for example, found that although three quarters of neglectful mothers in her study reported having partners, they also reported feeling less companionship, less instrumental support, and less exchange of resources from their partners, in comparison with non-neglectful mothers.

In instances where partner conflict may turn violent, families face especially heightened risk for child maltreatment (Edelson, 1999). Studies, for example, have found an inordinately high co-occurrence of domestic violence in cases of child maltreatment. Hangen's (1994) study reported that 32% of reviewed child protective services cases indicated the presence of domestic violence in the home. Similarly, studies of children suspected of being maltreated conducted from hospital settings have reported that between 45% and 59% of their mothers showed evidence of being battered by their partners (McKibben, De Vos, & Newberger, 1991; Stark & Flitcraft, 1988). Of most profound concern, domestic violence has been linked with the most severe forms of child maltreatment. For example, domestic violence was found to be present in 41% of cases of critical and fatal child maltreatment in a state of Oregon review (Oregon Children's Services Division, 1993) and in 40% to 43% of child maltreatment fatalities in child fatality reviews from New York City and the state of Massachusetts (Child Fatality Review Panel, 1993; Felix & McCarthy, 1994). Given such findings, it is not surprising that male partners or fathers are overrepresented as perpetrators in cases of fatal child abuse in early childhood (Brewster et al., 1998; Krugman, 1985; Margolin, 1990, 1992).

Aside from heightened risk of direct abuse and neglect against the child, partner violence has been linked with additional detrimental psychosocial sequelae in children, including increased aggression, depression, cognitive delays, and symptoms of post-traumatic stress disorder (Shipman, Rossman, & West, 1999). Given such consequences, children's mere exposure to partner violence (independent of their direct victimization) has increasingly been incorporated in legal definitions of child neglect (Magen, 1999). Although further study is needed to understand the unfolding of physical child abuse and neglect in instances where domestic violence is present, it is clear that effective prevention efforts must assiduously attend to risks of domestic violence, particularly given that such violence raises worries about the possible perpetration of the most lethal forms of child maltreatment.

HOME VISITATION AND SOCIAL NETWORK SUPPORTS: THE CURRENT STATE

What has been the role of early home visitation services in addressing the complicated yet important social network influences that shape child maltreatment risk? Traditionally, early home visitation services have themselves been promoted as a formalized vehicle for providing social support to families, or as a bridge to enhance social supports. For example, as Ross Thompson (1995) has noted,

> By going to the recipient's home and offering many kinds of supportive assistance, home visitors hope to compensate for the absence of this (social supportive) aid from neighbors, friends, and extended kin. . . . Some home visitation programs employ a social support model, in which the visitor's efforts are focused on providing counseling, emotional reassurance, friendly advice, parenting guidance, concrete aid . . . and other kinds of assistance to enhance the emotional well-being and coping skills of the parent. . . . The overall goal of this approach to home visitation, therefore, is to provide the family with many kinds of supportive assistance that will ease the transition to parenting (for first time parents), strengthen parental competencies and/or coping, and otherwise contribute to family well-being by reducing the family's limited social embeddedness. (pp. 125-126)

In a similar vein, Heather Weiss (1993) has noted,

> Home visits, especially if they are relatively frequent and skillfully done, afford the opportunity to build a supportive and continuing one-to-one relationship between visitor and parent that promotes adult and parenting

growth and change. This special relationship can become a powerful bridge for intensive transmission of social support in the form of emotional, informational, and instrumental assistance. . . . For some families, especially those distrustful of services, building a trusting relationship through home visits is an essential first step to subsequently persuading parents to participate in any other center-based programs or parent groups. (pp. 118-119)

To what degree have home visitation services been able to successfully reduce families' limited social embeddedness, serving as a "bridge" for the transmission of social support? As noted in Chapter 4, home visitation programs ordinarily include case management activities that link families with needed formal supports, such as health care, public assistance, or mental health services (e.g., Black et al., 1994; Brayden et al., 1993; Caruso, 1989; Daro et al., 1998; Olds, Henderson, Chamberlin, et al., 1986; Olds, Henderson, Tatelbaum, et al., 1986; Siegel et al., 1980). As an example of this "bridge" function, Healthy Start-type programs regularly link families with a "medical home," where health care services such as well-baby visits are coordinated between home visitor and the health care organization (Breakey & Pratt, 1991). Home visitation programs, however, have less frequently acted in similarly systematic ways to help parents address the complex yet potent influences of strong and weak informal social ties (see Larson, 1980; Olds, 1997).

One of the more clearly documented examples of attending to informal network relations in the course of early home visitation services, particularly with regard to fathers and grandmothers, is provided in the Prenatal/Early Infancy Project (PEIP; Olds, 1982). While engaging families during the prenatal period, nurse home visitors in the PEIP, for example, seek to include boyfriends or husbands as well as other key family members, such as grandmothers or sisters. During this period, informal network members are encouraged to accompany the mother-to-be to the obstetrician's office and childbirth classes and to practice exercises and relaxation techniques with her. A designated coach is encouraged to assist with labor and delivery as well as with household chores to reduce the woman's strain as she nears birth. Mothers-to-be are asked to identify a "life-line" support person to whom they may turn when they are having troubles with parenting the infant.

Postnatally, fathers or other support members are asked to participate at several specific points, through the end of services. At around the fourth month postnatally, a home visit is arranged that seeks to include the father or support person in discussion of early child-development concerns. Around the eighth month, nurse visitors again attempt to include the support person in discussions about child discipline and the infant's developing autonomy, and they broach the topic of how the parents themselves were raised, to help them anticipate and address potential conflicts in child-rearing styles. Fathers and support members are again invited to participate in child-rearing discussions at 12 and 16 months (Olds, 1982). Despite the PEIP's focus on one or two specific support people and their limited participation in services, particularly postnatally, the PEIP's protocol to include support members at strategic service points remains unusual within the early home visitation field.

More commonly, home visitation services have addressed social support needs either via the home visitor's own direct provision of social support to the family or through adjunct parent support-group activities held in parallel with home visiting services. Across program models, home visitors are often viewed as directly providing what Dawson et al. (1989, 1990) have labeled "informal social support" in the form of emotional aid and availability, concrete help with transportation or lunches, information on pregnancy and infant care, and suggestions for improving relationships with friends and family.

A number of early home visitation programs have also reported attempts at mounting parent support groups that are an adjunct to home visits (Brayden et al., 1993; Caruso, 1989; Center on Child Abuse Prevention Research, 1996; Dawson et al., 1989, 1990; Marcenko et al., 1996; McCormick et al., 1998). Although there has been little examination of the role, function, or structure of parent support groups within the context of early home visitation, such groups have typically focused on content involving parent-child interaction, health, nutrition, and safety domains rather than on the explicit expansion and/or improvement of families' social supports (e.g., Center on Child Abuse Prevention Research, 1996; McCormick et al., 1998). Programs that include group services have persistently reported that such groups are substantially underattended (Brayden et al., 1993; Caruso, 1989; Dawson et al., 1989, 1990; Liaw et al., 1995; McCurdy, in press; Wagner & Clayton, 1999). As a typical example, McCurdy (in press) noted that in the Hawaii Healthy Start Program, only one third of the mothers attended any support group sessions, and those attending sessions participated in an average of only four sessions throughout a year's time. Likewise, Wagner and

Clayton (1999) reported that less than 15% of mothers ever attended any of the group sessions offered in the Parents as Teachers program.

Given that early home visitation programs have, by and large, attended to families' social support needs either through home visitors' direct provision of surrogate support or by substantially underused parent support groups, it is no surprise that such programs have rarely demonstrated their capacity to improve families' indigenous support networks. The PEIP trial in Elmira, New York, exerting perhaps the most explicit efforts to work with select informal network members during home visitation, found that home-visited fathers showed greater interest during pregnancy and that mothers were accompanied to the labor room more frequently than those in control group families. However, aside from one subgroup finding indicating greater family help with child care at 10 months postpartum (only among nurse-visited, older, poor, unmarried women), no postnatal social support differences appear linked with home visitation services (Olds et al., 1988).[3]

Similarly, Marcenko and colleagues (Marcenko & Spence, 1994; Marcenko et al., 1996) reported that although home-visited families showed some gains in their social support networks at 10 months after initiation of services, these gains were lost at 16 months when services ended, and indeed, support levels ended slightly below the level reported at the start of services. Furthermore, although parents reported some increased social support at the 10-month point of service delivery, Marcenko and Spence (1994) note that the higher social support scores were "probably directly attributable to the relationship between the women in the study and their peer home visitors" (p. 476), rather than to meaningful increases in indigenous supports received by home-visited mothers.

Evaluations of the Healthy Start model of home visitation have consistently reported virtually no discernable program effects on families' social support networks, and indeed, home-visited families have occasionally reported slightly lower (although not statistically significant) social support in select domains when compared against control group families at follow-up (Daro & Harding, 1999; Duggan et al., 1999; McCurdy, in press).

Taken as a whole, these findings point out that although home visitation services have been promoted as a potential vehicle for enhancing families' informal social supports, they have on the whole yet to show a positive impact in this area during the postnatal period and beyond. Furthermore, findings from Marcenko and colleagues (Marcenko & Spence, 1994; Marcenko et al., 1996) and from evaluations of Healthy Start programs have raised the possibility that the home visitor's role as a surrogate support person may, in fact, create unanticipated hindrances to improving families' own indigenous support systems. For example, by providing direct social support ingredients to compensate for families' indigenous support deficits, home visitors may also serve to diminish families' motivation and efforts to identify and develop their own indigenous support pathways over the longer term.

PRACTICE PRINCIPLE 7.1: To promote long-term positive change in parenting and address potent social network influences in child maltreatment risk, early home visitation services must advance beyond serving as a form of surrogate social support toward providing fully developed assessment, engagement, and intervention activities targeting families' own indigenous support systems.

EMERGING DIRECTIONS IN EFFECTIVELY TAPPING SOCIAL NETWORKS VIA HOME VISITATION SERVICES

How might home visitation services move beyond serving as a surrogate social support system to enhance families' own indigenous supports in the parenting process? What specific activities might directly serve to promote families' more self-sufficient reliance on helpful support systems and to assist them in effectively negotiating troubling or conflictual relationships? Although the field of early home visitation services has yet to fully address families' informal social networks in ways that reduce child maltreatment risk, evidence from allied service domains points out the clear potential to forge advances in this area. Several key strategies are identifiable from programs serving maltreating families or high-risk families facing other related problems. These strategies include:

- *Assessment of families' social networks* in ways that identify their existing strengths, sources of conflict, unmet needs, and areas where services may assist in mobilizing ongoing support for parents

- *Social skills-building activities* that serve to enhance families' capacities to identify their needs, tap needed supports, and manage difficult network relations
- *Direct intervention in and work with informal social network sources* to enhance the support families receive, to negotiate more productive exchanges, or to mobilize untapped supports
- *Organizing "quasi-informal" self-help groups* of similar families to enhance reciprocal learning, a sense of shared challenges, and indigenous supports on a longer-term basis

ASSESSING FAMILIES' SOCIAL NEWORKS AND INTERVENTION PLANNING IN RELATION TO MALTREATMENT RISK

PRACTICE PRINCIPLE 7.2: As a first step, home visitation services should systematically assess families' informal social networks over time, examining the roles they play in supporting families and the ways they may directly reduce or heighten maltreatment risk.

As a standard feature of social support activities within the context of home visitation services, careful assessment of families' informal social networks is critical. Although home visitation programs often carefully assess families' needs for formalized supports, programs also require means to systematically assess the complex web of informal relationships with immediate family members, kin, friends, and neighbors in ways that can guide their work with families. Do parents have the necessary skills to recognize their support needs and then to scan the environment to look for sources of assistance meeting those needs? Who in the family validates parents in their roles or provides useful feedback about parents' efforts to respond to their infant's needs? Are there members of the family who can provide needed concrete assistance, such as transportation, child care, money, or assistance with chores, during especially stressful times? Do some network ties exacerbate parents' felt stresses by criticizing or undermining their efforts to respond to children's needs? To what degree can network members become engaged in ways that minimize their potentially negative influences on the family or that maximize positive support they may provide? Can parents recognize problems in network relationships and consider how to manage them? Such questions must be weighed carefully before seeking to articulate goals for intervention.

Although not yet visibly applied within home visitation services, social network assessment tools addressing some of these questions are available and adaptable for use. Psychometrically tested social network assessment tools for families with young children include the Systematic Assessment of Social Support Inventory (Dunst & Trivette, 1990), the Maternal Social Support Index (Pascoe, Loda, Jeffries, & Earp, 1981), the Arizona Social Support Inventory (Barrera, 1980), and the Inventory of Socially Supportive Behaviors (Barrera, Sandler, & Ramsay, 1981; see Dunst & Trivette, 1990, for discussion of some of the most widely used scales). Many of these scales hold psychometric rigor and yield information on overall support levels; however, they may not provide the level of clinical detail necessary to understand network dilemmas or complexities and to guide intervention planning. Other available social network assessment tools may provide greater practice utility by providing venues for a family and home visitor to depict and discuss family needs in relation to their existing social network, promoting goal setting for improvements. These include the Eco-map (Hartman, 1978), the Social Network Map (Tracy & Whittaker, 1990), and the Social Network Diagram (Guterman, 1997c). With the exception of the Social Network Map, however, these applied tools developed for clinical practice require further research demonstrating their empirical validity and reliability. Mapping tools such as these, nonetheless, serve as means to lay out the terrain for families and workers in ways that identify social network sources, the supports received, and the degree to which families' support needs are satisfied or unmet. By identifying networks graphically, these assessment techniques also provide a concrete means to help families and workers collaboratively identify goals and activities for improvement, as well as means to evaluate their progress in seeking to improve network supports.

Once parents and their home visitors develop an understanding of how a family's social network is functioning in relation to a family's expressed needs, home visitors can begin to develop intervention strategies aimed at enhancing informal supports. In considering strategies for intervention, home visitors must consider not only supports or social stresses in the environment but also families' capacities to manage their network ties. Home visitors may consider a variety of strategies to mobilize and/or enhance the functioning of supportive networks on behalf of families. These means may include directly intervening with network members, providing social skills training (e.g., through role playing, role modeling, or rehearsal with families) to promote more satisfying social interactions, or merely assisting families to identify and think through their own goals for improvement.

PRACTICE PRINCIPLE 7.3: To consider social network interventions that will most likely benefit families over the long term, home visitation service providers should consider not only properties of the social networks in which families are embedded but also families' own capacities to manage network challenges.

Home visitors may adopt varying intervention strategies and degrees of directiveness in their approach depending on families' own capacities, skills, and motivations for managing their own social network challenges. Families with sound skills in assertiveness, problem solving, and social reciprocity may merely need psychoeducational assistance to adjust to the changing demands made on their network during early infancy and to devise ways to assist network members to adjust their support to meet families' evolving needs. Families at risk for child maltreatment most commonly show problematic social skills, for example, in the areas of assertiveness, initiation of interactions, self-disclosure, and empathy (e.g., Kropp & Haynes, 1987; Scott, Baer, Christoff, & Kelley, 1984). With such families, greater assistance is required not only in recognizing the stressful transitions that accompany pregnancy and early childhood but also in exercising such skills as identifying their own unmet needs and seeking help from potential support members (e.g., Gaudin, 1993). Still other families may be so overwhelmed with the stresses of this sensitive period that they may also benefit from direct intervention in their interactions with other network members or even direct intervention with those network members to help them understand and respond to families' needs (see Figure 7.1).

As home visitation services take place during only a small portion of the week and ultimately withdraw their supports over time, programs must promote families' own capacities to meet their needs, seeking opportunities for families to learn skills and to develop a sense of efficacy in managing their own challenges (see also Chapter 9). For these

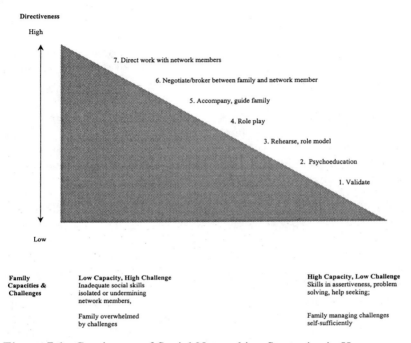

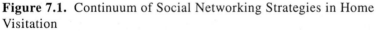

Figure 7.1. Continuum of Social Networking Strategies in Home Visitation

reasons, group-based interventions have been promoted as a vehicle to connect families with one another. Parent support groups designed expressly to expand and improve social supports and social skills (rather than to teach parenting skills and knowledge) may open avenues to develop longer-term relationships with other parents, promote families' "collective efficacy" (Bandura, 1997) in solving challenges, and provide opportunities to reciprocally exercise skills.

SOCIAL NETWORK GROUPS

Group-based services have frequently been used for child abuse and neglect intervention and prevention, but most often, these approaches have focused on delivering parent training or education. Less frequently, they have been used for the explicit purpose of enhancing families' support networks (e.g., Whipple & Wilson, 1996; see Wekerle & Wolfe, 1993). However, group-based support modalities integrated with in-home services can provide a number of distinct advantages over home-based services alone in addressing social network concerns. Support groups specifically aimed at enhancing families' social networks form a constructed network of similar parents, affording opportunities for parents to link with one another, share experiences, and reduce feelings of loneliness that many parents at risk for maltreatment report (Polansky et al., 1985; Smith et al., 1974). Participation in group sessions aimed at expanding social networks provides parents unique opportunities to reach out to others and to enact the major support-building strategies identified in Figure 7.1 in ways that are both time- and cost-efficient. Group activities afford opportunities for families to observe and role model from other parents' help-seeking efforts in order to practice and exercise skills in managing difficult relationships, to strategize with one another about how to resolve network difficulties, and to learn reciprocal efforts at help giving and help receiving, so often noted as a prevalent theme in child maltreamtent risk (Coohey, 1996; DePanfilis, 1996; Polansky et al., 1985). Furthermore, if groups are structured appropriately, their members can continue contact with one another outside of group meetings, affording real-world opportunities to provide one another direct assistance in handling difficult challenges and to exercise social skills such as help seeking. As group members proceed to identify common goals and challenges, a sense of connectedness can develop among members along with shared norms and expectations. When sensitively guided by a professional, such developments may provide parents with an alternative reference group that can convey appropriate expectations in the parenting role and promote the development of a sense of collective efficacy (Sampson, 1991).

At present, the evidence base on which to judge optimal approaches to enhance social supports within a support group modality is limited. Social skills groups training for enhancing supports among young mothers has received some support. For example, support group interventions focused on training in help-seeking and negotiation skills have shown promise for pregnant and parenting teen women at risk of child maltreatment (Barth & Schinke, 1984; Schinke, Schilling, Barth, Gilchrist, & Maxwell, 1986). At the completion of group sessions, participating women reported improvements in social skills and in their social support networks, although it is unclear to what degree such changes were lasting and resulted in actual improvements in parenting. In addition to social skills training, the Social Network Intervention Project (SNIP) reported by Gaudin and colleagues linked neglectful families with mutual aid groups and neighborhood helpers, providing direct advocacy activities. Such efforts resulted in improvements not only in social networks but also in a broad range of parenting attitudes that are linked with child neglect (Gaudin, Wodarski, Arkinson, & Avery, 1990-1991).

Other findings demonstrate that social support groups may not produce uniformly positive outcomes, underscoring the complexity of improving at-risk families' social support. The Social Support Skills Training (SSST) groups for parents already identified as maltreating young children (Lovell & Richey, 1991, 1995, 1997) engaged families in developing a "relationship road map," helping them to identify strengths and gaps in their networks, and encouraging the development of conversational and assertiveness skills to link up more effectively with needed supports. This model has reported limited success: increased interactions with professional service providers and community organizations and increases in network size, but reductions in network intensity. Somewhat parallel, a self-help support group for self-referred mothers to a family support center documented mothers' reduction in feelings of social isolation, along with a reduction in the size of their informal support networks (Telleen, Herzog, & Kilbane, 1989).

Finally, although not yet applied in a systematic way within the field of early prevention, multiple-family group approaches have reported promising outcomes in maltreating families and in families with disruptive children (McKay, Gonzales, Quintana, Kim, & Abdul-Adil, 1999; Meezan & O'Keefe, 1998). Multiple-family group approaches bring all involved family members to a group setting to share information, address common concerns, and develop supportive networks (McKay, Gonzales, Stone, Ryland, & Kohner, 1995; O'Shea & Phelps, 1985). Although the focus of such groups is typically placed on shared concerns in the domain of parent-child interaction, some explicit focus has also been placed on developing supportive ties with other adults and support sources. Studies of multiple-family group approaches have shown increased rates of family participation in services offered in conjunction with groups, reduced child maltreatment potential, and increased satisfaction with informal and formal supports in maltreating families (McKay et al., 1999; Meezan & O'Keefe, 1998). However, improvements in informal social supports have been deemed to be largely attributable to interactions with other group members, rather than to ongoing improvement of interactions with indigenous supports (Meezan & O'Keefe, 1998).

Several authors have suggested that involvement in professionally sponsored support groups may account for some of the observed positive changes reported in social supports, and findings suggest that such involvement may unintentionally promote reductions in support from indigenous network members (e.g., Telleen et al., 1989).

PRACTICE PRINCIPLE 7.4: Group-based social support activities as an adjunct to home visitation services provide a promising vehicle to help families manage their social network challenges. At the same time, using such groups for the purpose of effectively tapping social supports must be done with care, mindful that existing evidence has been mixed and suggests that families may come to rely on groups as a replacement for longer term indigenous supports. Involving multiple family members within a support group modality appears to hold promise in improving engagement and retention of families in conjunctive services.

In sum, efforts to employ social network interventions must aim to catalyze and work with indigenous supports, considering ways to sustain such supports over the long term after the withdrawal of formal services. One program model that appears to catalyze supports external to the support group in a longer-term fashion is the Parents Together program described in Practice Exemplar 7.1.

PRACTICE EXEMPLAR 7.1

The Parents Together Program

Parents Together is a pilot program that aims to enhance the supportiveness of the indigenous social networks of mothers with young children. The program draws from social support and ecological theory, empowerment theory, and cognitive-behavioral theory (Bandura, 1997; Bronfenbrenner, 1977, 1979; Gutierrez & Lewis, 1999; Thompson, 1995; Zimmerman, 1990). It is adapted from social networking interventions developed for substance-abusing women and was first implemented with this population (e.g., El-Bassel, Ivanoff, Schilling, Borne, & Chen, 1995; Guterman, 1997c).

The program is implemented in a group setting and was designed as an independent component to be integrated with other ongoing formalized services. The structured curriculum can be delivered in 7 to 15 professionally led sessions, with ongoing parent-led sessions continuing afterward. Group activities are designed to give parents opportunities for new skill development with other parents, to promote mutual learning and help giving, and to launch parents' own self-sustaining, long-term support network after a professional helper has stepped away from providing formal guidance. The structured curriculum begins by providing parents psychoeducational guidance emphasizing the key role of social supports in parenting, helping parents to learn to assess the strengths and needs of their existing social networks through social network mapping exercises, and identifying specific individuals who provide them with positive support in the parenting role.

With each other, parents conduct social skills exercises and paired role-plays, and they later form family-to-family dyads, contacting one another and providing mutual assistance as they attempt to attain goals they set during group sessions. As the group sessions progress, parents discuss and test means to deepen their ties with supportive others, to manage and/or attenuate relationships with difficult others in their networks, and to identify possible network sources that can help them contend with unmet needs. They also identify barriers to successfully attaining needed support and learn problem-solving skills to aid them in overcoming such identified barriers.

During later sessions, parents begin to exercise and share leadership of the group sessions, setting group goals and agendas. They begin to prepare and discuss how they will continue the group as the professional leader steps away from facilitation. Discussions and exercises are also structured to handle tensions that may arise between formal helpers and informal network members, and ways are sought to help parents mutually align support systems—formal and informal—so that they are working in tandem, providing consistent messages.

As the formally structured sessions of the group wind down, parents begin to run group sessions, setting future agendas and goals and consulting with the facilitator and other professionals as needed. Parents set their own ground rules and make mutual commitments to one another about their ongoing participation.

In an initial evaluation of Parents Together, substance-abusing mothers with young children reported substantial pretest to posttest reductions in their perceived stress in the parenting role, improvements in their sense of personal control, and substantial positive changes in their social networks. For example, parents reported increases in conversations with others about their children, increases in help with chores and errands from family and friends, and a substantial decline in the number of network members in their lives that were labeled negative.

On network maps completed at pretest and at posttest, parents reported a fourfold decrease in negatively viewed network sources, a fivefold increase in the proportion of positively to negatively viewed network members, and a threefold increase in the proportion of positive to negative interactions with network members. In addition, they reported greater closeness with positive network members and a substantial decline in interactions with difficult members of their social networks (Guterman, 1997c). Mothers continued to hold ongoing mutual support meetings with one another for months after the withdrawal of the professional facilitator and beyond the period in which researchers collected data.

Parents Together is presently undergoing its second field-test, embedded in an early home visitation program, and will later be tested in a randomized efficacy trial where promising findings can more carefully be evaluated.

ADDRESSING THE ROLE OF FATHERS
IN HOME VISITATION SERVICES

Although fathers or male partners clearly play a critical role in maltreatment risk (particularly in its most severe forms) and are integral members of a majority of families engaged in early home visitation services, the field of early home visitation services has largely overlooked fathers as core service recipients (Guterman, 1997a). This oversight is particularly troubling, given their clear influence on mothers' participation in services and the degree to which they benefit (e.g., Birkel & Repucci, 1983; Dumas & Wahler, 1983; Spoth et al., 1996; Webster-Stratton, 1985). Thus, one of the clear missing pieces in the field of early home visitation remains how to effectively engage and work in tandem with such primary ties as the fathers of target children.

PRACTICE PRINCIPLE 7.5: Given the mulitfaceted influence of strong-tie relationships such as those with fathers or male partners, programs must fully consider and incorporate practice strategies that promote their positive partnership and, when relevant, that minimize ways such ties complicate parents' efforts to succeed with their children.

Empirical evidence has challenged not only the notion that fathers are uninvolved in child rearing but also the preconception that fathers are somehow unengageable and/or unavailable to benefit from formalized early prevention services. Several prototype programs have reported promising strategies for engaging and educating prospective fathers before the birth of their first children. Parallel to the experience of mothers-to-be, the prenatal period has been viewed as an opportune one for young men, given their own vulnerabilities in the transition to fatherhood. Programs that educate young fathers-to-be about the prenatal phase and infant care and that promote father-infant attachments have reported positive outcomes in promoting greater father involvement, improved knowledge of child development, and greater support for the mother and infant (Honig & Pfannenstiel, 1991; Scholz & Samuels, 1992; Westney, Cole, & Munford, 1988).

Including fathers as primary targets of early home visitation services appears to be an emerging issue, and little empirical evidence is available to guide programs struggling to accomplish this aim. Some programs, such as the Prenatal/Early Infancy Project (PEIP), solicit fathers' participation in a limited number of home-based discussions of parenting topics and activities, whereas other programs such as AVANCE or selected Healthy Start sites (Rau et al., 1999; Rodriguez & Cortez, 1988; Walker et al., 1995) have mounted father education groups and support groups to promote men's positive role in the family, as well as to address specific psychosocial risks such as coping with stress and violence potential. Perhaps the most comprehensive efforts to involve fathers in early home visitation services can be found in the U.S. military. Although not widely studied and reported in professional journals, the New Parent Support Programs of the U.S. military operate on a large scale, and the emphasis on reaching out to involve fathers in home visitation services may be viewed as unique (see Practice Exemplar 7.2).

PRACTICE EXEMPLAR 7.2

The U.S. Department of Defense's New Parent Support Programs

In 1984, the U.S. military initiated a home visitation program to prevent child maltreatment, which was replicated by the late 1980s throughout the four branches of the military. By 1998, the program was reported to involve more than 60,000 families, representing more than 80% of eligible military families (U.S. Department of Defense, 1999). Stemming from the Department of Defense's aim of strengthening and supporting the role of fathers in military families, the New Parent Support Programs established standards aiming for equal participation of fathers in home visitation services (U.S. Department of Defense, 1995). Toward this end, home visitors include fathers stationed with families in service activities, and in particular, they offer parent education and support group activities specifically tailored to fathers. By including fathers as co-equal parents, New Parent Support Programs aim to boost fathers' esteem and sense of accomplishment, supporting their development of an active and involved role in the family. Programs may encourage fathers' involvement by helping them to gather baby supplies and equipment, encouraging them to accompany mothers to ultrasound appointments, and teaching them to read and respond to infants' cues such as crying or fussiness (Salas & Besetsney, in press). New Parent Support Programs are tailored to address the special needs of military families, for example, by helping fathers and mothers cope when they may be stationed away from their home communities and family support networks.

Special attention is given to instances when a woman is pregnant or has given birth while her husband is deployed for active military duty. Some New Parent Support Programs have detailed educational activities in child development, helping fathers to understand the needs of an infant and normal developmental milestones and encouraging them to think about a reunion with the family after returning from deployment. For example, the Return and Reunion program developed at the Family Service Centers in San Diego supports fathers who have been deployed away from home while their wives have given birth, helping them to understand and respect family patterns and routines that may have been set up in their absence, to discuss with their partners ways to reintegrate themselves into family routines, and to allow themselves time to learn unfamiliar caregiving tasks such as diapering or bathing, ones with which their wives may already be familiar (U.S. Department of Defense, 1995). Initial evaluations of the New Parent Support Programs conducted without comparison groups report high degrees of father participation and substantial reductions from pretest to posttest in assessed child maltreatment risk and depression, particularly those families deemed at highest risk (U.S. Department of Defense, 1999).

The particular context of the U.S. military has helped spawn greater attention to fathers in early home visitation services. Given this, lessons learned from the New Parent Support Programs must be translated to programs for civilian populations with some discretion. The New Parent Support Programs within the U.S. military, however, demonstrate the importance of setting policies that recognize the key role fathers play in family life during early childhood, policies that can lead to meaningful involvement of fathers as recipients of home visitation services. At present, the New Parent Support Programs stand out as beacons in their commitment to address the strong-tie role fathers play in maltreatment risk and its reduction.

It is critical to recognize that home visitation services, although often promoted as longer term services, only provide support to families during a relatively narrow but critical window of time in the developing life of the family. Given that this window of time is a relatively small one, home visitation programs must have their sights set on the longer term horizon of childhood, seeking catalytic changes that promote families' capacities to assist themselves and that promote alterations in their social ecology that will likely germinate longer-term sustainable supports. Toward this end, the next chapter takes a close look at emerging strategies that seek to empower families, advancing their internal capacities and the capacities of their surrounding ecological contexts to support them in their ongoing parenting challenges.

NOTES

1. As it is beyond the scope of this chapter to exhaustively examine the many theoretical dimensions identified in the study of social networks, the reader is referred to Thompson (1995) for a more thorough review and analysis, particularly as it is relevant to understanding child maltreatment and its prevention.

2. Methodologically controlling for economic impoverishment can be accomplished by matching samples on socioeconomic status or including indicators of socioeconomic status in statistical models of prediction. To date, the large majority of studies in this area has drawn samples from low socioeconomic status populations, and thus, they have often assumed a uniform effect of these indicators in attempting to parse out social network effects.

3. As reported in a forthcoming article by Olds, Kitzman, and colleagues, PEIP fathers and boyfriends in the Elmira, New York, trial appear to report favorable employment trajectories when compared to controls (Kitzman, personal communication, October 23, 1999; Olds, personal communication, October 29, 1999). Social support findings from the PEIP trial in Elmira should be interpreted with some caution, given that nurse-visited and comparison group mothers differed on a number of important social support elements and in apparently complex ways, prior to the onset of the intervention. For example, Olds et al. note that at the onset of services, nurse-visited women, in comparison to control group women, had fewer family members in their helping networks and reported less confidence that someone would accompany them to labor and delivery. At the same time, the unmarried teens in the nurse-visited group reported greater boyfriend support than those not nurse-visited (cf. Olds, Henderson, Chamberlin, et al., 1986; Olds, Henderson, Tatelbaum, et al., 1986; Olds et al., 1988). Although boyfriend/husband support was entered as a covariate to statistically control for its effects on reported outcomes, the pre-intervention differences reported, as well as the complexity of accurately measuring social networks, raise questions as to the ways network changes reported at follow-up are empirically attributable to the effects of the intervention or rather to other pre-existing differences between intervention and control groups (cf. Olds et al., 1994, for further discussion of study limitations).

Chapter 8

EMPOWERING PARENTS IN HOME VISITATION

Neil B. Guterman
with Hyeouk C. Hahm

Tammy, an 18-year-old African American woman, gave birth to her first child having received no prenatal care. Tammy was an only child whose father died before she was born. Tammy's mother had used heroin as far back as Tammy could remember, and she was incarcerated when Tammy was 5 years old. Tammy went to live with an aunt, who often disciplined her with an extension cord. In school, Tammy was labeled as learning disabled and placed in special education, later dropping out of school in the 10th grade. At 15 years of age, Tammy was raped and sodomized at gunpoint by an older man whom she often later saw in the neighborhood. She stated that around this time, she began to smoke marijuana to cope with her anxiety. Tammy met her 21-year-old boyfriend 2 months before she became pregnant, and on learning about her pregnancy, he told her that he was not ready to be a father.

When the home visitor first met Tammy in the hospital shortly after her delivery, she offered to help Tammy enroll her child on Medicaid, locate job training and employment possibilities, and learn parenting techniques. The home visitor learned that Tammy was living with her mother, who continued to use heroin. Tammy stated that her mother often insulted her and was especially critical of her capacity to care for the child and find work. Tammy told the home visitor that she loved her mother dearly and that she sometimes felt like "self-destructing." She said that the relationship with her boyfriend was stressful and that, at times, he had slapped her and threatened to leave her. When the home visitor attempted to schedule an initial home visit, Tammy said she would have to talk with her mother about a convenient time. After several attempts to call Tammy, the home visitor was able to arrange a meeting with Tammy in the late morning. When the home visitor arrived at the public housing apartment where Tammy lived no one answered the door. The worker tried several additional times to contact Tammy by phone and was able to schedule a second home visit. When she arrived at Tammy's home, the home visitor found Tammy alone with her newborn in an apartment strewn with garbage and infested with cockroaches. Observing multiple mattresses on the floor, the home visitor concluded that Tammy lived with a number of other adults. Tammy missed several subsequent scheduled meetings intended to provide her information about Medicaid and help her with attachment behaviors toward her infant. Finally, after 3 months of trying to contact Tammy, the worker learned that her phone number had been changed. After receiving no response to attempts to contact Tammy by mail, the home visitor regretfully closed the case.

Aversive relationships, the lack of resources to meet basic needs, past traumas and perceived failures, the lack of opportunities to connect with others for assistance—taken together, these may have posed insurmountable obstacles for both Tammy and her home visitor as they sought to engage in activities that would assist her as a new parent. Among the most profound of all challenges for home visitors and the programs that deploy them are those over which the individual worker and the target family appear to hold little control. These include contending with economic impoverishment, a lack of availability of and access to needed health care or specialized services, and a long-standing web of relationships characterized by coercion and/or ongoing substance abuse. It has long been known that these seemingly uncontrollable contexts of parenting, as well as parents' own "out of control" responses, are a core theme in the makeup of child maltreatment risk (Garbarino, 1980; Garbarino & Gilliam, 1980; Helfer, 1987).

It can be argued that parental control plays such a fundamental role in child maltreatment that it may comprise one of its *defining* elements. For example, child maltreatment is often operationally defined as parents' "fail(ure), by their acts or omissions, to meet the needs of their children"; that is, behavioral lapses deemed within their charge, placing a child's safety and well-being at risk (DePanfilis & Salus, 1992). When parents are expected to exercise control, according to sociocultural norms and standards of behavior, and then fail to do so, the labels *abuse* or *neglect* are applied as the harmful consequences to their children become known (e.g., National Research Council, 1993; Sedlack & Broadhurst, 1996). For example, physical child abuse may be present when a parent "loses control," disciplining a child in inappropriate ways that result in their physical injury. Child neglect may be identified when a parent fails to exercise "appropriate control" in assuring adequate childcare supervision or in preventing a child's exposure to hazardous home conditions. In contrast, although children may suffer equally from victimization in schools or neighborhoods, or from exposure to toxic environmental hazards *outside* the home, such harm is typically not labeled *child abuse* or *child neglect,* given that the detriment incurred is deemed to be outside of parental control, and therefore, outside of parental culpability.

Ironically, as Chapter 2 has pointed out, factors that often transcend and threaten parents' individual capacity to exercise their control are among the most potent and consistently identified ones heightening risk of physical child abuse and neglect. As Chapter 2 emphasized, these ecologically based influences heighten maltreatment risk, particularly in ways that serve to *disempower* parents, because the lack or loss of control serves as a motivator for abusive or neglectful responses toward children.

Early home visitation services as a field represents an advance by engaging families within their own ecological context. To date, however, little consideration has yet been given to their capacity to effectively address parents' struggles with their power and control in relation to ecological challenges (Guterman, 1997a). At present, the relative paucity of attention given in the field to this core challenge may provide one of the central explanations for the relatively small to sometimes negligible impact that such services have demonstrated in child-maltreatment risk reduction. Given that parental disempowerment forms a core causal pathway in child maltreatment risk, the efficacy of home visitation services as a field may be demonstrably amplified by the degree to which such services can begin to assist families in overcoming their struggles with disempowerment.

This chapter revisits the role of parental powerlessness and control in shaping child maltreatment risk, focusing on the potential for early home visitation services to more effectively address the power-based dilemmas that families face. Although the terms *powerlessness* and *disempowerment,* along with the antithesis term, *empowerment,* have been widely used in social sciences and public health literatures over the last decade or more, the lack of theoretical precision and careful measurement (Swift & Levin, 1987; Wallerstein, 1992; Zimmerman, Israel, Schulz, & Checkoway, 1992) in their use puts them at risk of becoming popular buzzwords, not clearly prescriptive for intervention efforts. Some have argued that more carefully conceptualized and measured terms such as *self-efficacy* have greater precision and, therefore, ultimately guide intervention more reliably (e.g., Bandura, 1997). Nonetheless, as noted in Chapter 2, the terms powerlessness and empowerment more fully capture the etiological processes involved in child maltreatment than other related terms, given that they acknowledge the potency of macro- and mesosystemic processes. Given the critical importance of these still somewhat imprecise concepts, this chapter examines the role of parental powerlessness, as well as the closely related concepts of parental control and self-efficacy as they inform child maltreatment risk and its reduction through early home visitation services. This chapter assesses the present state of home visitation services in ways that attend to parental empowerment and control and points out several promising directions in which early home visitation services may progress to more adequately address the power-based sources of child maltreatment risk.

POWERLESSNESS AND CHILD MALTREATMENT

As Chapter 2 has shown, physical abuse and neglect are inextricably interwoven with parents' problematic use of their power in relation to their children as well as with parents' struggles to feel in control in relation to their social environments (e.g., Chilamkurti & Milner, 1993; Nurius et al., 1988; Oldershaw et al., 1986; Schellenbach et al., 1991; Stringer & LaGreca, 1985). Although stressors can contribute to maltreatment risk, when parents perceive that their stresses are *uncon-*

trollable, their capacities to cope particularly begin to break down (Brosschot et al., 1998; Folkman, 1984; Goldberg et al., 1997; Greenberger et al., 1989; Lefcourt, 1992; Pearlin, 1999; Peeters et al., 1995; Thompson, 1981), leading to maltreating parenting.

As Chapters 2 and 7 have discussed, macro-, meso-, and exosystemic factors such as parents' economic impoverishment, minority group status, community social impoverishment and disorganization, coercive webs of relationships, and isolation from necessary supports may serve to reduce their sense of control by constraining life opportunities and access to necessary resources for handling parenting challenges (e.g., Coohey, 1996; Coulton et al., 1995; DePanfilis, 1996; Drake & Pandey, 1996; Garbarino & Kostelny, 1992; Garbarino & Sherman, 1980; Korbin, 1994; Kruttschnitt, McLeod, & Dornfeld, 1994; Lindsey, 1994; Richters & Martinez, 1993; Zuravin, 1989a). Also, such factors may serve to heighten painful and alienating experiences of discrimination, inequity, and/or community-level violence and, by heightening distrust and isolation from others, prevent the transmission of parenting norms and sanctions supporting culturally acceptable child rearing. Without supportive social networks, parents may lack essential resources, information, and skills, along with validation that they are capable and competent, undermining their capacity to cope successfully with daily challenges.

Such experiences tend to erode parents' confidence that they can act to attain their aspirations, promoting learned helplessness and undermining self-efficacy beliefs. Such a loss or lack of control can motivate coercive parent-to-child behavior (in an effort to establish or regain control) or, conversely, can motivate disengaged, apathetic, or escapist behavior in relation to parenting, amid resigned beliefs of helplessness (e.g., Bugental et al., 1999; see Chapter 2). Given that parents' lack or loss of power serves as a prime motivator for physical child abuse and neglect, home visitation services that address parents' power-based challenges can interrupt a key causal pathway leading to child maltreatment.

PRACTICE PRINCIPLE 8.1: To reduce child maltreatment risks over the long term, home visitation programs must consider and adequately attend to power-based challenges in the parenting role, given that parental powerlessness forms a core etiological process in the unfolding development of child abuse and neglect.

EARLY HOME VISITATION AND
PARENTS' POWERLESSNESS

Given that parental powerlessness forms a core etiological theme in maltreatment risk, in what ways have early home visitation services directly attended to this important causal pathway? Although home visitation services try to teach parents skills in interacting with their young child and to help them connect with formalized supports, their predominant focus is placed on individual coping with and adapting to life with their new child rather than on addressing the disempowering contexts in which family life is embedded. The strengths of visiting in the home— individualizing services and reaching out to specific difficult-to-reach families—also present simultaneous dilemmas in tackling many of the ecologically based factors that undermine parents' power and heighten the risks of child maltreatment: Namely, efforts to reduce aversive experiences and increase parents' supports and opportunities within the context of their neighborhoods, networks, or larger community institutions often require broader organized efforts, ones that concern groups or constituencies of families, transcending the realm of individualized service delivery to families. Yet, such activities have not formed a core strategy within home visitation programs, nor have they been well executed within the vehicle of home visitation. For example, as Chapter 7 noted, attempts to augment early home visitation services with group-based activities have had a spotty record at best, and such activities have largely been confined to transmitting parenting knowledge rather than to addressing larger environmentally located concerns that collectively challenge parents in their struggles to cope.

Existing program models of home visitation services have provided only incipient attention to parents' powerlessness as a broad etiological theme in reducing maltreatment risk. Such treatment has to date been manifested in several ways. Some programs have drawn on empowerment language to describe an overarching philosophy to their intervention approaches (e.g., Marcenko & Spence, 1994; Olds & Korfmacher, 1998). Furthermore, a broad array of programs have tried to promote skill development to enhance parental competencies or have engaged in activities aimed at improving social supports, although, as noted in Chapter 7, programs have been largely unsuccessful in this latter domain. Finally, one home visitation program targeting substance-abusing mothers, reported by Black et al. (1994), "encouraged women to become advocates for themselves and their children" (p. 442).

Since its inception, the Olds Prenatal/Early Infancy program (PEIP) model has increasingly considered the importance of "maternal sense of control" in observed service outcomes (Olds, Kitzman, et al., 1997). Among the earliest findings reported in the initial Elmira, New York, trial of the PEIP were those that discerned a key role for maternal sense of control as a conditioner of program effects on child maltreatment. Namely, Olds and colleagues found that among poor, unmarried teenage mothers, their sense of control was linked with the magnitude of the observed effects that home visitation services demonstrated on child maltreatment outcomes (see Figure 8.1). As Olds and colleagues have shown, program effects were most noticeable in mothers with a low sense of control (Olds, Henderson, Chamberlin, et al., 1986; Olds, Henderson, Tatelbaum, et al., 1986; Olds et al., 1999). In their interpretation of the findings, Olds and colleagues emphasized that women with a lower sense of control received more home visits than those with a higher sense of control,[1] thereby inferring that women's sense of control was an indication of their level of need. According to Olds and colleagues, nurse home visitors assessed families with lower control as having higher need and, therefore, provided more intensive home visiting activities for such families. Furthermore, as Olds and Korfmacher (1998) have noted that

> the mothers in Elmira with lower feelings of control did not appear to be proactive in seeking contact; they actually spent less time on the phone in self-initiated calls to the nurse. It appears, instead, that the nurses perceived the increased need for visitation by these mothers and responded with greater effort to see that the protocol was met with this particular group. (p. 33)

Some have taken findings linking the magnitude of program effects with maternal sense of control as demonstrating that the early home visitation program had a greater impact on mothers with a lower sense of control than mothers with a higher sense of control, thereby implying that programs should target services to "low control" mothers (Olds et al., 1999). However, this interpretation of these key findings overlooks the fact that *all* nurse-visited mothers, regardless of their level of personal control, exhibited about the same low rate of maltreatment after home visitation services, as is observable in findings graphed by Olds and colleagues (Olds, Henderson, Tatelbaum, et al., 1986; see Figure 8.1). The findings, therefore, indicate that targeting services only to low-control mothers should result in the same level of child maltreatment out-

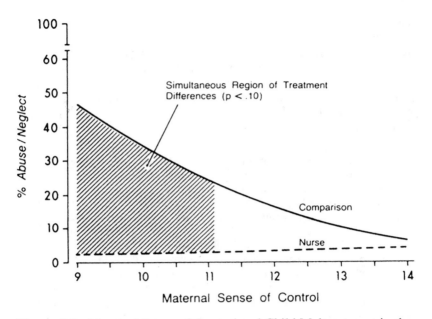

Figure 8.1. Maternal Sense of Control and Child Maltreatment in the Prenatal/Early Infancy Nurse Home Visitation Program (Elmira, New York)

SOURCE: Reprinted from *Pediatrics, 78,* D. L. Olds, C. R. Henderson, R. Chamberlin, & R. Tatelbaum, "Preventing Child Abuse and Neglect: A Randomized Trial of Nurse Home Visitation," pp. 65-78. Copyright 1986, with permission from Elsevier Science.

comes as if services were targeted to high-control mothers. It is only when comparing the relatively low levels of maltreatment found across all home-visited mothers (holding low or high control) with maltreatment among the mothers who were *not* home-visited that treatment effects for lower-control mothers appear comparatively more robust. Thus, these key findings reported by Olds and colleagues most saliently indicate that as non-home-visited mothers' sense of control increased across subjects, their maltreatment risk level declined, approaching the same relatively low risk level of nurse-visited mothers. Conversely, as non-home-visited mothers' sense of control decreased across subjects, their maltreatment risk increased.[2] In this light, rather than answering questions about appropriate targeting of services to family needs, such findings raise the significant possibility that if mothers' sense of control can be improved, this might directly reduce child maltreatment risk and even perhaps curtail the need for ongoing intensive home visitation services.

Recognizing the key role of maternal control on the outcomes observed in the Elmira study, particularly with regard to child maltreatment, Olds and colleagues have increasingly incorporated an understanding of its role in more recent PEIP trials. As Olds, Kitzman, et al. (1997) have noted,

> Self-efficacy theory was not emphasized explicitly as a theoretical foundation in [the first trial in] Elmira, however, to the same degree as it was in [later trials conducted in] Memphis and Denver. The increased focus on self-efficacy in the later trials grew out of our observation that several of the most important program effects in Elmira (in particular the reduction in child maltreatment and emergency-department encounters for injuries) were concentrated among women who at registration had little sense of control over their life circumstances. We hypothesized that the promotion of self-efficacy played a central role in enabling at-risk women to reduce . . . their dysfunctional care of their children. In reviewing these findings, we reasoned that in Elmira the nurses' emphasis on helping women gain control over specific life circumstances such as these promoted women's generalized sense of control over a wider range of life circumstances. (Olds et al., 1997, p. 17)

The PEIP home visitation model remains notable in its efforts to explicitly include strategies aiming to enhance parents' sense of control. From its inception, the program has included psychoeducational content, most notably during pregnancy, assisting mothers to understand the connections between their behaviors and the well-being of their children and seeking to influence their expectations about what their behavior could succeed in achieving for themselves and their children (Olds, 1982). For example, women are praised when they enact healthy behaviors such as keeping prenatal appointments or avoiding the use of alcohol or drugs during pregnancy (Olds, Kitzman, et al., 1997), and explicit questions assess mothers' outcome expectations and areas where their confidence may be improved. Furthermore, nurse home visitors explicitly seek to role-model effective caregiving, demonstrating how specific parenting techniques can be successfully implemented, without taking over parents' responsibilities in ways that might undermine their own confidence. In later trials, the PEIP project has also included activities to set small, realistically attainable goals promoting mothers' experiences of success, an element deemed crucial in facilitating a sense of self-efficacy (Bandura, 1997). Also, later trials have included specific skills development activities in problem-solving and solution-focused strategies, assisting mothers to envision and consider how their goals may become achieved (O'Brian & Baca, 1997). The more recent findings reported from the Memphis, Tennessee, randomized trial of the PEIP project found that home visited mothers significantly increased their generalized sense of mastery (a widely used proxy measure of personal control) when compared against control group mothers (Kitzman et al., 1997). Such findings demonstrate that mothers' sense of control appears responsive to intervention strategies aimed at its improvement.

As emphasized earlier and acknowledged by Olds, Kitzman, and colleagues (1997), however, the social environment is a potent force in providing specific opportunities for success or failure. The constraints, contradictions, and connections that the environment may present are significant influences as parents access and develop skills, knowledge, and resources necessary for effective parenting. As an example, analyses of the Memphis PEIP trial data have found that home visitation services were less successful in shaping the quality of maternal caregiving and the home environment when mothers lived in larger extended households and had limited control of household resources. Such findings underscore the limits of merely targeting the enhancement of intrapersonal perceptions of self-efficacy, as it is predominantly an individually focused strategy that must be supplemented with environmentally oriented strategies that increase the responsiveness of the environment to family needs. Emphasizing the limitations of the individually focused vehicle of home visitation services provided by Olds and colleagues, Felton Earls (1998) has emphasized,

> Policy considerations should place nurse home visitation within the larger context of the social integrity of neighborhoods and the availability and quality of medical, social, and child care services in which the lives of poor families are situated. One can only speculate on how much stronger the effects of this early intervention would have been if the program had continued beyond the child's second year of life or if efforts had been made to engage the wider social settings in which families lived. (p. 1272)

Indeed, home visitation services have yet to address these "wider social settings" adequately as they seek to alter the underlying etiological conditions that most potently breed child maltreatment.

EXPANDING HOME VISITATION SERVICES
TO EMPOWER FAMILIES

Given that the vehicle of home visitation services is a largely individually focused strategy, how might such services be augmented to more effectively target the underlying power-based struggles that characterize families at risk of child maltreatment? Here, we must re-examine general understandings of how to promote empowerment within families. The term *empowerment,* which requires further theoretical refinement, reflects an omnibus concept encompassing processes and outcomes occurring at intrapersonal, interpersonal, organizational, community, and societal levels (Bandura, 1997; Gutierrez & Lewis, 1999; Schulz, Israel, Zimmerman, & Checkoway, 1995). At its core, empowerment concerns the power and control individuals hold in their lives, the ways such power is attained, and interactions with the surrounding environment that shape and are shaped by those with or without power. Psychological levels of empowerment and powerlessness involve cognitive, affective, and behavioral components and intimately involve the nature of one's interactions with the social environment. Integrating much of the recent theory on empowerment, Gutierrez and Lewis (1999) have proposed that the process of empowering individuals includes three intra- and interpersonal elements: "consciousness, confidence, and connection" (p. 6).

In their terminology, confidence is reflective of an increasing sense of self-efficacy, as earlier discussed. Developing beliefs that one can overcome situations that earlier appeared insurmountable contributes to empowerment. Perceived success as a result of one's efforts is most influential in promoting this confidence. Secondarily, self-efficacy may be promoted through the observed successes of others as well as by attempts through social persuasion (Bandura, 1997). The PEIP has best documented its attention to this element of empowerment, particularly with regard to prenatal health habits. It is important to emphasize, however, that evidence indicates the development of self-efficacy is predominantly domain-specific (Bandura, 1997)—that is, individuals develop confidence from successful performance in specific spheres of life such as personal health habits, parenting, or peer relationships, and such confidence does not tend to generalize well across differing spheres of life. For example, although home visitation services may promote parents' sense of confidence in caring for their young children through parent skills activities, such confidence will not hold up well when parents face challenges in other life domains such as efforts to obtain employment or to manage stressful relations with neighbors or public bureaucracies. Given this, efforts to promote parents' self-efficacy must cut across life domains and most especially must entail experiences of success in relation to challenges posed by the social environment, because such external challenges have been most clearly predictive of maltreatment risk and are likely to engender in parents the most fundamental experiences of powerlessness.

PRACTICE PRINCIPLE 8.2: To overcome the effects of parents' powerlessness, home visitation services should promote personal experiences of success across spheres of functioning and particularly in relation to social-environmental challenges, such as managing social network relations or accessing necessary resources.

To initiate and successfully handle complicated social-environmental challenges such as employability or the improvement of coercive relationships, parents need more than a cognitive frame to motivate efforts at improvement. Parents must also have the necessary skills, resources, and supports in place to effectively enact steps in their advancement. Indeed, control beliefs coupled with inadequate skills or supports may heighten the likelihood of attempts that result in failure, promoting subsequent self-attributions of failure, self-blame, and resignation (e.g., Folkman, 1984). Parents must also, then, be provided with access to practical knowledge, resources, and skills in tandem with a growing sense of confidence to empower them to more effectively handle social environmental challenges. As examples, skills training procedures for parents in problem solving, assertiveness, conflict management, or effective communication have been well developed and supported empirically (e.g., Barth, Schinke, & Maxwell, 1985; Booth, Mitchell, Barnard, & Spieker, 1989; Fantuzzo, 1986; Palinkas, Atkins, Miller, & Ferreira, 1996; Pfiffner, Jouriles, Brown, & Etscheidt, 1990; Schinke et al., 1986), and these can be readily incorporated into home visiting protocols. Rehearsal or role-plays prior to attempts at solving real-world challenges can provide opportunities to exercise new skills and promote parents' confidence that they can, indeed, succeed in their efforts. Once successfully enacted, newly acquired skills can advance parents' efficacy beliefs and begin to undo feelings of learned helplessness—indeed promoting what

Zimmerman (1990) has called "learned hopefulness," where parents begin to increase their confidence and anticipation that their own capacities can serve them to overcome challenges once thought insurmountable. As parents enrolled in home visitation services may present a wide array of needs for skill development including social skills, literacy and language skills, job readiness skills, and/or skills in personal health care, home visitors must carefully assess needed skill domains and be well trained in guiding parents to expand their competencies, either through direct skill-development activities or coordination with community resources providing such guidance.

PRACTICE PRINCIPLE 8.3: Home visitors should carefully assess the adequacy of parents' skills that may promote their functioning in the social environment over the long term. Especially important to assess are those skill spheres that may open still further opportunities to enhance their competency and support in the future. Home visitation programs should then be prepared to directly engage families in skill-building activities or to serve as a bridge to community resources that also offer opportunities for parents to experience successes connected with their own participation.

Revisiting such "first generation" early-intervention models as Head Start, selected family support programs have often sought to promote parents' social and problem-solving skills by engaging them directly in the process of a program's development. Parents can be involved in ways that advance a program through a variety of means: by participating in committees or advisory boards, acting as mentors or peer supports to other parents, organizing special program-related events, or engaging in program advocacy efforts. Involving parents as participants in program development activities can serve multiple purposes in synergistic ways. When parents are provided with a safe context for exercising participatory social skills, they can begin to receive supportive feedback that organizations may, indeed, respond to their efforts. To the extent that parents' participation results in actual benefits for themselves as well as for others, skills in self-advocacy and the attendant beliefs in their own power to shape further organizational and community processes can be expanded (Kiefer, 1984; Zimmerman et al., 1992). As involvement in program development can enhance a sense of ownership of and identification with a program, such a strategy may also increase parents' commitment to and engagement in services, thereby enhancing the delivery of intended benefits to families and children. Indeed, allied studies have shown that efficacy beliefs linked to participation in larger organizations can promote improved organizational performance and that such improved performance can, in a positive turn, continue to expand efficacy beliefs of participants (e.g., Bandura, 1993; Lindsley, Brass, & Thomas, 1995; Prussia & Kinicki, 1996). Programs may yield further benefit as their services become more sensitively attuned and responsive to the needs of families served by the program, as has been shown in the case of Head Start (Phillips & Cabrera, 1996).

One current example of an early intervention model that has adopted parents' participation in program development in substantial ways is the Parent Services Project, an empowerment-oriented family support program lodged within state-subsidized child care programs. Although not an early home visitation program, the Parent Services Project can be viewed as a family support "cousin," and its involvement of parents in the program holds important lessons for how early home visitation services might seek to empower families served by their programs (see Practice Exemplar 8.1).

PRACTICE EXEMPLAR 8.1

The Parent Services Project

In 1980, the Parent Services Project was initiated to provide comprehensive supports and mental health services for families using publicly subsidized child care centers in the San Francisco Bay area. The project specifically sought to provide services and resources for families in child care centers, settings increasingly tapped by impoverished families with infants and young children, given the advent of welfare-to-work arrangements in public assistance (Kisker & Ross, 1997). Child care settings were chosen as they were deemed opportune settings in which to intervene with families early and voluntarily: Essential supports, practical skills, and leadership training could be provided in a cost-efficient and easily accessible location. In addition to child care services, Parent Services Project sites provide educational and skills development activities for parents, concrete assistance including financial aid, and recreational activities solely for parents, as well as for parents with their children.

Parent Services Project sites are notable for involving parents as partners in working on behalf of the young children served by the child care center. In particular, Parents Services Project sites include parent leadership opportunities whereby parents participate in program and community development activities. Parents often participate in parent planning groups that help set the agency's agenda for allocation of resources on a yearly basis. Also, parents help develop baby-sitting co-op networks, they handle community public relations for the project, and they plan specific events for families served by the project such as holiday celebrations, nutrition workshops, or clothing and toy exchanges. Parents may also become involved in project policy councils and in larger community-based advocacy, for example, through involvement with state child care coalitions and conferences (Link, Beggs, & Seiderman, 1997).

According to a 1997 report, the Parent Services Project has grown from four centers serving 400 families in 1980 to collaboration with over 500 early childhood providers serving over 19,000 families across six states. The findings of an unpublished pretest-posttest comparison group evaluation of the Parent Services Project conducted in 1988 reported that after 15 months of services, parents showed an increase in their social supports and a decrease in their reported stresses and psychological symptoms relative to a comparison group. At 30 months, although serviced families appeared to have stabilized, comparison group families reported deepening stresses, declining supports, and increased symptoms (Stein & Haggard, 1988).

Although further study directly examining parent participatory strategies in early home visitation programs is necessary, the initial successes of programs such as the Parent Services Project suggest that empowering parents through program involvement is highly promising. Participating in program development can help families link up with others in a common purpose, exercise new skills in effecting social-environmental improvements, and therefore, promote leadership skills that may translate to other related challenges parents may face.

EMPOWERMENT THROUGH PEER LEARNING
AND ROLE MODELING

In situations where parents are uncertain of their capabilities or hesitant to begin participating in programmatic changes that might expand their self-advocacy skills, self-efficacy theory suggests that observing the successes of others can increase beliefs in one's personal capacity to succeed. Such vicarious experiences can increase the likelihood of enacting later attempts to accomplish goals. Bandura (1997) points out that key to enhancing personal efficacy through vicarious observation are social comparison processes:

> Seeing or visualizing people similar to oneself perform successfully typically raises efficacy beliefs in observers that they themselves possess the capabilities to master comparable activities. They persuade themselves that if others can do it, they too have the capabilities to raise their performance. . . . The greater the assumed similarity, the more persuasive are the models' successes and failures. If people see the models as very different from themselves, their beliefs of personal efficacy are not much influenced by the models' behavior and the results in produces. (p. 87)

Given that the persuasiveness of modeling from the successes of others depends on the degree of perceived similarity to the role model, home visitation programs can seek to enhance the efficacy of parents by exposure to successful similar others through a variety of means.

PRACTICE PRINCIPLE 8.4: Home visitation services may seek to empower parents by providing specific opportunities for learning with peers and similar others, for example, through the use of paraprofessionals matched for similarity, peer or mutual aid groups, and/or mentoring.

Evidence from role modeling and social comparison theory has provided the rationale for mentoring-based interventions, particularly for young mothers. Young mothers' relationships with mentors appear to promote greater life optimism and lower depression, and specially expanded educational and career aspirations (Klaw & Rhodes, 1995; Rhodes, Contreras, & Mangelsdorf, 1994; Rhodes, Ebert, & Fischer, 1992; Zippay, 1995). Role modeling and social comparison influences also provide one of the most persuasive rationales for deploying paraprofessional home visitors who are ethnically and geographically matched to the families they serve. Lessened social distance and dissimilarity between parents and home visitors (Thompson, 1995), combined with perceptions that the home visitor is successful in valued life domains, can facilitate the role-modeling process. This can subsequently encourage parents' beliefs about their own capabilities to succeed in new behaviors previously viewed as beyond their reach. Role models from the same ethnic and geographic community as parents may inspire greater credibility and motivation to enact new behavioral repertoires than role models viewed as more socially distant, although social distance may be overcome if the skills being modeled and taught are viewed as important to the parent (Bandura, 1997).

The importance of learning from peers and similar others underscores what Gutierrez and Lewis (1999) highlight as the two other major facets of empowerment—connection and consciousness. By connection, Gutierrez and Lewis mean developing supportive networks of others (considered in Chapter 8) and, in particular, addressing powerlessness by linking up with others facing similar circumstances and challenges. Individuals collectively confronting common obstacles and problems may learn to develop what Gutierrez and Lewis (1999) and others have termed consciousness, perceptions that one's concerns are shared by a larger group and that these shared difficulties, in part, derive from larger social problems transcending individual challenges (Barrett, 1978; Friere, 1970; Gurin, 1985; Gurin, Miller, & Gurin, 1980; Lieberman, Solow, Bond, & Reibstein, 1979; Lopez, Gurin, & Nagda, 1998; Zubrow, 1993). These two elements of empowerment, connection and consciousness, when combined with confidence, shape individuals' motivations to take personal and collective action to effect improvements in their environment (Gutierrez & Lewis, 1999).

Empowerment-oriented, group-based activities become particularly relevant in this regard as they deliberately bring together similar others around a shared set of problems. By focusing on parents' collective handling of challenges in their social environments, empowerment-oriented groups hold the potential to provide a host of unique peer-based benefits not directly available in any individual family's home setting (see Table 8.1). Empowerment-oriented groups do more than aid in breaking down feelings of isolation and affirming that struggles with early parenting are shared. They may also provide specific opportunities for reciprocally giving and receiving support, for exercising skills in managing social-environmental challenges, and for transferring enabling information and guidance (e.g., opinions on day care options, places to acquire family goods, or referrals to responsive social services settings), helping to lower barriers to needed resources and supports in the community. Furthermore, empowerment-oriented groups can provide opportunities for parents to begin to see the links between their own personal struggles and broader social and community problems, such as dangerous neighborhoods, restrictive or discriminatory housing practices, unresponsive service systems, or a lack of affordable quality child care options. Such groups offer the opportunity for parents to become involved in an alternative support network with its own norms and expectations for parenting and social behavior, conveying a sense of membership in a parenting mission that transcends the concerns of any single parent.

As noted in Chapter 7, especially in the Parents Together Practice Exemplar 7.1, to accomplish such goals, group activity must transcend mere skill development focused within the microsystem of the parent-child relationship. Rather, empowerment-oriented activities assist parents through the shared exercise of skills and problem solving centered on accessing and using needed supports and resources. Also, empowerment-oriented groups may provide venues to try out new competencies in managing difficult network relationships or constraining environmental realities, providing positive feedback for attempts successfully enacted. Such efforts can promote individual and collective efficacy and firm up parents' skills in seeking needed assistance (see Table 8.1).

Outcome studies of empowerment-oriented group interventions for the early prevention of child maltreatment are still necessary to establish their efficacy within this population and problem area. However, studies with other populations and problems have reported that empowerment-group approaches are linked with increased help-seeking from additional community organizations (Koroloff, Elliott, Koren, & Friesen, 1996), increased participation in community supports such as schooling (Collins, Bybee, & Mowbray, 1998), and increased interest and activity in group-based advocacy to change community conditions (Gutierrez & Ortega, 1991; Singh et al., 1997; Yeich & Levine, 1994). This budding knowledge base underscores that empowerment-oriented group interventions hold the potential to enhance the responsiveness of community supports to the needs of parents and to expand parents' capacities to access and utilize community services, including those of home visitation. In this way, empowerment approaches are likely to improve engage-

Table 8.1

Unique Benefits and Challenges of
Empowerment-Oriented Group Support in Home Visitation Services

Potential Benefits	Potential Challenges
Positive role modeling and peer learning are promoted	Negative role modeling and peer learning may also occur
Feelings of loneliness and isolation as a parent are reduced	Initial engagement to discuss personal struggles in a group setting may be difficult
Opportunities are offered to learn and try out new skills in the company of similar others	Geography, group scheduling, and transportation obstacles may hinder participation
Means are provided to establish and convey alternative and influential prosocial parenting norms that may countervail problematic indigenous influences	Dissonance/conflict may arise between the group's parenting norms and norms of members' indigenous networks
Parents have opportunities to engage in reciprocal help-giving and -receiving activities	Provision of child care during group meetings may be required
Groups offer parents the potential to share concrete resources, supports (e.g., child care, baby clothes)	Collective space must be found for group meetings
Parents may develop "critical consciousness," linking personal struggles with larger social problems	
"Success" feedback can promote self-efficacy	
A long-term peer-support network may evolve	
A self-sustaining network to conduct group advocacy may develop	
Parents have opportunities to learn leadership development skills in the group context	
Cost efficiencies are achieved by delivering services to multiple families simultaneously	

ment and participation of families in home visitation by helping families overcome common internal and external barriers to service use, while also ultimately contributing to the responsiveness and relevance of such services to family needs (cf. Elliott, Koroloff, Koren, & Friesen, 1998; Singh et al., 1997). By improving parents' personal sense of efficacy, participation in empowerment-group activities may also directly serve to interrupt the chain of events leading to maltreating parenting by minimizing the out-of-control feelings that motivate abusive or neglectful parental responses.

PRACTICE PRINCIPLE 8.5: Augmenting home visitation services with empowerment-oriented group support should directly reduce child maltreatment risk by reducing parents' out-of-control feelings, by increasing parents' participation in community and services, and by increasing parents' efforts to improve community conditions that shape family life.

Findings linked with the use of empowerment-oriented groups suggest that they can enhance parents' sense of "collective efficacy"—that is, their willingness to act together to achieve a common goal in the context of shared values and mutual trust (Bandura, 1997; Sampson et al., 1997). Paralleling the positive spiraling noted in the development of self-efficacy at the individual level, development of collective efficacy can promote further participatory activity leading to desired community-level changes (e.g., Phillips & Cabrera, 1996), fueling still further increases in collective efficacy perceptions. It has been observed that the development of collective efficacy may trickle down, enhancing individual perceptions of self-efficacy as well (Zimmerman et al., 1992). If such is indeed the case, empowerment-oriented group activities may reduce child maltreatment risk via multiple important pathways: through the enhancement of personal self-efficacy and acquisition of needed skills, the reduction of isolation and increased use of ecologically based supports, the increased access to instrumental and concrete resources, and the increased responsiveness of community institutions to parents' needs.

Self-help groups originating and sustained from parent interest rather than from professional management have been especially noteworthy as important vehicles to promote parents' sense of empowerment and control (e.g., Battaglino, 1987; Bly, 1988; Chesler & Chesney, 1988; Dickerson, 1998; Gidron, Guterman, & Hartman, 1990; Neighbors,

Braithwaite, & Thompson, 1995; Segal, Silverman, & Temkin, 1993). Self-help groups are parent-owned and parent-run, although parents may consult or coordinate other supports with professional organizations. Thus, when parents perceive benefits as a result of participation, they are more likely to attribute gains made as resulting from their own actions, directly promoting personal and collective efficacy beliefs. Self-help groups are often initiated for the purpose of meeting the needs of members in the group, and they provide opportunities for members to interact and share in problem solving centered on common concerns.

Although self-help groups often initially focus on meeting the immediate needs of participants, they often arise and form a response to dissatisfaction with (or lack of) available formalized supports. Given this, they may commonly focus their activities on increasing the responsiveness of formalized helping systems to their needs, often developing an explicit and ongoing group advocacy agenda. At the same time, self-help groups, on the whole, appear to promote improved use of formalized supports, often serving as a gateway or mediating influence between parents' informal networks and professional supports (e.g., Emerick, 1990; Powell, 1990). The paradigm of the self-help movement, therefore, provides a hopeful if underexplored avenue within the field of early home visitation, through which parents with young children can seek to enhance their own empowerment—and thereby directly reduce their maltreatment risk—while simultaneously addressing environmental impediments as they strive to parent in the early years. The popularity of birthing classes attests to the potential for quasi-informal self-help groups to tap pregnant mothers' and new parents' motivation for group-based support. Furthermore, the widespread presence of Parents Anonymous groups (see Practice Exemplar 8.2) across the United States, supporting parents who voluntarily identify their maltreating behavior, clearly indicates the potential for parents in home visitation programs to become actively involved in self-help, seeking broader scale environmental changes on their own behalf.

Although self-help groups targeting new or young parents have been largely unexamined in well-controlled studies, their widespread presence and their underlying change approach hold important implications for the expanding field of early home visitation services. First, given the successful expansion of Parents Anonymous groups for maltreating parents or for parents at high risk for maltreatment, self-help groups are likely to hold clear appeal to new parents struggling with common concerns and challenges. Whereas home visitation services can pinpoint and

PRACTICE EXEMPLAR 8.2

Parents Anonymous

Although few links have been forged between early home visitation services and self-help, the Parents Anonymous movement may hold important lessons for expanding early home visitation services in ways that empower parents in the prevention of child abuse and neglect. Established in 1970, Parents Anonymous is a national self-help organization "of, by and for" parents who may be at risk of abusing their children. Originally founded by a parent in traditional clinical therapy with the aid of a social worker, Parents Anonymous developed into parent-led, professionally facilitated self-help group meetings, expanding across the United States (and to several additional nations) and providing support to an estimated 100,000 parents per year. Those involved in Parents Anonymous groups reflect a highly diverse ethnic profile, and about two thirds are female (Rafael & Pion-Berlin, 1999).

By design, Parents Anonymous groups aim to provide alternatives to maltreating parenting, to provide mutual support and a sense of shared community among participants, and to develop parents' leadership and responsibility in the group's work. Parents Anonymous groups promote personal growth by providing parents with a trusting atmosphere where they determine session agendas and topics, often addressing such concerns as child developmental expectations, effective strategies to promote children's growth, family communication skills, and parents' stress management and self-control. Parents are encouraged to practice new behaviors at home, and they exchange phone numbers so that they can make 24-hour support available for one another in times of need. Parents Anonymous groups also assist parents in understanding the role of their own upbringing as it influences their own parenting behaviors.

Parents Anonymous groups work in collaboration with other community organizations, and seek to promote parents' reciprocal support-giving to one another and the use of available resources in the community. An articulated aim of Parents Anonymous is to aid parents in gaining a sense of their own power and to enact it in a responsive and responsible way, supporting parenting practices that promote healthy child outcomes. Through leadership activities, parents become involved in owning and operating groups, providing child care, and serving on community boards concerned about children's well-being. The organization has developed into a national network that provides technical assistance, materials, advocacy, and media exposure for the organization. Parents Anonymous now advocates at all levels of government to promote the development of community-based programs, to foster changes in child protection and child welfare programming across the nation, and to ensure that the voices of parents are heard on issues relevant to families and children. Representatives of the organization estimate that about 30,000 Parents Anonymous volunteers donate an estimated $10 million of services each year (Rafael & Pion-Berlin, 1999).

As with other self-help movements in the United States, there is a paucity of carefully controlled outcome data on the effectiveness of Parents Anonymous in reducing child maltreatment. In 1976, Behavior Associates found that participants reported (from pretest to posttest) improvements in their parenting behaviors, more appropriate developmental expectations, self-reported reductions in child abuse, and improvements in help seeking and reliance on others for support in the parenting role. Recognizing the need for more careful information about the effectiveness of Parents Anonymous, the U.S. Office of Juvenile Justice and Delinquency Prevention recently initiated an effort to study Parents Anonymous under more carefully controlled conditions (Rafael & Pion-Berlin, 1999).

promote positive parent-child interactional patterns in the home, self-help groups may, if appropriately configured, serve a complementary function of providing an empowering network of similar parents who can share experiences, resources, and knowledge, transmitting social norms and expectations about parenting. Also, participating parents can advocate as a group for improvements in community, health, and social services systems enhancing the responsiveness of local ecological contexts to family needs. The national expansion and advocacy work of self-help groups such as Parents Anonymous or other self-help organizations such as the National Alliance of the Mentally Ill (NAMI) has shown that they hold the potential to stimulate significant improvements in services, supports, and policies affecting parents, even shaping the national agenda on the problem. Advocacy efforts of NAMI, for example, are instructive as they have helped to redefine public and professional attitudes about the sources of mental illnesses away from family blame, thereby reducing public stigma and reticence to support families struggling with mentally ill children. By developing "national report cards" spotlighting service deficits, commissioning evaluations of services, lobbying legislators, and holding national agenda-setting conferences with federal agencies, self-help organizations such as Parents Anonymous and NAMI have become integral players in setting and shaping policies and the resulting services that support vulnerable families (cf. Corrigan et al., 1999; Dixon, Goldman, & Hirad, 1999; Evans & McGee, 1998; Havel, 1992; Lefley & Johnson, 1990; Sommer, 1990).

Empowerment group-based activities, whether they are led by professions or parents themselves, are not fundamentally incompatible with ongoing home visitation support; in fact, they can be orchestrated in a complementary fashion (e.g., Powell, 1990). Home visitors, for example, can serve as referral sources, consultants, or facilitators for ongoing groups, serving a bridge function between in-home professional services and empowerment groups. Home visitation programs can also participate in launching or expanding professionally led empowerment-group or self-help programs, contributing directly to both maltreatment risk reduction in families served and to local community capacity development for young families. Given the reciprocal and participatory nature of the help-giving process within empowerment-oriented groups (whether self-help or professionally led), parents' participation in self-help can improve their help-seeking and self-advocacy skills, contributing to their ability to tap home visitation services for their benefit. Indeed, the presence of local self-help groups for families with young children may place productive pressures on home visitation programs to adopt changes that are more responsive to the local needs of young families.

The low participation rates observed when home visitation programs have sought to mount parent support groups, although providing a precautionary note, hold limited lessons for empowerment-oriented group approaches. To date, such groups have generally been focused on providing parenting guidance, a service parents may have viewed as duplicative of that provided in the home. If families are receiving such services in their homes, it is to be expected that few would also venture out to receive similar support in a group. Also, program models have, as a rule, mounted group-based services as ancillary ones, not core to the mission of the program. Yet, if programs convey to parents the centrality of empowerment-oriented group services and provide opportunities to overcome common barriers to center-based supports (such as transportation or convenient meeting times and places), such groups may hold the potential to increase overall service participation, as multiple-family group approaches have shown (McKay et al., 1999; Meezan & O'Keefe, 1998). No carefully studied home visitation program has yet reported efforts to integrate home visiting services with group-based supports targeting social-ecological challenges. Thus, the potential to expand home visitation to more directly address parents' power-based dilemmas through group-based activities remains a promising opportunity that the field has yet to tap or carefully study. The present lack of knowledge and practice in this area serves as a reminder that the field of early home visitation, although it has made meaningful inroads to address the problem of child maltreatment, still requires further advancement along a number of critical horizons, especially in those domains of child maltreatment etiology thought to be both among the most significant and intractable.

NOTES

1. Olds and colleagues have noted that, in fact, the relationship between maternal sense of control and the number of completed home visits is somewhat curvilinear. Namely, home visits decrease as maternal control increases, except for women with a "very high sense of internal control," who tended also to receive comparatively more home visits. This pattern of an upward "tail" for high-control women was found in both the Elmira and Memphis trials of the program (Olds & Korfmacher, 1998).

2. A similar pattern has been documented in numerous nonintervention studies showing an empirical association between parents' personal control and maltreatment risk, as reviewed in Chapter 2.

Chapter 9

REVISITING HOME VISITING

Can we stop child maltreatment before it starts? This book has argued that we can and must do so. We not only face a moral imperative to work to end this all-too-common form of victimization and deprivation of our youngest citizens. We also face a societal imperative, confronting us with the reality that child abuse and neglect, particularly experienced early in life, form the taproot of some of the most destructive and costly social problems of our day, including substance and alcohol abuse, problematic school performance, juvenile delinquency and crime, later-life depression, and domestic violence (National Research Council, 1993).

Can early home visitation services stop child maltreatment before it starts? Selected findings have clearly shown the promise of early home visitation services in reducing risk of child maltreatment. At the same time, unlike the first question, which underscores the moral and societal imperative to stop child maltreatment, answers to this latter question are more complex. A number of home visitation studies report equivocal outcomes, suggesting the need for a careful examination of early home visitation services, one that moves beyond overall questions of effectiveness and a "one size fits all" approach. In Chapters 3 and 4, I have underscored that early home visitation services are, perhaps, the brightest star on the child maltreatment prevention horizon. Yet, concerned professionals in the field must resist selective inattention to the empirical base, only acknowledging those studies that report positive outcomes with regard to child maltreatment. As Heather Weiss (1993) has observed, "there is a long history of setting up home visiting as a silver bullet—the panacea for poverty—and of subsequent disappointment, reconsideration, and revamping of the role home visits can play in ameliorating the effects of poverty" (pp. 115-116). Caution must be exercised to avoid repeating the historical cycle of oversell and backlash that has characterized home visitation from its inception. As summarized in Chapter 4, the fieldwide findings on the overall capacity for early home visitation services to reduce child maltreatment risk reveal a relatively small yet positive trend. At the same time, such findings are far from uniform across studies. Taken as a whole, such findings point out that although early home visitation services remain promising, we must seek to identify specific active ingredients that produce positive outcomes across programs. Furthermore, given the modest inroads early home visitation has made in reducing maltreatment risk so far, we must continue to search for strategies that extend and enlarge their impact.

An understandable sense of urgency underlies the forward press to find and quickly implement solutions to the difficult problem of child maltreatment. Such urgency, however, must be balanced out with the hard realities presented from careful empirically grounded study. Given their promising start, home visitation services have been increasingly relied on by decision makers as a vehicle to address child maltreatment and a widening circle of problems and populations—indeed, wider than those for which such services were originally designed and tested. For example, home visiting service models are presently being tested for mothers in the Temporary Assistance to Needy Families (TANF) program across a number of states. In addition, home visitation services are now being relied on as a possible solution for families identified as maltreating in open protective services cases and even for foster parents who have new foster children in their homes (cf. Graham et al., 1997).

Yet, especially in cases where families are mandated to receive services, fundamental questions arise as to whether and how home visitation services can be appropriately altered and adapted for their benefit. Early home visitation services were originally conceptualized and designed as proactive, family supportive, and voluntary, where families engage in services because of their own internally felt needs. Adapting early home visitation services to nonvoluntary situations raises an array of thorny and unanswered questions: To what degree will families continue to effectively engage on their home turf if services are mandated and any lack of involvement may lead to negative consequences? To what degree will families engage in a meaningful working relationship with their home visitor if that same person is viewed as someone who might take away custody of their child? To what degree can home visitors engage parents and facilitate changes in families when parents find themselves in situations not in accordance with the mandating source's requirements—for example, by their undocumented immigrant status, by their use of an illegal psychoactive substance, or by the ongoing presence of the father in the home? Answers to these questions will be important as proponents of early home visitation seek to expand their application to arenas for which they were not originally designed or tested. The scant empirical evidence available assessing the effectiveness of mandated home visitation services is wholly unclear (e.g., Barth, 1991; Duerr Berrick & Duerr, 1993; Huxley & Warner, 1993).

Earlier scholars have certainly cautioned against taking program models developed within a specific context with one set of principles and then altering or adapting them for similar but fundamentally different situations. Indeed, after its experimental phase ended, the Prenatal/Early Infancy Program (PEIP) model in Elmira, New York, was altered and shortened by a local funding source, resulting in a program that ultimately produced "rotten outcomes" (Schorr & Schorr, 1988). Such experiences underscore the critical need to carefully study and consider ways that programs can be adapted and altered to meet changing circumstances, problems, and populations.

From another angle, the issue is the degree to which an intervention developed for before-the-fact prevention purposes is applicable for after-the-fact treatment—that is, aiming to lessen the consequences of a problem by applying an intervention designed to prevent it. Here, medical analogies may provoke some thought: To what degree are such early prevention strategies such as water fluoridation, early childhood immunizations, or exercise regimens appropriate for redeployment in treating such target problems as dental decay, childhood diseases, or heart disease *after* those target problems have already occurred? Although the desire to transfer early home visitation services to mandated cases underscores the exciting interest that early home visitation has generated, such transfers raise delicate and complicated questions about if and in what ways such transfers can be appropriate.

Fundamentally at issue is the match between the intervention and the problem or condition of concern, and here, we revisit a theme that is threaded throughout this book. Namely, to what extent do early home visitation services appropriately fit the known etiology of physical child abuse and neglect, the population served by early home visitation programs, and the evolving needs of individual families served by home visitors? Although home visitors individualize their services on a case-by-case and moment-by-moment basis in practice, the empirical base allows us to examine in a broad way the extent to which programs are appropriately fitted to problems and populations they are targeted to address. In this regard, the developing knowledge base about the etiology of child maltreatment has revealed the potency of multiple influences within an ecological context that shape parenting and ultimately child maltreatment. Especially noted in this text are many of the power-based challenges that confront parents in their role and that directly motivate maltreating behavior. By delivering services within families' home contexts, by seeking to promote enhanced parent-child interaction, and by fostering a more positive system of formal supports for parents, early home visitation programs have clearly targeted a number of important, ecologically rooted influences in the etiology of child maltreatment. At the same time, as this text has discussed in the last three chapters, early home visitation services have still further to travel if they are to more closely match their service activities and supports to several of the most potent influences shaping child maltreatment risk. As this text has pointed out in multiple ways, by enhancing this fit, programs should see meaningful improvements in family participation in home visitation services and, ultimately, more robust reduction in child maltreatment risk over the longer term.

This text has attempted to provide some signposts as home visitation services advance to contend with substance and alcohol abuse in families, as they more fully attend to families' informal supports, and as they seek to create greater programmatic fidelity in their efforts to empower families. Yet, these domains are nascent ones within the field of early home visitation, and the programmatic and practice strategies offered rest on a still developing empirical base requiring far more careful and systematic elaboration.

Although the knowledge base in the field has been dominated by *outcome* evaluation information, what may be most helpful for programs is *process* evaluation data. Process evaluation approaches can begin to shed light on program services in ways that point out directions for their improvement. For example, what service factors predict family participation or drop-out from programs? What happens when programs adapt "best practice" principles or service models to fit specific populations and community niches? On what basis do programs determine how to optimally adapt programs to meet new circumstances? Intervention design and development research methods (e.g., Rothman & Thomas, 1994) are particularly useful in addressing such process questions, because they provide systematic steps in launching new intervention practices, whereby new or altered practice strategies are translated into protocols, pilot-tested, and empirically monitored on the microlevel, undergoing progressive refinement and enlargement over time to form an optimal fit to the presenting needs of service recipients.

This text has most especially attempted to underscore the pressing need for early home visitation programs to forge programmatic and practice advances that better address social-ecological forces pressing in on parents and promoting their powerlessness, given the central role of parental powerlessness in the etiology of child maltreatment. The overall strategy of delivering services in the home, although imminently sensible for promoting child-rearing skills and especially helpful for families who may be hard to reach, also holds limitations when considering parents' powerlessness, given that the sources of such powerlessness are often outside the home.

To reduce child maltreatment on a broad scale and over the long term, home visitation services must do more than seek to empower parents by addressing micro- and mesolevel challenges. They must ultimately also consider empowerment-oriented activities that address macrostructural elements such as socioeconomic status, as these have been repeatedly demonstrated to be among the most robust predictors of child maltreatment risk. Summarizing the wide body of findings on socioeconomic distress and child maltreatment, Leroy Pelton (1994) has noted,

> There is overwhelming and remarkably consistent evidence—across a variety of definitions and methodologies and from studies performed at different times—that poverty and low income are strongly related to child abuse and neglect and to the severity of child maltreatment. Children from impoverished families are vastly overrepresented in the incidence of child abuse and neglect. . . . Approximately 40-50% of all child abuse and neglect incidents occur within the less than 15% of all U.S. families with children who live below the poverty level. More than 90% of all incidents occur in families below the median income. . . . Perhaps an "empowered" and superiorly competent person can ward off poverty, its deficits, and/or the stresses that can arise therefrom. But the environment is real, not just a matter of perception, and can overwhelm people. . . . In short, we must

address the poverty conditions that leave children abused, neglected, or otherwise harmed in the short run if we are to increase individual competencies and inner resources in the long run. (pp. 166-172)

Environmentally oriented interventions must, therefore, strive not only to forge changes in parents' competencies and the mesosystemic niches in which parents conduct their daily activities, but also to address macrostructural factors of class, culture, and even history. As Stephanie Riger has asserted,

> Neighborhood groups are embedded in larger forces and institutions that are nonlocal and often not susceptible to local influence. . . . [Such forces] often affect neighborhood dynamics in ways that are difficult if not impossible for local grass-roots groups to influence. . . . If interventions aimed to empower do not address these larger sociopolitical forces, they may be doomed to transitory or ineffective actions. (Riger, 1993, p. 283)

Many of the practice principles outlined in this text are individual, family, or group interventions. The strategies identified in this book that hold some capacity to alter macrostructural factors are empowerment-oriented, group-based ones, which have been shown to catalyze broader social advocacy, such as initiation of self-help groups or involvement of parents in programmatic and advocacy efforts. However, further work is clearly necessary to forge closer links between home visitation practices and the macrosystemic influences that shape maltreatment risk. Further study is also essential to clarify through what causal pathways such factors as socioeconomic status shape child maltreatment risk. For example, far from being monolithic, poverty is multifaceted and can result from a variety of circumstances, ranging from job loss, poor education, the departure of a primary breadwinner, a disability, or parental characteristics. Also, the experience of poverty can be shaped by a variety of factors, as noted earlier in this text, such as community cohesion and organization, social supports, and parents' own sense of efficacy. How such experiences shape parents' coping and their parenting behaviors may vary widely, yet, we know all too little about these dynamic processes, given the lack of longitudinal studies examining these factors over time. As we begin to trace in a more sophisticated fashion the ways in which economic impoverishment and child maltreatment are linked, intervention strategies to address these links can be devised with greater fidelity.

This text has sought to highlight the importance of another broad social influence in stopping child maltreatment by pointing out the key role that scientific knowledge has played in advancing the early home visitation field. Scientific and technological advance can clearly alter the broad societal landscape undergirding family life in the United States. In fact, such advances have helped to catalyze the early home visitation movement. At the same time, it is also crucial to note that a scientific evidentiary basis is important but by no means the only way to muster broad social will to alter the contexts of family life and to advance home visitation services in the United States. Clearly, the will to advance such services and to address social conditions shaping child maltreatment risk can be stirred in other ways. Here, it is instructive to note that universal home visitation services are a given in a number of northern European countries. Within these national contexts, such services are available to all, and they are viewed as an established and accepted part of ongoing health care for families with young children, similar to the way we in the United States view well-baby care, childhood immunizations, and education as established necessities. In Britain, for example, universally available home visitation services have been mandated for many years. As Sheila Kamerman and Alfred Kahn (1993) note,

> Very different perspectives and premises affect policy making in the United States compared with most European countries. In Europe, home visiting programs have existed for more than a century; they are a well-accepted part of life that is integrated into broad government-funded health and social services systems. Despite growing concern about limited resources to expend on social programs in many European countries, their home visiting programs continue to be universal (available to all families), popular, generously supported and viewed as effective. . . . Debate here about whether to expand home visiting programs often begins with questions about their proven effectiveness with specific targeted populations, questions simply not asked in Europe's history with these programs. (pp. 39-40)

The state of such established home visitation services in other nations reminds us that although empirical findings may influence the development and expansion of such services here in the United States, underlying the present crossroads facing the home visitation movement are public values considerations about the relative importance of early support for children and families to our nation's survival and growth.

Thus, early home visitation services must be viewed as one among a variety of strategies aimed at supporting young families and children, their extended families, communities, and wider social circles. A wider net must be cast and reinforced if we as a nation are to recognize our future and substantially reduce the problem of child maltreatment in America. Otherwise, our public values and actions, which presently give priority to economic, technological, and scientific advance, will continue to spawn devastating results for us as individuals, families, communities, and a nation.

Perhaps one way to muster the will is through advancement of policies on a broad scale that ensure the safety of young children and their families. Another way is through local community-by-community efforts, group-by-group efforts, and parent-by-parent efforts to assert the essential importance of intervening early to help families get off to a good start and to empower them in their struggles to face seemingly insurmountable odds. In so doing, we will aid families to grow and nurture the next generation, and we will ultimately realize a clear promise of early home visitation services: to stop child maltreatment before it ever starts.

REFERENCES

Aber, J. L. (1994). Poverty, violence, and child development: Untangling family and community level effects. In C. A. Nelson (Ed.), *Threats to optimal development: Integrating biological, psychological, and social risk factors* (pp. 229-272). Hillsdale, NJ: Lawrence Erlbaum.

Aber, J. L., Allen, J. P., Carlson, V., & Cicchetti, D. (1990). The effects of maltreatment on development during early childhood: Recent studies and their theoretical, clinical, and policy implementations. In D. Cicchetti & V. Carlson (Eds.), *Child maltreatment: Theory and research on causes and consequences* (pp. 579-619). New York: Cambridge University Press.

Abramson, L. Y., Seligman, M. E., & Teasdale, J. D. (1978). Learned helplessness in humans: Critique and reformulation. *Journal of Abnormal Psychology, 87*(1), 49-74.

Acebo, C., & Thoman, E. B. (1995). Role of infant crying in the early mother-infant dialogue. *Physiology & Behavior, 57*(3), 541-547.

Adamakos, H., Ryan, K., Ullman, D. G., Pascoe, J., Diaz, R., & Chessare, J. (1986). Maternal social support as a predictor of mother-child stress and stimulation. *Child Abuse and Neglect, 10,* 463-470.

Affleck, G., Tennen, H., Rowe, J., Roscher, B., & Walker, L. (1989). Effects of formal support on mothers' adaptation to the hospital-to-home transition of high-risk infants: The benefits and costs of helping. *Child Development, 60,* 488-501.

Ainsworth, M. D. S. (1967). *Infancy in Uganda: Infant care and the growth of love.* Baltimore, MD: Johns Hopkins University Press.

Ainsworth, M. D. S., Blehar, M. C., Waters, E., & Wall, S. (1978). *Patterns of attachment: A psychological study of the strange situation.* Hillsdale, NJ: Lawrence Erlbaum.

Albarracin, D., Repetto, M. J., & Albarracin, M. (1997). Social support in child abuse and neglect: Support functions, sources, and contexts. *Child Abuse and Neglect, 21*(7), 607-615.

Albee, G. (1980). Primary prevention and social problems. In G. Gerbner, C. J. Ross, & E. Zigler (Eds.), *Child abuse and neglect: An agenda for action* (pp. 106-117). New York: Oxford University Press.

Albee, G. (1986). Toward a just society: Lessons from observations on the primary prevention of psychopathology. *American Psychologist, 41*(8), 891-898.

Albert, V., Klein, D., Noble, A., Zahand, E., & Holtby, S. (2000). Identifying substance-abusing delivering women: Consequences for child maltreatment reports. *Child Abuse and Neglect, 24*(2), 173-183.

Allen, D., & Tarnowski, K. (1989). Depressive characteristics of physically abused children. *Journal of Abnormal Child Psychology, 17,* 1-11.

Allen, R. E., & Oliver, J. M. (1982). The effects of child maltreatment on long-term development. *Child Abuse and Neglect, 6,* 299-305.

Allen, R. E., & Wasserman, G. A. (1985). Origins of language delay in abused infants. *Child Abuse and Neglect, 9,* 335-340.

Altemeier, W. A., O'Connor, S., Vietze, P., Sandler, H., & Sherrod, K. (1984). Prediction of child abuse: A prospective study of feasibility. *Child Abuse and Neglect, 8,* 393-400.

Altemeier, W. A., Vietze, P. M., Sherrod, K. B., Sandler, H. M., Falsey, S., & O'Connor, S. (1979). Prediction of child maltreatment during pregnancy. *Journal of the American Academy of Child and Adolescent Psychiatry, 18,* 205-218.

American Academy of Pediatrics, Council on Child and Adolescent Health. (1998). The role of home visitation programs in improving health outcomes for children and families. *Pediatrics, 101*(3), 486-489.

American Association for Protecting Children. (1987). *Highlights of official child abuse and neglect reporting, 1986.* Denver, CO: American Humane Association.

American Association for Protecting Children. (1988). *Highlights of official child abuse and neglect reporting—1987.* Denver, CO: American Humane Association.

Ammerman, R. T., Kolko, D. J., Kirisci, L., Blackson, T. C., & Dawes, M. A. (1999). Child abuse potential in parents with histories of substance use disorder. *Child Abuse and Neglect, 23,* 1225-1238.

Anastasiow, N. J. (1990). Implications of the neurobiological model for early intervention. In S. M. Meisels & J. P. Shonkoff (Eds.), *Handbook of early childhood intervention.* New York: Cambridge University Press.

Andersen, R. M. (1995). Revisiting the behavioral model and access to medical care: Does it matter? *Journal of Health and Social Behavior, 36,* 1-10.

Anisfeld, E., & Guillen, S. (1999, May 28). *Addressing substance abuse within an HFA home visiting program.* Paper presented at the 9th Annual National Abandoned Infants Grantee's Conference, Washington, DC.

Anisfeld, E., Guterman, N. B., & Estrada-Nadal, L. (2000, May 24). *The effectiveness of home visiting with substance-abusing families: Preliminary results of a randomized trial.* Paper presented at the 10th Annual National Abandoned Infants Assistance Grantees' Conference, Washington, DC.

Antler, J., & Antler, S. (1980). From child rescue to family protection: The evolution of child protection movement in the United States. *Children and Youth Services Review, 1*(2), 177-204.

Ards, S. (1989). Estimating local child abuse. *Evaluation Review, 13,* 484-515.

Ards, S., Chung, C., & Myers, S. L. (1998). The effects of sample selection bias on racial differences in child abuse reporting. *Child Abuse & Neglect, 22*(2), 103-115.

Armstrong, K. (1981). A treatment and education program for parents and children who are at-risk of abuse and neglect. *Child Abuse and Neglect, 5,* 167-175.

Armstrong, K. (1983). Economic analysis of a child abuse and neglect treatment program. *Child Welfare, 62*(1), 3-13.

Aylward, G. P. (1997). *Infant and early childhood neuropsychology.* New York: Plenum.

Azar, S. T., Barnes, K. T., & Twentyman, C. T. (1988). Developmental outcomes in abused children: Consequences of parental abuse or a more general breakdown in caregiver behavior? *Behavior Therapist, 11,* 27-32.

Bandura, A. (1977). Self-efficacy: Toward a unifying theory of behavior change. *Psychological Review, 84,* 191-215.

Bandura, A. (1993). Perceived self-efficacy in cognitive development and functioning. *Educational Psychologist, 28,* 117-148.

Bandura, A. (1997). *Self-efficacy: The exercise of control.* New York: W. H. Freeman.

Barber, J. G. (1995). Working with resistant drug abusers. *Social Work, 40*(1), 17-23.

Barkauskas, V. H. (1983). Effectiveness of public health nurse home visits to primaparous mothers and their infants. *American Journal of Public Health, 73*(5), 573-580.

Barnard, K. E. (1979). *Nursing child assessment satellite teaching manual.* Seattle: University of Washington.

Barnard, K. E. (1986). *Nursing Child Assessment Satellite Training: Learning resource manual.* Seattle: University of Washington.

Barnard, K. E. (1990). *Keys to caregiving.* Seattle: University of Washington.

Barnard, K. E., Magyary, D., Sumner, G., Booth, C. L., Mitchell, S. K., & Spieker, S. (1988). Prevention of parenting alterations for women with low social support. *Psychiatry, 51,* 248-253.

Barrera, M. (1980). A method for the assessment of social support networks in community survey research. *Connections, 3,* 8-13.

Barrera, M. (1981). Social support in the adjustment of pregnant adolescents: Assessment issues. In B. H. Gottleib (Ed.), *Social networks and social support* (pp. 69-96). Beverly Hills, CA: Sage.

Barrera, M., Sandler, I. N., & Ramsay, T. B. (1981). Preliminary development of a scale of social support: Studies on college students. *American Journal of Community Psychology, 9,* 435-447.

Barrett, C. J. (1978). Effectiveness of widows' groups in facilitating change. *Journal of Consulting & Clinical Psychology, 46*(1), 20-31.

Barry, F. D. (1994). A neighborhood-based approach: What is it? In G. B. Melton & F. D. Barry (Eds.), *Protecting children from abuse and neglect: Foundations for a new national strategy* (pp. 14-39). New York: Guilford.

Barth, R. (1991). An experimental evaluation of in-home child abuse prevention services. *Child Abuse and Neglect, 15,* 363-375.

Barth, R., Ash, J. R., & Hacking, S. (1986). Identifying, screening, and engaging high-risk clients in private non-profit child abuse prevention programs. *Child Abuse and Neglect, 10,* 99-109.

Barth, R. P., & Blythe, B. J. (1983, September). The contribution of stress to child abuse. *Social Service Review,* pp. 477-489.

Barth, R., Hacking, S., & Ash, J. R. (1988). Preventing child abuse: An experimental evaluation of the Child Parent Enrichment Project. *Journal of Primary Prevention, 8*(4), 201-217.

Barth, R. P., & Schinke, S. P. (1984). Enhancing the social supports of teenage mothers. *Social Casework: The Journal of Contemporary Social Work, 65*(9), 523-531.

Barth, R. P., Schinke, S. P., & Maxwell, J. S. (1985). Coping skills training for school-age mothers. *Journal of Social Service Research, 8*(2), 75-94.

Battaglino, L. (1987). Family empowerment through self-help groups. *New Directions for Mental Health Services, 34,* 43-51.

Bavolek, S. J. (1998). *Research and validation report of the nurturing programs.* Park City, UT: Family Development Resources, Inc.

Bavolek, S. J., & Bavolek, J. D. (1988). *Nurturing program for parents and children: Birth to five years.* Park City, UT: Family Development Resources, Inc.

Bayatpour, M., Wells, R. D., & Holford S. (1992). Physical and sexual abuse as predictors of substance use and suicide among pregnant teenagers. *Journal of Adolescent Health, 13*(2), 128-132.

Bayley, N. (1993). *Bayley Scales of Infant Development* (2nd ed.). New York: The Psychological Corporation.

Beeman, S. K. (1997). Reconceptualizing social support and its relationship to child neglect. *Social Service Review, 71,* 421-440.

Behavior Associates. (1976). *Parents Anonymous self-help for child-abusing parents project: Evaluation report for version May 1, 1974-April 30, 1976.* Tucson, AZ: Author.

Bell, S. H., Burnstein, N. R., & Orr, L. L. (1987). *Overview of evaluation results: Evaluation of the AFDC home-maker health aide demonstrations.* Cambridge, MA: ABT Associates.

Bell, S. M., & Ainsworth, M. D. (1972). Infant crying and maternal responsiveness. *Child Development, 43*(4), 1171-1190.

Belsky, J. (1980). Child maltreatment: An ecological integration. *American Psychologist, 35*(4), 320-335.

Belsky, J. (1994). *Transition to parenthood: How a first child changes a marriage.* New York: Delacorte.

Belsky, J., Lang, M. E., & Rovine, M. (1985). Stability and change in marriage across the transition to parenthood. *Journal of Personality and Social Psychology, 50,* 517-522.

Belsky, J., Sanier, G. B., & Rovine, M. (1983). Stability and change in marriage across the transition to parenthood. *Journal of Marriage and the Family, 45,* 553-556.

Bennett, E. M., & Kemper, K. J. (1994). Is abuse during childhood a risk factor for developing substance abuse problems as an adult? *Journal of Developmental & Behavioral Pediatrics, 15*(6), 426-429.

Berlin, L. J., O'Neal, C. R., & Brooks-Gunn, J. (1998, February-March). What makes early intervention programs work? The program, its participants, and their interaction. *Zero to Three,* pp. 4-14.

Bernstein, N. (1999a, July 23). Agency head defends effort for children. *New York Times,* pp. B1, B6.

Bernstein, N. (1999b, May 20). Bronx woman convicted in starving of her breast-fed son. *New York Times,* pp. B1, B8.

Birkel, R. C., & Repucci, N. D. (1983). Social networks, information-seeking, and the utilization of services. *American Journal of Community Psychology, 11*(2), 185-205.

Bishop, S. J., & Leadbeater, B. J. (1999). Maternal social support patterns and child maltreatment: Comparison of maltreating and nonmaltreating mothers. *American Journal of Orthopsychiatry, 69,* 172-181.

Black, M. M., Nair, P., Kight, C., Wachtel, R., Roby, P., & Schuler, M. (1994). Parenting and early development among children of drug-abusing women: Effects of home intervention. *Pediatrics, 94*(4), 440-448.

Black, R., & Mayer, J. (1980). Parents with special problems: Alcoholism and opiate addiction. *Child Abuse and Neglect, 4,* 45-54.

Bly, L. N. (1988). Self-help and child abuse: Victims, victimizers, and the development of self-control. *Contemporary Family Therapy, 10,* 243-255.

Bogat, G. A., Caldwell, R. A., Guzman, B., Galasso, L., & Davidson, W. S. (1998). Structure and stability of maternal support among pregnant and parenting adolescents. *Journal of Community Psychology, 26*(6), 549-568.

Bonnier, C., Nassogne, M. C., & Evrard, P. (1995). Outcome and prognosis of whiplash shaken infant syndrome: Late consequences after a symptom-free interval. *Developmental Medicine & Child Neurology, 37*(11), 943-956.

Booth, C. L., Mitchell, S. K., Barnard, K. E., & Spieker, S. J. (1989). Development of maternal social skills in multiproblem families: Effects on the mother-child relationship. *Developmental Psychology, 25*(3), 403-412.

Bor, W., Najman, J. M., Andersen, M. J., O'Callaghan, M., Williams, G. M., & Behrens, B. C. (1997). The relationship between low family income and psychological disturbance in young children: An Australian longitudinal study. *Australian & New Zealand Journal of Psychiatry, 31*(5), 664-675.

Bordieu, P. (1985). The forms of capital. In J. G. Richardson (Ed.), *Handbook of theory and research for the sociology of education* (pp. 241-258). New York: Greenwood.

Bowlby, J. (1951). *Maternal care and mental health.* Geneva: World Health Organization.

Bowlby, J. (1969). *Attachment and loss: Vol. 1. Attachment.* New York: Basic Books.

Bradley, R. H., Witeside, L., Mundfrom, D. J., Casey, P. H., Caldwell, B. M., & Barrett, K. (1994). Impact of the Infant Health and Development Program (IHDP) on the home environments of infants born prematurely and with low birth weight. *Journal of Educational Psychology, 86*(4), 531-541.

Brayden, R. M., Altemeier, W. A., Dietrich, M. S., Tucker, D. D., Christensen, M. J., McLaughlin, F. J., & Sherrod, K. B. (1993). A prospective study of secondary prevention of child maltreatment. *The Journal of Pediatrics, 122*(4), 511-516.

Breakey, G., & Pratt, B. (1991). Healthy growth for Hawaii's "Healthy Start": Toward a systematic statewide approach to the prevention of child abuse and neglect. *Zero to Three, 11*(4), 16-22.

Bremner, R. (Ed). (1971). *Children and youth in America: A documentary history: Volume 2. 1866-1932.* Cambridge, MA: Harvard University Press.

Brenner, S. L., Fischer, H., & Mann-Gray, S. (1989). Race and the shaken baby syndrome: Experience at one hospital. *Journal of the National Medical Association, 81*(2), 183-184.

Brewster, A. L., Nelson, J. P., Hymel, K. P., Colby, D. R., Lucas, D. R., McCanne, T. R., & Milner, J. S. (1998). Victim, perpetrator, family, and incident characteristics of 32 infant maltreatment deaths in the United States Air Force. *Child Abuse and Neglect, 22,* 91-101.

Bronfenbrenner, U. (1977). Toward an experimental ecology of human development. *American Psychologist, 32*(7), 513-531.

Bronfenbrenner, U. (1979). *The ecology of human development: Experiments by nature and design.* Cambridge, MA: Harvard University Press.

Brooks-Gunn, J., Duncan, G. J., Klebanov, P. K., & Sealand, N. (1993). Do neighborhoods influence child and adolescent development? *American Journal of Sociology, 99*(2), 353-395.

Brooks-Gunn, J., Klebanov, P. K., & Liaw, F. (1995). The learning, physical, and emotional environment of the home in the context of poverty: The Infant Health and Development Program. *Children and Youth Services Review, 17,* 251-276.

Brosschot, J. F., Godaert, G. L., Benschop, R. J., Olff, M., Ballieux, R. E., & Heijnen, C. J. (1998). Experimental stress and immunological reactivity: A closer look at perceived uncontrollability. *Psychosomatic Medicine, 60*(3), 359-361.

Browne, D. H. (1988). The role of stress in the commission of subsequent acts of child abuse and neglect. *Early Child Development & Care, 31*(1-4), 27-33.

Browne, K., & Saqi, S. (1988). Approaches to screening for child abuse and neglect. In K. Browne & C. Davies (Eds.), *Early prediction and prevention of child abuse* (pp. 57-85). UK: John Wiley.

Bruer, J. T. (1999). *The myth of the first three years: A new understanding of early brain development and lifelong learning*. New York: Free Press.

Brunelli, S. A., Wasserman, G. A., Rauh, V. A., & Alvarado, L. E. (1995). Mothers' reports of parental support: Associations with maternal child-rearing attitudes. *Merrill-Palmer Quarterly, 41*(2), 152-171.

Bugental, D., Blunt, L., Judith, E., Lin, E. K., McGrath, E. P., & Bimbela, A. (1999). Children "tune out" in response to the ambiguous communication style of powerless adults. *Child Development, 70*(1), 214-230.

Burns, K., Melamed, J., Burns, W. J., Chasnoff, I., & Hatcher, R. (1985). Chemical dependency and depression in pregnancy. *Journal of Clinical Psychology, 41*, 851-854.

Butterfield, P. M. (1996). The partners in parenting education program: A new option in parenting education. *Zero to Three, 17*, 3-10.

Byrd, R. S., Neistadt, A. M., Howard, C. R., Brownstein-Evans, C., & Weitzman, M. (1999). Why screen newborns for cocaine: Service patterns and social outcomes at age one year. *Child Abuse and Neglect, 23*, 523-530.

Caffey, J. (1946). Multiple fractures in the long bones of infants suffering from chronic subdural hematoma. *American Journal of Roentgenology, 56*(2), 163-173.

Caldwell, B., & Bradley, R. (1978). *Administration manual: Home observation for measurement of the environment*. Little Rock: University of Arkansas.

Caldwell, B., & Bradley, R. (1984). *Home Observation for Measurement of the Environment* (revised). Little Rock: University of Arkansas.

Caldwell, R. A., Bogat, G. A., & Davidson, W. S. (1988). The assessment of child abuse potential and the prevention of child abuse and neglect: A policy analysis. *American Journal of Community Psychology, 16*(5), 609-624.

Caliso, J. A., & Milner, J. S. (1994). Childhood physical abuse, childhood social support, and adult child abuse potential. *Journal of Interpersonal Violence, 9*(1), 27-44.

Campbell, A. (1993). *Men, women, and aggression*. New York: Basic Books.

Caplan, G. (1964). *Principles of preventive psychiatry*. New York: Basic Books.

Carlson, E. A., Jacobvitz, D., & Sroufe, L. A. (1995). A developmental investigation of inattentiveness and hyperactivity. *Child Development, 66*(1), 37-54.

Carlson, V., Cicchetti, D., Barnett, D., & Braunwald, K. (1989). Disorganized/disoriented attachment relationships in maltreated infants. *Developmental Psychology, 25*(4), 525-531.

Carr, A., & Gelles, R. J. (1978). *Reporting child maltreatment in Florida: The operation of public child protective service systems* (Report to the National Center on Child Abuse and Neglect). Washington, DC: U.S. Department of Health and Human Services.

Caruso, G. L. (1989). Optimum growth project: Support for families with young children. *Prevention in Human Services, 6*(2), 123-139.

Casaer, P. (1993). Old and new facts about perinatal brain development. *Journal of Child Psychology and Psychiatry and Allied Disciplines, 34*(1), 101-109.

Cazenave, N., & Straus, M. (1979). Race, class, network embeddedness, and family violence: A search for potent support systems. *Journal of Comparative Family Studies, 10*(3), 282-300.

Center on Child Abuse Prevention Research. (1996). *Intensive home visitation: A randomized trial, follow-up and risk assessment study of Hawaii's Healthy Start program* (Final report prepared for the National Center on Child Abuse and Neglect). Chicago: National Committee to Prevent Child Abuse.

Centers for Disease Control and Prevention. (1997). *Facts about fetal alcohol syndrome.* Atlanta, GA: Author.

Chaffin, M., Kelleher, K., & Hollenberg, J. (1996). Onset of physical abuse and neglect: Psychiatric, substance abuse, and social risk factors from prospective community data. *Child Abuse and Neglect, 20*(3), 191-203.

Chalk, R., & King, P. A. (1998). *Violence in families: Assessing prevention and treatment programs.* Washington, DC: National Academy Press.

Chan, Y. C. (1994). Parenting stress and social support of mothers who physically abuse their children in Hong Kong. *Child Abuse and Neglect, 18*(3), 261-269.

Chasnoff, I. J., Anson, A., Hatcher, R., Stenson, H., Laukea, K., & Randolph, L. A. (1998). Prenatal exposure to cocaine and other drugs: Outcome at four to six years. In J. A. Harvey & B. E. Kosofsky (Eds.), *Cocaine effects on the developing brain* (pp. 314-328). New York: New York Academy of Sciences.

Chavkin, W., Paone, D., Friedman, P., & Wilets, I. (1993). Psychiatric histories of drug using mothers: Treatment implications. *Journal of Substance Abuse Treatment, 10*(5), 445-448.

Cheah, I. G., Kasim, M. S., Shafie, H. M., & Khoo, T. H. (1994). Intracranial haemorrhage and child abuse. *Annals of Tropical Paediatrics, 14*(4), 325-328.

Chen, S. C., Telleen, S., & Chen, E. H. (1995). Family and community support of urban pregnant students: Support person, function, and parity. *Journal of Community Psychology, 23*(1), 28-33.

Chesler, M. A., & Chesney, B. K. (1988). Self-help groups: Empowerment attitudes and behaviors of disabled or chronically ill persons. In H. E. Yuker (Ed.), *Attitudes toward persons with disabilities* (pp. 230-245). New York: Springer.

Chilamkurti, C., & Milner, J. S. (1993). Perceptions and evaluations of child transgressions and disciplinary techniques in high- and low-risk mothers and their children. *Child Development, 64*, 1801-1814.

Child Fatality Review Panel. (1993). *Child Fatality Review Panel annual report for 1993.* New York: New York City Human Resources Administration.

Children's Bureau. (1998). *Child maltreatment 1996: Reports from the states to the National Child Abuse and Neglect Data System.* Washington, DC: Government Printing Office.

Child Welfare League of America. (1997). At-risk kids at greater risk. *Children's Voice, 6*(2), 21.

Cicchetti, D., & Beeghly, M. (1987). Symbolic development in maltreated youngsters: An organizational perspective. *New Directions for Child Development, 36*, 47-68.

Cicchetti, D., Toth, S. L., & Lynch, M. (1993). The developmental sequelae of child maltreatment: Implications for war-related trauma. In L. A. Leavitt & N. A. Fox (Eds.), *The psychological effects of war and violence on children* (pp. 41-71). Hillsdale, NJ: Lawrence Erlbaum.

Cicchinelli, L. F. (1995). Risk assessment: Expectations and realities. *APSAC Advisor, 8*(4), 3-8.

Cohen, J. (1977). *Statistical power analysis for the behavioral sciences.* Hillsdale, NJ: Lawrence Erlbaum.

Cohen, P., & Hesselbart, C. S. (1993). Demographic factors in the use of children's mental health services. *American Journal of Public Health, 83,* 49-52.

Cohen, S., & Wills, T. A. (1985). Stress, social support, and the buffering hypothesis. *Psychological Bulletin, 98,* 310-357.

Cohn, A. H. (1979). Effective treatment of child abuse and neglect. *Social Work, 24,* 513-519.

Cohn, A. H. (1982). Stopping abuse before it occurs: Different solutions for different population groups. *Child Abuse and Neglect, 6,* 473-483.

Cohn, A. H., & Daro, D. (1987). Is treatment too late? What ten years of evaluative research tell us. *Child Abuse and Neglect, 11,* 433-440.

Coleman, J. S. (1990). *Foundations of social theory.* Cambridge, MA: Belknap Press of Harvard University Press.

Colletta, N. D., Hadler, S., & Gregg, C. H. (1981). How adolescents cope with the problems of early motherhood. *Adolescence, 16,* 499-512.

Collins, M. E., Bybee, D., & Mowbray, C. T. (1998). Effectiveness of supported education for individuals with psychiatric disabilities: Results from an experimental study. *Community Mental Health Journal, 34*(6), 595-613.

Collins, P. H. (1990). *Black feminist thought: Knowledge, consciousness, and the politics of empowerment.* London: HarperCollins Academic.

Conger, J. A., & Kanungo, R. N. (1988). The empowerment process: Integrating theory and practice. *Academy of Management Review, 13,* 471-482.

Connelly, C. D., & Straus, M. A. (1992). Mother's age and risk for physical abuse. *Child Abuse and Neglect, 16*(5), 709-718.

Coohey, C. (1996). Child maltreatment: Testing the social isolation hypothesis. *Child Abuse and Neglect, 20*(3), 241-251.

Corrigan, P. W., River, L. P., Lundin, R. K., Wasowski, K. U., Campion, J., Mathisen, J., Goldstein, H., Gagnon, C., Bergman, M., & Kubiak, M. A. (1999). Predictors of participation in campaigns against mental illness stigma. *Journal of Nervous & Mental Disease, 187*(6), 378-380.

Corse, S. J., Schmid, K., & Trickett, P. K. (1990). Social network characteristics of mothers in abusing and nonabusing families and their relationships to parenting beliefs. *Journal of Community Psychology, 18*(1), 44-59.

Costin, L. B. (1980). The historical context of child welfare. In A. Hartman & J. Laird (Eds.), *A handbook of child welfare: Context, knowledge, and practice* (pp. 34-60). New York: Free Press.

Costin, L. B., Karger, H. J., & Stoesz, D. (1996). *The politics of child abuse in America.* New York: Oxford University Press.

Coulton, C. J., Korbin, J. E., & Su, M. (1996). Measuring neighborhood context for young children in an urban area. *American Journal of Community Psychology, 24*(1), 5-32.

Coulton, C. J., Korbin, J. E., & Su, M. (1999). Neighborhoods and child maltreatment: A multi-level study. *Child Abuse and Neglect, 23*(11), 1019-1040.

Coulton, C. J., Korbin, J. E., Su, M., & Chow, J. (1995). Community level factors and child maltreatment rates. *Child Development, 66,* 1262-1276.

Courtney, M. E. (1998). The costs of child protection in the context of welfare reform. *The Future of Children, 8*(1), 88-103.

Courtney, M. E., Barth, R. P., Berrick, J. D., Brooks, D., Needell, B., & Park, L. (1996). Race and child welfare services: Past research and future directions. *Child Welfare, 75*(2), 99-137.

Cowan, P. A., & Cowan, C. P. (1988). Changes in marriage during the transition to parenthood: Must we blame the baby? In G. Y. Michaels & W. A. Goldberg (Eds.), *The transition to parenthood: Current theory and research* (pp. 114-154). Cambridge, UK: Cambridge University Press.

Cox, A. D., Puckering, C., Pound, A., & Mills, M. (1987). The impact of maternal depression in young children. *Journal of Child Psychology, Psychiatry, and Allied Disciplines, 28*(6), 917-928.

Crittenden, P. M. (1981). Abusing, neglecting, problematic, and adequate dyads: Differentiating by patterns of interaction. *Merrill-Palmer Quarterly, 27*(3), 201-218.

Crittenden, P. M. (1985). Social networks, quality of child rearing, and child development. *Child Development, 56,* 1299-1313.

Crittenden, P. M. (1998). Dangerous behavior and dangerous contexts: A 35-year perspective on research on the developmental effects of child physical abuse. In P. K. Trickett & C. J. Schellenbach (Eds.), *Violence against children in the family and the community* (pp. 11-38). Washington, DC: American Psychological Associaton Press.

Crnic, K. A., Greenberg, M. T., Robinson, N. M., & Ragozin, A. S. (1984). Maternal stress and social support: Effects on the mother-infant relationship from birth to 18 months. *American Journal of Orthopsychiatry, 54,* 224-235.

Crockenberg, S. (1987). Support for adolescent mothers during the postnatal period: Theory and practice. In C. F. Boukydis (Ed.), *Research on support for parents and infants in the postnatal period* (pp. 3-24). Norwood, NJ: Ablex.

Crockenberg, S. B., & Smith, P. (1983). Antecedents of mother-infant interaction and infant irritability in the first three months of life. *Annual Progress in Child Psychiatry & Child Development,* 126-143.

Crohan, S. E. (1996). Marital quality and conflict across the transition to parenthood in African American and White couples. *Journal of Marriage and the Family, 58*(4), 933-944.

Cronkite, R. C., & Moos, R. H. (1980). Determinants of the post treatment functioning of alcoholic patients: A conceptual framework. *Journal of Consulting and Clinical Psychology, 48,* 305-316.

Cummings, E. M., Hennessy, K. D., Rabideau, G. J., & Cicchetti, D. (1994). Responses of physically abused boys to interadult anger involving their mother. *Development & Psychopathology, 6,* 31-41.

Cutrona, C. E., Hessling, R. M., Bacon, P. L., & Russell, D. W. (1998). Predictors and correlates of continuing involvement with the baby's father among adolescent mothers. *Journal of Family Psychology, 12*(3), 369-387.

Danoff, N. L., Kemper, K. J., & Sherry, B. (1994). Risk factors for dropping out of a parenting education program. *Child Abuse and Neglect, 18,* 599-606.

Danziger, S. K., & Radin, N. (1990). Absent does not equal uninvolved: Predictors of fathering in teen mother families. *Journal of Marriage and the Family, 52,* 636-642.

Daro, D. (1988). *Confronting child abuse: Research for effective program design.* New York: Free Press.

Daro, D. (1993). Child maltreatment research: Implications for program design. In D. Cicchetti & S. L. Toth (Eds.), *Child abuse, child development, and social policy: Advances in applied developmental psychology* (Vol. 8, pp. 331-367). Norwood, NJ: Ablex.

Daro, D. (1999). *Public opinion and behaviors regarding child abuse prevention: 1999 survey.* Chicago: National Center of Child Abuse Prevention Research.

Daro, D., & Harding, K. (1999). Healthy Families America: Using research to enhance practice. *The Future of Children, 9*(1), 152-176.

Daro, D., & McCurdy, K. (1994). Preventing child abuse and neglect: Programmatic interventions. *Child Welfare, 73*(5), 405-430.

Daro, D., McCurdy, K., & Harding, K. (1998). *The role of home visiting in preventing child abuse: An evaluation of the Hawaii Healthy Start program.* Chicago: National Committee to Prevent Child Abuse.

Daro, D., & Winje, C. (1998). *Healthy Families America: Profile of pilot sites.* Chicago: National Committee to Prevent Child Abuse.

Davis, S. (1994). Effects of chemical dependency in parenting women. In R. Watson (Ed.), *Drug and alcohol abuse reviews: Vol. 5. Addictive behaviors in women* (pp. 381-413). Totowa, NJ: Humana Press.

Dawson, G., Hessl, D., & Frey, K. (1994). Social influences on early developing biological and behavioral systems related to risk for affective disorder. *Development and Psychopathology, 6,* 759-779.

Dawson, P. M., Robinson, J. L., Butterfield, P. M., van Doornick, W. J., Gaensbauer, T. J., & Harmon, R. J. (1990). Supporting new parents through home visits: Effects on mother-infant interaction. *Topics in Early Childhood Special Education, 10*(4), 29-44.

Dawson, P., Van Doorninck, W. J., & Robinson, J. L. (1989). Effects of home-based, informal social support on child health. *Developmental and Behavior Pediatrics, 10,* 63-67.

De Bellis, M. D., Keshavan, M. S., Clark, D. B., Casey, B. J., Giedd, J. N., Boring, A. M., Frustaci, K., & Ryan, N. D. (1999). Developmental traumatology: II. Brain development. *Biological Psychiatry, 45*(10), 1271-1284.

DePanfilis, D. (1996). Social isolation and neglectful families: A review of social support assessment and intervention models. *Child Maltreatment, 1*(1), 37-52.

DePanfilis, D., & Salus, M. K. (1992). *Child Protective Services: A guide for caseworkers.* Washington, DC: U.S. Department of Health and Human Services.

Deren, S. (1986). Children of substance abusers: A review of the literature. *Journal of Substance Abuse Treatment, 3,* 77-94.

Diamond, D., Heinicke, C., & Mintz, J. (1996). Separation-individuation as a family transactional process in the transition to parenthood. *Infant Mental Health Journal, 17*(1), 24-42.

Dickerson, F. B. (1998). Strategies that foster empowerment. *Cognitive & Behavioral Practice, 5*(2), 255-275.

Dickie, J. R., & Gerber, S. C. (1980). Training in social competence: The effect on mothers, fathers, and infants. *Child Development, 51,* 1248-1251.

Dickinson, N. S., & Cudaback, D. J. (1992). Parent education for adolescent mothers. *The Journal of Primary Prevention, 13*(1), 23-35.

Disbrow, M. A., Coerr, H., & Caufield, C. (1977). Measuring the components of parents potential for child abuse and neglect. *Child Abuse and Neglect, 1,* 279-296.

Dixon, L., Goldman, H., & Hirad, A. (1999). State policy and funding of services to families of adults with serious and persistent mental illness. *Psychiatric Services, 50*(4), 551-552.

Dobash, E. R., & Dobash, P. (1979). *Violence against wives: A case against the patriarchy.* New York: Free Press.

Dodge, K. A., Pettit, G. S., & Bates, J. E. (1994). Effects of physical maltreatment on the development of peer relations. *Development and Psychopathology, 6*(10), 43-56.

Donovan, W. L., & Leavitt, L. A. (1989). Maternal self-efficacy and infant attachment: Integrating physiology, perceptions, and behavior. *Child Development, 60*(2), 460-472.

Donovan, W. L., Leavitt, L. A., & Walsh, R. O. (1998). Conflict and depression predict maternal sensitivity to infant cries. *Infant Behavior and Development, 21*(3), 505-507.

Drake, B., & Pandey, S. (1996). Understanding the relationship between neighborhood poverty and specific types of child maltreatment. *Child Abuse and Neglect, 20*(11), 1003-1018.

Drotar, D. (1992). Prevention of neglect and nonorganic failure to thrive. In D. J. Willis, E. W. Holden, & M. Rosenberg (Eds.), *Prevention of child maltreatment: Developmental and ecological perspectives* (pp. 115-149). New York: John Wiley.

Dubowitz, H. (1999, June 3). *Fathers and child neglect.* Paper presented at the 7th National Colloquium of the American Professional Society on the Abuse of Children, San Antonio, TX.

Duerr Berrick, J., & Duerr, M. (1993). Preventing child neglect: A study of an in-home program for children and families. In R. Barth, J. Duerr Berrick, & N. Gilbert (Eds.), *Child welfare research review* (Vol. 1, pp. 63-83). New York: Columbia University Press.

Duerr Berrick, J., Needell, B., Barth, R. P., & Jonson-Reid, M. (1998). *The tender years: Toward developmentally sensitive child welfare services for very young children.* New York: Oxford University Press.

Duggan, A. K., McFarlane, E. C., Windham, A. M., Rohde, C. A., Salkever, D. S., Fuddy, L., Rosenberg, L. A., Buchbinder, S. B., & Sia, C. J. (1999). Evaluation of Hawaii's Healthy Start program. *The Future of Children, 9*(1), 66-91.

Dumas, J. E. (1986). Indirect influence of maternal social contacts on mother-child interactions: A setting event analysis. *Journal of Abnormal Child Psychology, 14*(2), 205-216.

Dumas, J., & Wahler, R. (1983). Predictors of treatment outcome in parent training: Mother insularity and socioeconomic disadvantage. *Behavioral Assessment, 5,* 301-313.

Dumka, L. E., Garza, C. A., Roosa, M. W., & Stoerzinger, H. D. (1997). Recruitment and retention of high-risk families into a preventive parent training program. *Journal of Primary Prevention, 18*(1), 25-39.

Duncan, G. J., Brooks-Gunn, J., & Klebanov, P. K. (1994). Economic deprivation and early childhood development. *Child Development, 65*(2), 296-318.

Dunst, C. J., & Trivette, C. M. (1990). Assessment of social support in early intervention programs. In J. Shonkoff & S. Meisels (Eds.), *Handbook of early childhood intervention* (pp. 326-349). New York: Cambridge University Press.

Dykes, L. (1986). The whiplash shaken infant syndrome: What has been learned? *Child Abuse & Neglect, 10,* 211-221.

Dykman, R. A., McPherson, B., Ackerman, P. T., Newton, J. E., Mooney, D. M., Wherry, J., & Chaffin, M. (1997). Internalizing and externalizing characteristics of sexually and/or physically abused children. *Integrative Physiological & Behavioral Science, 32*(1), 62-74.

Earle, R. B. (1995). *Helping to prevent child abuse—and future criminal consequences: Hawai'i Healthy Start.* Washington, DC: National Institute of Justice.

Earls, F. (1998). Positive effects of prenatal and early childhood interventions. *Journal of the American Medical Association, 280*(4), 1271-1273.

Edelson, J. L. (1999). The overlap between child maltreatment and woman battering. *Violence Against Women, 5,* 134-154.

Egeland, B., Breitenbucher, M., & Rosenberg, D. (1980). A prospective study of the significance of life stress in the etiology of child abuse. *Journal of Consulting and Clinical Psychology, 48,* 195-205.

Egeland, B., Jacovitz, D., & Sroufe, L. A. (1988). Breaking the cycle of abuse. *Child Development, 59,* 1080-1088.

Egeland, B., & Sroufe, L. A. (1981). Attachment and early maltreatment. *Child Development, 52,* 44-52.

Eisenberg, A., Murkoff, H. E., & Hathaway, S. E. (1991). *What to expect when you're expecting.* New York: Workman.

El-Bassel, N., Ivanoff, A., Schilling, R., Borne, D., & Chen, D. (1995). Preventing HIV/AIDS in drug-abusing incarcerated women through skills building and social support enhancement: Preliminary outcomes. *Social Work Research, 19,* 131-141.

Elder, G. H., Jr., Eccles, J. S., Ardelt, M., & Lord, S. (1995). Inner-city parents under economic pressure: Perspectives on the strategies of parenting. *The Journal of Marriage and the Family, 57,* 771-784.

Elliott, D. J., Koroloff, N. M., Koren, P. E., & Friesen, B. J. (1998). Improving access to children's mental health services: The Family Associate approach. In M. H. Epstein & K. Kutash (Eds.), *Outcomes for children and youth with emotional and behavioral disorders and their families: Programs and evaluation best practices* (pp. 581-609). Austin, TX: Pro-Ed.

Ellis, R. H., & Milner, J. S. (1981). Child abuse and locus of control. *Psychological Reports, 48*(2), 507-510.

Ellwood, A. (1988). Prove to me that MELD makes a difference. In H. B. Weiss (Ed.), *Evaluating family programs: Modern applications of social work* (pp. 303-313). Hawthorne, NY: Aldine De Gruyter.

Ellwood, D. T. (1988). *Poor support: Poverty in the American family.* New York: Basic Books.

Elmer, E. (1967). *Children in jeopardy.* Pittsburgh, PA: University of Pittsburgh Press.

Emerick, R. E. (1990). Self-help groups for former patients: Relations with mental health professionals. *Hospital & Community Psychiatry, 41*(4), 401-407.

Engfer, A., & Schneewind, K. A. (1982). Causes and consequences of harsh parental punishment: An empirical investigation of a representative sample of 570 German families. *Child Abuse and Neglect, 6,* 129-139.

English, D. J. (1999). The extent and consequences of child maltreatment. *The Future of Children, 8*(1), 39-53.

Esposito, G., & Fine, M. (1985). The field of child welfare as a world of work. In J. Laird & A. Hartman (Eds.), *A handbook of child welfare: Context, knowledge, and practice* (pp. 727-740). New York: Free Press.

Espy, K. A., Riese, M. L., & Francis, D. J. (1997). Neurobehavior in preterm neonates exposed to cocaine, alcohol, and tobacco. *Infant Behavior and Development, 20*(3), 297-309.

Ethier, K. A. (1996). Becoming a mother: Identity acquisition during the transition to parenthood. *Dissertation Abstracts International,* B, 56(10-B), 5832.

Evans, C. J., & McGee, C. (1998). Collaboration between a state alliance for the mentally ill and a state mental health authority in monitoring the consequences of downsizing. Evidence-Based Medicine Working Group. (1992). Evidence-based medicine: A new approach to teaching the practice of medicine. *Journal of the American Medical Association, 268*(17), 2420-2425.

Evans, C. J., & McGee, C. (1998). Collaboration between a state alliance for the mentally ill and a state mental health authority in monitoring the consequences of downsizing. *Journal of Behavioral Health Services & Research, 25*(1), 43-50.

Ewigman, B., Kivlahan, C., & Land, G. (1993). The Missouri child fatality study: Underreporting of maltreatment fatalities among children younger than five years of age, 1983 through 1986. *Pediatrics, 91*(2), 330-337.

Faller, K. C. (1981). *Social structural variables in families that abuse and neglect their children.* Unpublished doctoral dissertation, University of Michigan, Ann Arbor.

Famularo, R., Kinscherff, R., & Fenton, T. (1992). Parental substance abuse and the nature of child maltreatment. *Child Abuse and Neglect, 16,* 475-483.

Fanshel, D. (1975). Parental failure and consequences for children: The drug abusing mother whose children are in foster care. *American Journal of Public Health, 65*(6), 604-612.

Fantuzzo, J. W. (1986). Parent and social-skills training for mentally retarded mothers identified as child maltreaters. *American Journal of Mental Deficiency, 91*(2), 135-140.

Fantuzzo, J. W. (1990). Behavioral treatment of the victims of child abuse and neglect. *Behavior Modification, 14,* 316-339.

Feig, L. (1990). *Drug-exposed infants and children: Service needs and policy questions.* Washington, DC: U.S. Department of Health and Human Services.

Feldman, R., Greenbaum, C. W., Mayes, L. C., & Erlich, S. H. (1997). Change in mother-infant interactive behavior: Relations to change in the mother, the infant, and the social context. *Infant Behavior and Development, 20*(2), 151-163.

Felix, A. C., & McCarthy, K. F. (1994). *An analysis of child fatalities, 1992.* Boston: Commonwealth of Massachusetts Department of Social Services.

Field, T. (1984). Peer separation of children attending new schools. *Developmental Psychology, 20,* 786-792.

Field, T. (1992). Infants of depressed mothers. *Development and Psychopathology, 4*(1), 49-66.

Field, T. (1998). Maternal depression effects on infants and early interventions. *Preventive Medicine: An International Devoted to Practice and Theory, 27*(2), 200-203.

Field, T. M., Scafidi, F., Pickens, J., Prodromidis, M., Pelaez-Nogueras, M., Torquati, J., Wilcox, H., Malphurs, J., Schanberg, S., & Kuhn, C. (1998). Polydrug-using adolescent mothers and their infants receiving early intervention. *Adolescence, 33*(129), 117-143.

Field, T., Widmayer, S., Greenberg, R., & Stoller, S. (1982). Effects of parent training on teenage mothers and their infants. *Pediatrics, 69*(6), 703-707.

Field, T. M., Widmayer, S. M., Stringer, S., & Ignatoff, E. (1980). Teenage, lower class, black mothers and their pre-term infants: An intervention and developmental follow-up study. *Child Development, 51,* 426-436.

Fink, A., & McCloskey (1990). Moving child abuse and neglect prevention programs forward: Improving program evaluations, *Child Abuse and Neglect, 14,* 187-206.

Fink, A. E., Wilson, E. E., & Conover, M. B. (1963). *The field of social work.* New York: Holt, Rinehart & Winston.

Finkelhor, D., & Korbin, J. (1988). Child abuse as an international issue. *Child Abuse & Neglect, 12*(1), 3-23.

Finkelstein, N. (1994). Treatment issues for alcohol- and drug-dependent pregnant and parenting women. *Health and Social Work, 19*(1), 7-15.

Firestone, P., & Witt, J. E. (1982). Characteristics of families completing and prematurely discontinuing a behavioral parent-training program. *Journal of Pediatric Psychology, 7*(2), 209-222.

Fischler, R. S. (1985). Child abuse and neglect in American Indian communities. *Child Abuse and Neglect, 9,* 95-106.

Folkman, S. (1984). Personal control and stress and coping processes: A theoretical analysis. *Journal of Personality and Social Psychology, 46,* 839-852.

Fontana, C. A., Fleischman, A. R., McCarton, C., Meltzer, A., & Ruff, J. (1988). A neonatal preventive intervention study: Issues of recruitment and retention. *Journal of Primary Prevention, 9,* 164-176.

Forgays, D. G. (1983). Primary prevention of psychopathology. In M. Hersen, A. E. Kazdin, & A. S. Bellack (Eds.), *The clinical psychology handbook* (pp. 701-734). New York: Pergamon.

Fox, N. A., Calkins, S. D., & Bell, M. A. (1994). Neural plasticity and development in the first two years of life: Evidence from cognitive and socioemotional domains of research. *Development and Psychopathology, 6,* 677-696.

Fox, N. A., Kimmerly, N. L., & Schafer, W. D. (1991). Attachment to mother/attachment to father: A meta-analysis. *Child Development, 62*(1), 210-225.

Fraiberg, S. (1980). *Clinical studies in infant mental health: The first year of life.* New York: Basic Books.

Frank, Y., Zimmerman, R., & Leeds, N. M. (1985). Neurological manifestations in abused children who have been shaken. *Developmental Medicine & Child Neurology, 27*(3), 312-316.

Fraser, M., & Hawkins, J. D. (1984). The social networks of opioid abusers. *International Journal of the Addictions, 19,* 903-917.

Friere, P. (1970). *Pedagogy of the oppressed.* New York: Seabury.

Furstenberg, F. F. (1993). How families manage risk and opportunity in dangerous neighborhoods. In W. J. Wilson (Ed.), *Sociology and the public agenda* (pp. 231-258). Newbury Park, CA: Sage.

Gabinet, L. (1979). Prevention of child abuse and neglect in an inner-city population: II. The program and results. *Child Abuse and Neglect, 3,* 809-817.

Gaensbauer, T. J., & Mrazek, D. A. (1981). Differences in the patterning of affective expression in infants. *Journal of the American Academy of Child and Adolescent Psychiatry, 20,* 673-691.

Galanter, M. (1999). *Network therapy for alcohol and drug abuse.* New York: Guilford.

Garbarino, J. (1977, November). The human ecology of child maltreatment: A conceptual model for research. *Journal of Marriage and the Family,* pp. 721-735.

Garbarino, J. (1980). *Protecting children from abuse and neglect: Developing and maintaining effective support systems for families.* San Francisco: Jossey-Bass.

Garbarino, J., & Ebata, A. (1983, November). The significance of ethnic and cultural differences in child maltreatment. *Journal of Marriage and the Family,* pp. 773-783.

Garbarino, J., & Gilliam, G. (1980). *Understanding abusive families*. Lexington, MA: Lexington Books.

Garbarino, J., & Kostelny, K. (1992). Child maltreatment as a community problem. *Child Abuse and Neglect, 16,* 455-462.

Garbarino, J., & Sherman, D. (1980). High-risk neighborhoods and high-risk families: The human ecology of child maltreatment. *Child Development, 51,* 188-198.

Gaudin, J. M. (1993). Effective intervention with neglectful families. *Criminal Justice and Behavior, 20*(1), 66-89.

Gaudin, J., Polansky, N., Kilpatrick, A., & Shilton, P. (1993). Loneliness, depression, stress, and social support in neglectful families. *American Journal of Orthopsychiatry, 63*(4), 597-605.

Gaudin, J. M., & Pollane, L. (1983). Social networks, stress, and child abuse. *Children and Youth Services Review, 5*(1), 91-102.

Gaudin, J. M., Wodarski, J. S., Arkinson, M. K., & Avery, L. S. (1990-1991). Remedying child neglect: Effectiveness of social network interventions. *Journal of Applied Social Sciences, 15,* 97-123.

Gaventa, J. (1982). *Power and powerlessness*. Urbana and Chicago: University of Illinois Press.

Gecas, V. (1989). The social psychology of self-efficacy. *Annual Review of Sociology, 15,* 291-316.

Gelles, R. J. (1989). Child abuse and violence in single parent families: Parent absence and economic deprivation. *American Journal of Orthopsychiatry, 59,* 492-501.

Gelles, R. (1996). *The book of David: How preserving families can cost children's lives.* New York: Basic Books.

Gelles, R. J., & Cornell, C. P. (1983). *International perspectives on family violence.* Lexington, MA: Lexington Books.

George, C. (1996). A representational perspective of child abuse and prevention: Internal working models of attachment and caregiving. *Child Abuse and Neglect, 20*(5), 411-424.

George, C., & Main, M. (1979). Social interactions of young abused children: Approach, avoidance, and aggression. *Child Development, 50,* 306-318.

Gerstein, D., Johnson, R., Larison, C., Harwood, H., & Fountain, D. (1997). *Alcohol and drug abuse treatment for parents and welfare recipients: Outcomes, benefits, and costs.* Washington, DC: U.S. Department of Health and Human Services.

Gidron, B., Guterman, N. B., & Hartman, H. (1990). Participation in self-help groups and empowerment among parents of the mentally ill in Israel. In T. J. Powell (Ed.), *Working with self-help* (pp. 267-276). Silver Spring, MD: NASW Press.

Gil, D. (1970a). Societal violence and violence in families. In D. Gil (Ed.), *Child abuse and violence* (pp. 357-385). New York: AMS Press.

Gil, D. (1970b). *Violence against children: Physical abuse in the United States.* Cambridge, MA: Harvard University Press.

Gil, D. G. (1984). The ideological context of child welfare. *Children & Youth Services Review, 6*(4), 299-309.

Giovannoni, J. M. (1971). Parental mistreatment: Perpetrators and victims. *Journal of Marriage and the Family, 20,* 649-657.

Glanchan, M. (1990). Power: A dimension of family abuse. *Early Child Development and Care, 60,* 1-10.

Glass, G. V., McGaw, B., & Smith, M. L. (1981). *Meta-analysis in social research.* Beverly Hills, CA: Sage.

Goehl, L., Nunes, E., Quitkin, F., & Hilton, I. (1993). Social networks and methadone treatment outcome: The costs and benefits of social ties. *American Journal of Drug and Alcohol Abuse, 19*(3), 251-262.

Goerge, R., & Harden, A. (1993). *The impact of substance affected infants on Child Protection Services and substitute caseloads: 1985-1992.* Springfield, IL: Illinois Department of Children and Family Services.

Goldberg, J., Weisenberg, M., Drobkin, S., Blittner, M., & Gotestam, K. (1997). Effects of manipulated cognitive and attributional set on pain tolerance. *Cognitive Therapy & Research, 21*(5), 525-534.

Goldfarb, W. (1945). Psychological privation in infancy and subsequent adjustment. *American Journal of Orthopsychiatry, 15,* 247-255.

Goldstein, H. (1983, May). Starting where the client is. *Social Casework,* pp. 267-275.

Gomby, D. S., Culross, P. L., & Behrman, R. E. (1999). Home visiting: Recent program evaluations—Analysis and recommendations. *The Future of Children, 9*(1), 4-26.

Gondolf, E. W. (1985). *Men who batter: An integrated approach for stopping wife abuse.* Holmes Beach, FL: Learning Publications.

Gordon, A. J., & Zrull, M. (1991). Social networks and recovery: One year after inpatient treatment. *Journal of Substance Abuse Treatment, 8,* 143-152.

Gottlieb, B. H. (1983). *Social support strategies.* Beverly Hills, CA: Sage.

Gottwald, S. R., & Thurman, S. K. (1994). The effects of prenatal cocaine exposure on mother-infant interaction and infant arousal in the newborn period. *Topics of Early Childhood Special Education, 14,* 217-231.

Gouch, B., & Reavey, P. (1997). Parental accounts regarding the physical punishment of children: Discourses of dis/empowerment. *Child Neglect & Abuse, 21,* 417-430.

Graham, M., Stabile, I., Powell, A., Pruett, R., Hakes, A. Z., & Butler, B. (1997). Serving pregnant women within Early Head Start: Lessons from the Panhandle Health Start and Early Head Start. *Zero to Three, 17,* 31-36.

Granovetter, M. S. (1973). The strength of weak ties. *American Journal of Sociology, 78*(6), 1360-1380.

Gray, E. B. (1982). Perinatal support programs: A strategy for the primary prevention of child abuse. *Journal of Primary Prevention, 2*(3), 138-152.

Gray, E., & Cosgrove, J. (1985). Ethnocentric perception of childrearing practices in protective services. *Child Abuse & Neglect, 9,* 389-396.

Gray, J., Cutler, C., Dean, J., & Kempe, C. H. (1979). Prediction and prevention of child abuse and neglect. *Journal of Social Issues, 35*(2), 127-139.

Gray, S. W., & Klaus, R. A. (1970). The Early Training Project: A seventh year report. *Child Development, 41*(4), 909-924.

Gray, S. W., Ramsey, B. K., & Klaus, R. A. (1982). *From 3 to 20: The Early Training Project.* Baltimore, MD: University Park Press.

Greenberger, D. B., Strasser, S., Cummings, L. L., & Dunham, R. B. (1989). The impact of personal control on performance and satisfaction. *Organizational Behavior & Human Decision Processes, 43*(1), 29-51.

Greenough, W. T., Wallace, C. S., Alcantara, A. A., Anderson, M. S., Hawyrak, M. C., Sirevaag, A. M., Weiler, I. J., & Withers, G. S. (1993). Development of the brain: Experience affects the structure of neurons, glia, and blood vessels. In N. J. Anastasiow &

S. Harel (Eds.), *At-risk infants: Interventions, families, and research* (pp. 173-185). Baltimore, MD: Paul H. Brookes.

Gregoire, T. (1994). Assessing the benefits and increasing the utility of addiction training for public child welfare workers: A pilot study. *Child Welfare, 73*(1), 69-81.

Grief, G., & Drechsler, M. (1993). Common issues for parents in a methadone maintenance group. *Journal of Substance Abuse Treatment, 10,* 339-343.

Griffin, J. A., Cicchetti, D., & Leaf, P. J. (1993). Characteristics of youths identified from a psychiatric case register as first-time users of services. *Hospital & Community Psychiatry, 44*(1), 62-65.

Griffin, R. E. (1991). Assessing the drug involved client. *Families in Society, 72*(2), 87-94.

Grubb, W. N., & Lazerson, M. (1988). *Broken promises: How Americans fail their children.* Chicago: University of Chicago Press.

Gurin, P. (1985). Women's gender consciousness. *Public Opinion Quarterly, 49*(2), 143-163.

Gurin, P., Miller, A. H., & Gurin, G. (1980). Stratum identification and consciousness. *Social Psychology Quarterly, 43*(1), 30-47.

Guterman, N. B. (1990). *Social isolation and physical child abuse: A review and revision.* Unpublished manuscript.

Guterman, N. B. (1997a). Early prevention of physical child abuse and neglect: Existing evidence and future directions. *Child Maltreatment, 2*(1), 12-34.

Guterman, N. B. (1997b). Parental violence toward children. In N. K. Phillips & S. L. A. Straussner (Eds.), *Children in the urban environment: Linking social policy and clinical practice* (pp. 113-134). Springfield, IL: Charles C Thomas.

Guterman, N. B. (1997c). *Social network changes of participants in the "Parents Together" pilot.* Unpublished document available from author.

Guterman, N. B. (1999). *Preliminary outcome findings on Best Beginnings Plus.* Unpublished document available from Best Beginnings, New York, NY.

Guterman, N. B., & Jayaratne, S. (1994). "Responsibility at-risk:" Perceptions of stress, control, and professional effectiveness in child welfare direct practitioners. *Journal of Social Service Research, 20*(1/2), 99-120.

Gutierrez, L. M. (1988). *Coping with stressful life events: An empowerment perspective.* Unpublished manuscript, University of Michigan, Ann Arbor.

Gutierrez, L. M., & Lewis, E. A. (1999). *Empowering women of color.* New York: Columbia University Press.

Gutierrez, L. M., & Ortega, R. (1991). Developing methods to empower Latinos: The importance of groups. *Social Work With Groups, 14*(2), 23-43.

Gynn-Orenstein, J. S. (1981). The relationship between moral reasoning, locus of control, emotional empathy, and parenting profile in physically abusing mothers. *Dissertation Abstracts International, 42*(5-B), 2056-2057.

Halpern, R. (1993). Poverty and infant development. In C. H. Zeanah (Ed.), *Handbook of infant mental health* (pp. 73-86). New York: Guilford.

Hampton, R. L. (1987). Race, class, and child maltreatment. *Journal of Comparative Family Study, 18*(1), 113-126.

Hampton, R. L., & Newberger, E. H. (1985). Child abuse incidence and reporting by hospitals: Significance of severity, class, and race. *American Journal of Public Health, 75*(1), 56-60.

Hangen, E. (1994). *D.S.S. Interagency Domestic Violence Team Pilot Project: Program data evaluation.* Boston: Massachusetts Department of Social Services.

Hardy, J. B., & Streett, R. (1989). Family support and parenting education in the home: An effective extension of clinic-based preventive health care service for poor children. *Journal of Pediatrics, 115*(6), 927-931.

Harkavy, O., & Bond, J. T. (1992). Program operations: Time allocation and cost analysis. In M. Larner, R. Halpern, & O. Harkavy (Eds.), *Fair Start for children: Lessons learned from seven demonstration projects* (pp. 198-217). New Haven, CT: Yale University Press.

Harlow, H. F. (1958). The nature of love. *American Psychologist, 13,* 673-685.

Harrison, M. (1981). Home-Start: A voluntary home-visiting scheme for young families. *Child Abuse and Neglect, 5*(4), 441-447.

Hartman, A. (1978). Diagrammatic assessments of family relationships. *Social Casework, 59,* 465-476.

Hashima, P., & Amato, P. R. (1994). Poverty, social support, and parental behavior. *Child Development, 65,* 394-403.

Havel, J. T. (1992). Associations and public interest groups as advocates. *Administration & Policy in Mental Health, 20*(1), 27-44.

Hawaii Family Stress Center. (1994). *Healthy Start.* Honolulu, HI: Department of Health, Maternal and Child Health Branch.

Healthy Families America. (1993). *Healthy Families America first year progress report.* Chicago: National Committee to Prevent Child Abuse.

Healthy Families America. (1996). *Fourth year progress report.* Unpublished document, National Committee to Prevent Child Abuse, Chicago.

Hegar, R. L., Zuravin, S. J., & Orme, J. G. (1994). Factors predicting severity of physical child abuse injury: A review of the literature. *Journal of Interpersonal Violence, 9*(2), 170-183.

Helfer, R. E. (1987). The developmental basis of child abuse and neglect: An epidemiological approach. In R. E. Helfer & R. S. Kempe (Eds.), *The battered child* (4th ed., pp. 60-80). Chicago: University of Chicago Press.

Herman-Giddens, M. E., Brown, G., Verbiest, S., Carlson, P. J., Hooten, E. G., Howell, E., & Butts, J. D. (1999). Underascertainment of child abuse mortality in the United States. *Journal of the American Medical Association, 282*(5), 463-467.

Herrenkohl, R., & Herrenkohl, E. (1981). Some antecedents and developmental consequences of child maltreatment. In R. Rizley & D. Cicchetti (Eds.), *New directions for child development, development perspectives on child maltreatment* (Vol. 11, pp. 57-76). San Francisco: Jossey-Bass.

Herzog, E. P., Cherniss, D. S., & Menzel, B. J. (1986). Issues in engaging high-risk adolescent mothers in supportive work. *Infant Mental Health Journal, 7,* 59-68.

Heschel, A. J. (1996). *Moral grandeur and spiritual audacity: Essays.* New York: Farrar Straus Giroux.

Hiatt, S. W., Michalek, P., Younge, P., Miyoshi, T., & Fryer, E. (2000). Characteristics of volunteers and families in a neonatal home visitation project: The Kempe community caring program. *Child Abuse and Neglect, 24,* 85-97.

Hiatt, S. W., Sampson, D., & Baird, D. (1997). Paraprofessional home visitation: Conceptual and pragmatic considerations. *Journal of Community Psychology, 25*(1), 77-93.

Hillson, J. M. C., & Kupier, N. A. (1994). A stress and coping model of child maltreatment, *Clinical Psychology Review, 14*(4), 261-285.

Hodges, V. G., & Blythe, B. J. (1992). Improving service delivery to high-risk families: Home-based practice. *Families in Society, 73*(5), 259-265.

Hodges, W. F., Landis, T., Day, E., & Oderberg, N. (1991). Infant and toddlers and post divorce parental access: An initial exploration. *Journal of Divorce and Remarriage, 16*(3/4), 239-252.

Hodnett, E. D., & Roberts, I. (1999). Home-based social support for socially disadvantaged mothers. *Cochrane Review* [On-line]. Available: http://www.updateusa.com

Hoffman-Plotkin, D., & Twentyman, C. (1984). A multimodal assessment of behavioral cognitive deficits in abused and neglected preschoolers. *Child Development, 55,* 794-802.

Hong, G. K., & Hong, L. K. (1991). Comparative perspectives on child abuse and neglect: Chinese versus Hispanics and whites. *Child Welfare, 70*(4), 463-475.

Honig, A. S., & Pfannenstiel, A. E. (1991). Difficulties in reaching low-income new fathers: Issues and cases. *Early Child Development and Care, 77,* 115-125.

Hooker, C. E. (1976). Learned helplessness. *Social Work, 21,* 194-197.

Hossain, Z., Field, T., Gonzalez, J., & Malphurs, J. (1994). Infants of "depressed" mothers interact better with their nondepressed fathers. *Infant Mental Health Journal, 15*(4), 348-357.

Hossain, Z., Field, T., Pickens, J., Malphurs, J., & Del Valle, C. (1997). Fathers' caregiving in low-income African-American and Hispanic-American families. *Early Development and Parenting, 6*(2), 73-82.

House, J. H., Umberson, D., & Landis, K. R. (1988). Structures and processes of social support. In W. R. Scott & J. Blake (Eds.), *Annual review of sociology* (Vol. 14, pp. 293-318). Palo Alto, CA: Annual Reviews.

Householder, J., Hatcher, R. P., Burns, W. J., & Chasnoff, I. (1982). Infants born to narcotic-addicted mothers. *Psychological Bulletin, 92*(2), 453-468.

Howing, P., Wodarski, J., Kurtz, P., & Gaudin, J. (1989). Methodological issues in child maltreatment research. *Social Work Research and Abstracts, 23*(3), 3-7.

Huang, L., Cerbone, F., & Gfroerer, J. (1998). Children at risk because of parental substance abuse. In *Analyses of substance abuse and treatment need issues* (Analytic Series A-7). Rockville, MD: U.S. Department of Health and Human Services, Substance Abuse and Mental Health Services Administration.

Huxley, P., & Warner, R. (1993). Primary prevention of parenting dysfunction in high-risk cases. *American Journal of Orthopsychiatry, 63*(4), 582-588.

Infante-Rivard, C., Filion, G., Baumgarten, M., Bourassa, M., Labelle, J., & Messier, M. (1989). A public health home intervention among families of low socioeconomic status. *Children's Health Care, 18*(2), 102-107.

Infant Health and Development Program. (1990). Enhancing the outcomes of low-birthweight, premature infants. *Journal of the American Medical Association, 263*(22), 3035-3042.

INMED. (1999). International Medical Services for Health Web site. http://www.interaction.org/members/inmed.html.

Intagliata, J., & Doyle, N. (1984). Enhancing social support for parents of developmentally disabled children: Training in interpersonal problem solving skills. *Mental Retardation, 22*(1), 4-11.

Ito, Y., Teicher, M. H., Glod, C. A., & Harper, D. (1993). Increased prevalence of electrophysiological abnormalities in children with psychological, physical, and sexual abuse. *Journal of Neuropsychiatry & Clinical Neurosciences, 5*(4), 401-408.

Jansson, L. M., Svikis, D., Lee, J., Paluzzi, P., Rutigliano, P., & Hackerman, F. (1996). Pregnancy and addiction: A comprehensive care model. *Journal of Substance Abuse Treatment, 13,* 321-329.

Jason, J., Amereuh, N., Marks, J., & Tyler, C. (1982). Child abuse in Georgia: A method to evaluate risk factors and reporting bias. *American Journal of Public Health, 72*(12), 1353-1358.

Jaudes, P., Ekwo, E., & Van Voorhis, J. (1995). Association of drug abuse and child abuse. *Child Abuse and Neglect, 19,* 1065-1075.

Jayaratne, S., & Chess, W. A. (1984). Job satisfaction, burnout, and turnover: A national study. *Social Work, 29*(5), 449-454.

Joffe, J. M. (1988). The causes of the causes. In G. W. Albee, J. M. Joffe, & L. A. Dusenbury (Eds.), *Prevention, powerlessness, and politics* (pp. 57-79). Beverly Hills, CA: Sage.

Johnson, D. L., Walker, T. B., & Rodriguez, G. G. (1996). Teaching low-income mothers to teach their children. *Early Childhood Research Quarterly, 11*(1), 101-114.

Johnson, M. H. (1997). *Fundamentals of cognitive neuroscience.* Cambridge, MA: Blackwell.

Josten, L. E., Mullett, S. E., Savik, K., Campbell, R., & Vincent, P. (1995). Client characteristics associated with not keeping appointments for public health nursing home visits. *Public Health Nursing, 12*(5), 305-311.

Justice, B., Calvert, A., & Justice, R. (1985). Factors mediating child abuse as a response to stress. *Child Abuse and Neglect, 9*(3), 359-363.

Kadushin, A., & Martin, J. (1988). *Child welfare services* (4th ed.). New York: Macmillan.

Kagel, J. (1987). Secondary prevention of substance abuse. *Social Work, 32*(5), 446-448.

Kamerman, S. B. (1999). Child welfare and the under-threes: An overview. *Zero to Three, 19*(3), 1-7.

Kamerman, S. B., & Kahn, A. J. (1990, Winter). If CPS is driving child welfare—Where do we go from here? *Public Welfare,* pp. 9-13.

Kamerman, S. B., & Kahn, A. J. (1993). Home health visiting in Europe. *The Future of Children, 3*(3), 39-51.

Kandall, S. R., Gaines, J., Habel, L., Davidson, G., & Jessop, D. (1993). Relationship of maternal substance abuse to subsequent sudden infant death syndrome in offspring. *Journal of Pediatrics, 123*(1), 120-126.

Kanfer, F. H. (1986). Implications of a self-regulation model of therapy for treatment of addictive behaviors. In W. R. Miller & N. Heather (Eds.), *Treating addictive behaviors: Processes of change* (pp. 29-47). New York: Plenum.

Karoly, L. A., Greenwood, P. W., Everingham, P. W., Hoube, J., Kilburn, M. R., Rydell, C. P., Sanders, M., & Chiesa, J. (1998). *Investing in our children: What we know and don't know about the costs and benefits of early childhood interventions.* Santa Monica, CA: RAND.

Kaufman, J., & Cicchetti, D. (1989). The effects of maltreatment on school-age children's socioemotional development: Assessments in a day camp setting. *Developmental Psychology, 15,* 516-524.

Kaufman, J., & Zigler, E. (1992). The prevention of child maltreatment: Programming, research, and policy. In D. J. Willis, E. W. Holden, & M. Rosenberg (Eds.), *Prevention of child maltreatment: Developmental and ecological perspectives* (pp. 269-295). New York: John Wiley.

Kawachi, I., Kennedy, B. P., Lochner, K., & Prothrow-Stith, D. (1997). Social capital, income inequality, and mortality. *American Journal of Public Health, 87,* 1491-1498.

Kawachi, I., Kennedy, B. P., & Wilkenson, R. G. (1999). Crime: Social disorganization and relative deprivation. *Social Science and Medicine, 48,* 719-731.

Kazdin, A., & Mazurick, J. L. (1994). Dropping out of child psychotherapy: Distinguishing early and late dropouts over the course of treatment. *Journal of Consulting and Clinical Psychology, 62,* 1069-1074.

Kazdin, A., Moser, J., Colbus, D., & Bell, R. (1985). Depressive symptoms among physically abused and psychiatrically disturbed children. *Journal of Abnormal Psychology, 94,* 298-307.

Kelleher, K., Chaffin, M., Hollenberg, J., & Fischer, E. (1994). Alcohol and drug disorders among physically abusive and neglectful parents in a community-based sample. *American Journal of Public Health, 84*(10), 1586-1590.

Kelley, S. J. (1998). Stress and coping behaviors of substance-abusing mothers. *Journal of the Society of Pediatric Nurses, 3*(3), 103-110.

Kelly, S. J. (1999, June 6). *Substance abuse and child maltreatment: Understanding the connection.* Paper presented at the 7th National Colloquium of the American Professional Society on the Abuse of Children, San Antonio, TX.

Kempe, C. H. (1976). Approaches to preventing child abuse: The health visitor concept. *American Journal of Diseases of Children, 130,* 941-947.

Kempe, C. H., & Silver, H. (1959). The problem of parental criminal neglect and severe abuse of children. *AMA Journal of Diseases of Children, 98,* 528.

Kempe, C. H., Silverman, F., Stele, B., Droegmueller, W., & Silver, H. (1962). The battered-child syndrome. *Journal of the American Medical Association, 181,* 17-24.

Kennell, J., Voos, D., & Klaus, M. (1976). Parent-infant bonding. In R. E. Helfer & C. H. Kempe (Eds.), *Child abuse and neglect: The family and community* (pp. 25-53). Cambridge, MA: Ballinger.

Kestenbaum, R., Farber, E. A., & Sroufe, L. A. (1989). Individual differences in empathy among preschoolers: Relation to attachment history. *New Directions for Child Development, 44,* 51-64.

Keverne, E. B., Nevison, C. M., & Martel, F. L. (1997). Early learning and the social bond. In C. S. Carter & I. I. Lederhendler (Eds.), *The integrative neurobiology of affiliation: Annals of the New York Academy of Sciences* (Vol. 807, pp. 329-339). New York: New York Academy of Sciences.

Kiefer, C. (1984). Citizen empowerment: A developmental perspective. *Prevention in Human Services, 3,* 9-36.

Kiefer, L. M. (1990). Learned helplessness: A factor in women's depression. *Affilia, 5*(1), 21-31.

Kinard, E. M. (1979). The psychological consequences of abuse for the child. *Journal of Social Issues, 35,* 82-100.

Kinard, E. M. (1995). Perceived social support and competence in abused children: A longitudinal perspective. *Journal of Family Violence, 10*(1), 73-98.

Kirkham, M. A., Schinke, S. P., Schilling, R. F., & Meltzer, N. J. (1986). Cognitive-behavioral skills, social supports, and child abuse potential among mothers of handicapped children. *Journal of Family Violence, 1*(3), 235-245.

Kisker, E. E., & Ross, C. M. (1997). Arranging child care. *The Future of Children, 7*(1), 99-109.

Kitzman, H., Cole, R., & Yoos, L. (1997). Challenges experienced by home visitors: A qualitative study of program implementation. *Journal of Community Psychology, 25,* 95-109.

Kitzman, H., Olds, D. L., Henderson, C. R., Hanks, C., Cole, R., Tatelbaum, R., Mcconnochie, K. M., Sidora, K., Luckey, D. W., Shaver, D., Engelhart, K., James, D., & Barnard, K. (1997). Effect of prenatal and infancy home visitation by nurses on pregnancy outcomes, childhood injuries, and repeated childbearing. *Journal of the American Medical Association, 278*(8), 644-652.

Klaw, E. L., & Rhodes, J. E. (1995). Mentor relationships and the career development of pregnant and parenting African-American teenagers. *Psychology of Women Quarterly, 19*(4), 551-562.

Kobak, R., & Sceery, A. (1988). Attachment in later adolescence: Working models, affect regulation, and perception of self and others. *Child Development, 59,* 135-146.

Kochanska, G. (1998). Mother-child relationship, child fearfulness, and emerging attachment: A short-term longitudinal study. *Developmental Psychology, 34*(3), 480-490.

Kolko, D. (1992). Characteristics of child victims of physical violence: Research findings and clinical implications. *Journal of Interpersonal Violence, 7*(2), 244-276.

Kolko, D. J., Kazdin, A. E., Thomas, A. M., & Day, B. (1993). Heightened child physical abuse potential: Child, parent, and family dysfunction. *Journal of Interpersonal Violence, 8*(2), 169-192.

Kondrat, M. E. (1995). Concept, act, and interest in professional practice: Implications of an empowerment perspective. *Social Service Review, 69,* 405-427.

Korbin, J. (1987). Child maltreatment in cross-cultural perspective: Vulnerable children and circumstances. In R. J. Gelles & J. B. Lancaster (Eds.), *Child abuse and neglect: Biosocial dimensions* (pp. 31-55). New York: Aldine de Gruyter.

Korbin, J. (1994). Sociocultural factors in child maltreatment. In G. B. Melton & F. D. Barry (Eds.), *Protecting children from abuse and neglect: Foundations for a new national strategy* (pp. 182-223). New York: Guilford.

Korfmacher, J. (1998, February/March). Examining the service provider in early intervention. *Zero to Three,* pp. 17-22.

Korfmacher, J. (2000). The Kempe family stress inventory: A review. *Child Abuse and Neglect, 24*(1), 129-140.

Korfmacher, J., Kitzman, H. K., & Olds, D. L. (1998). Intervention processes as conditioners of home visitation program effects. *Journal of Community Psychology, 26,* 49-64.

Korfmacher, J., O'Brien, R., Hiatt, S., & Olds, D. (1999). Differences in program implementation between nurses and paraprofessionals providing home visits during pregnancy and infancy: A randomized trial. *American Journal of Public Health, 89,* 1847-1851.

Koroloff, N. M., Elliott, D. J., Koren, P. E., & Friesen, B. J. (1996). Linking low-income families to children's mental health services: An outcome study. *Journal of Emotional and Behavioral Disorders, 4*(1), 2-11.

Kotch, J. B., Browne, D. C., Dufort, V., & Winsor, J. (1999). Predicting child maltreatment in the first 4 years of life from characteristics assessed in the neonatal period. *Child Abuse and Neglect, 23*(4), 305-319.

Kotch, J. B., & Thomas, L. P. (1986). Family and social factors associated with substantiation of child abuse and neglect reports. *Journal of Family Violence, 1*(2), 167-179.

Kotelchuck, M. (1982). Child abuse and neglect: Prediction and misclassification. In R. Starr (Ed.), *Child abuse prediction: Policy implications* (pp. 67-104). Cambridge, MA: Ballinger.

Kouzekanani, K., & Neeley, M. A. (1996, November 6-9). *Coping styles of female cocaine addicts.* Paper presented at the 20th Annual AMERSA National Conference, Reston, VA.

Kroetsch, P., & Shamoian, C. A. (1983). Pain and depression. *Journal of Psychiatric Treatment & Evaluation, 5*(5), 417-420.

Kropp, J. P., & Haynes, O. M. (1987). Abusive and nonabusive mothers' ability to identify general and specific emotion signals of infants. *Child Development, 58,* 187-190.

Krugman, R. D. (1985). Fatal child abuse: Analysis of 24 cases. *Pediatrician, 12,* 68-72.

Krugman, R. D. (1993). Universal home visiting: A recommendation from the U.S. Advisory Board on Child Abuse and Neglect. *The Future of Children, 3*(3), 184-191.

Krugman, R. D. (1999, April 4). It's time to break the abuse cycle and protect the children, Exchange "chronic crisis" for solutions. *The Denver Post,* p. G-1.

Kruttschnitt, C., McLeod, J. D., & Dornfeld, M. (1994). The economic environment and child abuse. *Social Problems, 41*(2), 299-315.

Kumpfer, K. L., & Bayes, J. (1995). Child abuse and drugs. In J. H. Jaffe (Ed.), *The encyclopedia of drugs and alcohol* (Vol. 1, pp. 217-222). New York: Simon & Schuster.

Laken, M. R., McComish, J. F., & Ager, J. (1997). Predictors of prenatal substance use and birth weight during outpatient treatment. *Journal of Substance Abuse Treatment, 14*(4), 359-366.

Lancon, J. A., Haines, D. E., & Parent, A. D. (1998). Anatomy of the shaken baby syndrome. *Anatomical Record, 253*(1), 13-18.

Larner, M., Halpern, R., & Harkavy, O. (1992). The Fair Start story: An overview. In M. Oarner, R. Halpern, & O. Harkavy (Eds.), *Fair Start for children: Lessons learned from seven demonstration projects* (pp. 3-22). New Haven, CT: Yale University Press.

Larner, M. B., Stevenson, C. S., & Behrman, R. E. (1998). Protecting children from abuse and neglect: Analysis and recommendations. *The Future of Children, 8*(1), 4-22.

Larson, C. P. (1980). Efficacy of prenatal and postpartum visits on child health and development. *Pediatrics, 66*(2), 191-197.

Lauderdale, M., Valiunas, A., & Anderson, R. (1980). Race, ethnicity, and child maltreatment: An empirical analysis. *Child Abuse and Neglect, 4*(3), 163-169.

Lauer, B., Ten Broeck, J., & Grosman, M. (1974). Battered child syndrome: Review of 130 patients with controls. *Pediatrics, 54,* 67-70.

Lealman, G. T., Haigh, D., Phillips, J. M., Stone, J., & Ord-Smith, C. (1983). Prediction and prevention of child abuse: An empty hope? *Lancet, 25,* 1423-1424.

Lefcourt, H. M. (1992). Perceived control, personal effectiveness, and emotional states. In B. N. Carpenter (Ed.), *Personal coping: Theory, research, and application* (pp. 111-131). Westport, CT: Praeger/Greenwood.

Lefley, H. P., & Johnson, D. L. (Eds.). (1990). *Families as allies in treatment of the mentally ill: New directions for mental health professionals.* Washington, DC: American Psychiatric Press.

Leung, S. M. R., & Carter, J. E. (1983). Cross cultural study of child abuse among Chinese, Native Indians, and Anglo-Canadian children. *Journal of Psychiatric Treatment and Evaluation, 5,* 37-44.

Leventhal, J. M. (1988). Can child maltreatment be predicted during the perinatal period: Evidence from longitudinal cohort studies. *Journal of Reproductive and Infant Psychology, 6*(3), 139-161.

Leventhal, J. M. (1996). Twenty years later: We do know how to prevent child abuse and neglect. *Child Abuse and Neglect, 20*(8), 647-653.

Levitt, M. J., Weber, R. A., & Clark, M. C. (1986). Social network relationships as sources of maternal support and well-being. *Developmental Psychology, 22*(3), 310-316.

Lewis, D. O. (1992). From abuse to violence: Psychological consequences of maltreatment. *Journal of the American Academy of Child and Adolescent Psychiatry, 31*(3), 383-391.

Liaw, F., Meisels, S. J., & Brooks-Gunn, J. (1995). The effects of experience of early intervention on low birth weight, premature children: The Infant Health and Development Program. *Early Childhood Research Quarterly, 10*(4), 405-431.

Lieberman, M. A., Solow, N., Bond, G. R., & Reibstein, J. (1979). The psychotherapeutic impact of women's consciousness-raising groups. *Archives of General Psychiatry, 36*(2), 161-168.

Light, R. J., & Pillemer, D. B. (1984). *Summing up: The science of reviewing research.* Cambridge, MA: Harvard University Press.

Lindblad-Goldberg, M., & Dukes, J. (1985). Social support in black, low-income, single-parent families: Noramtive and dysfuctional patterns. *American Journal of Orthopsychiatry, 55*(1), 42-58.

Lindsey, D. (1994). *The welfare of children.* New York: Oxford University Press.

Lindsley, D. H., Brass, D. J., & Thomas, J. B. (1995). Efficacy-performance spirals: A multilevel perspective. *Academy of Management Review, 20*(3), 645-678.

Link, G., Beggs, M., & Seiderman, E. (1997). *Serving families.* Fairfax, CA: Parent Services Project.

Litty, C. G., Kowalski, R., & Minor, S. (1996). Moderating effects of physical abuse and perceived social support on the potential to abuse. *Child Abuse and Neglect, 20*(4), 305-314.

Lopez, G. E., Gurin, P., & Nagda, B. A. (1998). Education and understanding structural causes for group inequalities. *Political Psychology, 19*(2), 305-329.

Lorenz, K. (1965). *Evolution and modification of behavior.* Chicago: University of Chicago Press.

Lovell, M. L., & Hawkins, J. D. (1988). An evaluation of a group intervention to increase the personal social networks of abusive mothers. *Children and Youth Services Review, 10,* 175-188.

Lovell, M. L., & Richey, C. A. (1991). Implementing agency-based social support skill training. *Families in Society, 72,* 563-572.

Lovell, M. L., & Richey, C. A. (1995). The effectiveness of social support skill training with multiproblem families at risk for child maltreatment. *Canadian Journal of Community Mental Health, 14,* 29-48.

Lovell, M. L., & Richey, C. A. (1997). The impact of social support skill training on daily interactions among parents at risk for child maltreatment. *Children and Youth Services Review, 19,* 221-251.

Lung, C. T., & Daro, D. (1996). *Current trends in child abuse reporting and fatalities: The results of the 1995 Annual Fifty State Survey.* Chicago: NCPCA.

Lutzker, J., & Rice, J. (1984). Project 12-Ways: Measuring outcome of a large in-home service for treatment and prevention of child abuse and neglect. *Child Abuse and Neglect, 8,* 519-524.

Lutzker, J., & Rice, J. (1987). Using recidivism data to evaluate Project 12-Ways: An eco-behavioral approach to the treatment and prevention of child abuse and neglect. *Journal of Family Violence, 2*(4), 283-290.

Lyons, P., Doueck, H. J., & Wodarski, J. S. (1996). Risk assessment for child protective services: A review of the empirical literature on instrument performance. *Social Work Research, 20*(3), 143-155.

Lyons-Ruth, K., Alpern, L., & Repacholi, B. (1993). Disorganized infant attachment classification and maternal psychosocial problems as predictors of hostile-aggressive behavior in the preschool classroom. *Child Development, 64,* 572-585.

Lyons-Ruth, K., Zoll, D., Connell, D., & Grunebaum, H. U. (1986, Winter). The depressed mother and her one year-old infant: Environment, interaction, attachment, and infant development. *New Directions for Child Development, 34,* 61-82.

Magen, R. (1999). In the best interests of battered women: Reconceptualizing allegations of failure to protect. *Child Maltreatment, 4,* 127-135.

Magura, S., & Laudet, A. B. (1996). Parental substance abuse and child maltreatment: Review and implications for intervention. *Children & Youth Services Review, 18*(3), 193-220.

Main, M., & George, C. (1985). Response of abused and disadvantaged toddlers to distress in agitates: A study in the daycare setting. *Developmental Psychology, 21,* 407-412.

Main, M., & Goldwyn, R. (1984). Predicting rejection of her infant from mother's representation of her own experience: Implications for the abused-abusing intergenerational cycle. *Child Abuse and Neglect, 8*(2), 203-217.

Main, M., & Solomon, C. (1986). Discovery of a new insecure-disorganized, disoriented attachment pattern. In T. B. Brazelton & M. Yogman (Eds.), *Affective development in infancy* (pp. 95-12). Norwood, NJ: Ablex.

Malinosky-Rummell, R., & Hansen, D. J. (1993). Long-term consequences of childhood physical abuse. *Psychological Bulletin, 114*(1), 68-79.

Marcenko, M. O., & Spence, M. (1994). Home visitation services for at-risk pregnant and postpartum women: A randomized trial. *American Journal of Orthopsychiatry, 64*(3), 468-478.

Marcenko, M. O., Spence, M., & Samost, L. (1996). Outcomes of a home visitation trial for pregnant and postpartum women at-risk for child placement. *Children and Youth Services Review, 18*(3), 243-259.

Marchetti, D. (1998, February 12). A new focus on infants and toddlers. *The Chronicle of Philanthropy, 10*(8), 1, 9-12.

Marcus, D. K., & Nardone, M. E. (1992). Depression and interpersonal rejection. *Clinical Psychology Review, 12,* 433-449.

Margolin, L. (1990). Fatal child neglect. *Child Welfare, 69,* 309-319.

Margolin, L. (1992). Child abuse by mothers' boyfriends: Why the overrepresentation? *Child Abuse and Neglect, 16,* 541-551.

Marlatt, A. G. (1998). *Harm reduction: Pragmatic strategies for managing high-risk behaviors.* New York: Guilford.

Mash, E. J., Johnston, C., & Kovitz, K. (1983). A comparison of the mother-child interactions of physically abused and non-abused children during play and task situations. *Journal of Clinical Child Psychology, 12*(3), 337-346.

Maxfield, M. G., & Widom, C. S. (1996). The cycle of violence: Revisited 6 years later. *Archives of Pediatrics & Adolescent Medicine, 150*(4), 390-395.

McCarton, C., Brooks-Gunn, J., Wallace, I., Bauer, C. R., Bennett, F. C., Bernbaum, J. C., Broyles, R. S., Casey, P. H., McCormick, M. C., Scott, D. T., Tyson, J., Tonascia, J., & Meinert, C. L. (1997). Results at age 8 of early intervention for low-birth-weight premature infants: The Infant Health and Development Program. *Journal of the American Medical Association, 277*(2), 126-132.

McClain, P. W., Sacks, J. J., Foehlke, R. G., & Ewigman, B. G. (1993). Estimates of fatal child abuse and neglect, United States, 1979 through 1988. *Pediatrics, 91*(2), 338-343.

McClellan, D. C. (1975). *Power: The inner experience.* New York: Irvington.

McCormick, M. C., McCarton, C., Brooks-Gunn, J., Belt, P., & Gross, R. T. (1998). The Infant Health and Development Program, interim summary. *Developmental and Behavioral Pediatrics, 19*(5), 359-370.

McCroskey, J., & Meezan, W. (1998). Family-centered services: Approaches and effectiveness. *The Future of Children, 8*(1), 54-71.

McCurdy, K. (1995). Risk assessment in child abuse prevention programs. *Social Work Research, 19*(2), 77-87.

McCurdy, K. (in press). Can home visitation enhance maternal social support? *American Journal of Community Psychology.*

McCurdy, K., & Daro, D. (1993). *Current trends in child abuse reporting and fatalities: The results of the 1992 Annual Fifty State Survey.* Chicago: National Committee to Prevent Child Abuse.

McFadden, R. D. (1999, September 14). Mother of 3 is charged in daughter's death. *New York Times,* p. B3.

McGehee, C. L. (1983). Rethinking child abuse theory. *Victimology, 8,* 113-130.

McGovern, M. P., & Morrison, D. H., (1992). The Chemical Use, Abuse, and Dependence Scale (CUAD): Rationale, reliability, and validity. *Journal of Substance Abuse Treatment, 9*(1), 27-38.

McKay, M. M. (1994). The link between domestic violence and child abuse: Assessment and treatment considerations. *Child Welfare, 73*(1), 29-39.

McKay, M. M., Gonzales, J., Quintana, E., Kim, L., & Abdul-Adil, J. (1999). Multiple family groups: An alternative for reducing disruptive behavioral difficulties of urban children. *Research on Social Work Practice, 9,* 593-607.

McKay, M. M., Gonzales, J., Stone, S., Ryland, D., & Kohner, K. (1995). Multiple family therapy groups: A responsive intervention model for inner-city families. *Social Work With Groups, 18,* 77.

McKay, M. M., McCadam, K., & Gonzales, J. J. (1996). Addressing the barriers to mental health services for inner city children and their caretakers. *Community Mental Health Journal, 32*(4), 353-361.

McKay, M. M., Stoewe, J., McCadam, K., & Gonzales, J. (1998). Increasing access to child mental health services for urban children and their caregivers. *Health and Social Work, 23*(1), 9-15.

McKibben, L., De Vos, E., & Newberger, E. H. (1991). Victimization of mothers of abused children: A controlled study. In R. L. Hampton (Ed.), *Black family violence* (pp. 75-83). Lexington, MA: Lexington Books.

Meadow, R. (1999). Unnatural sudden infant death. *Archives of Disease in Childhood, 80*(1), 7-14.

Meezan, W., & O'Keefe, M. (1998). Evaluating the effectiveness of multifamily group therapy in child abuse and neglect. *Research on Social Work Practice, 8*(3), 330-353.

Meisels, S. J., Dichtelmiller, M., & Liaw, F. (1993). A multidimensional analysis of early childhood intervention programs. In C. H. Zeanah, Jr. (Ed.), *Handbook of infant mental health* (pp. 361-385). New York: Guilford.

Meisels, S. J., & Plunkett, J. W. (1988). Developmental consequences of preterm birth: Are there long-term effects? In P. B. Baltes, D. L. Featherman, & R. M. Lerner (Eds.), *Lifespan development and behavior* (pp. 87-128). Hillsdale, NJ: Lawrence Erlbaum.

Meisels, S. J., & Wasik, B. A. (1990). Who should be served? Indentifying children in need of early intervention. In S. J. Meisels & J. P. Shonkoff (Eds.), *Handbook of early childhood intervention* (pp. 605-632). New York: Cambridge University Press.

Melton, G. B., & Barry, F. D. (1994). Neighbors helping neighbors: The vision of the U.S. Advisory Board on Child Abuse and Neglect. In G. B. Melton & F. D. Barry (Eds.), *Protection from child abuse and neglect: Foundations for a new national strategy* (pp. 1-13). New York: Guilford.

Michaels, G. Y., & Goldberg, W. A. (1988). *The transition to parenthood: Current theory and research.* Cambridge, UK: Cambridge University Press.

Miller, W. R., & Rollnick, S. (Eds.). *Motivational interviewing: Preparing people to change addictive behaivor.* New York: Guilford.

Milner, J., & Chilamkurti, C. (1991). Physical child abuse perpetrator characteristics: A review of the literature. *Journal of Interpersonal Violence, 6*(3), 345-366.

Milner, J. S., & Gold, R. G. (1986). Screening spouse abusers for child abuse. *Journal of Clinical Psychology, 42*(1), 169-172.

Milner, J. S., Robertson, K. R., & Rogers, D. L. (1990). Childhood history of abuse and adult child abuse potential. *Journal of Family Violence, 5*(1), 15-34.

Minde, K. (1993). Prematurity and serious medical illness in infancy: Implicatons for development and intervention. In C. H. Zeanah (Ed.), *Handbook of infant mental health* (pp. 87-105). New York: Guilford.

Mitchel, L., & Cohn Donnelly, A. (1993). Healthy Families America: Building a national system. *The APSAC Advisor, 6*(4), 9-27.

Mitchell-Herzfeld, S., & Trudeau, L. (1999, March 2). *A study of program retention in New York's home visiting program.* Albany: New York State Office of Children and Family Services.

Moncher, F. J. (1995). Social isolation and child-abuse risk. *Families in Society, 76,* 421-433.

Money, J. (1977). The syndrome of abuse dwarfism (psychosocial dwarfism or reversible hyposomatotropism). *American Journal of Diseases of Children, 131*(5), 508-513.

Moreland, J. R., Schwebel, A. I., Beck, S., & Wells, R. (1982). Parents as therapists: A review of behavior therapy parent training literature—1975-1981. *Behavior Modification, 6*(2), 250-276.

Moss, H. B, Mezzich, A., Yao, J. K., Gavaler, J., & Martin, C. S. (1995). Aggressivity among sons of substance-abusing fathers: Association with psychiatric disorder in the father and son, paternal personality, pubertal development, and socioeconomic status. *American Journal of Drug and Alcohol Abuse, 2,* 195-208.

Mrazek, P. J. (1993). Maltreatment and infant development. In C. H. Zeanah, Jr. (Ed.), *Handbook of infant mental health* (pp. 159-170). New York: Guilford.

Mrazek, P. J., & Haggerty, R. J. (1994). *Reducing risks for mental disorders.* Washington, DC: National Academy Press.

Mullen, B. (1989). *Advanced BASIC meta-analysis.* Hillsdale, NJ: Lawrence Erlbaum.

Murphy, J. M., Jellinek, M., Quinn, D., Smith, G., Poitrast, F. G., & Goshko, M. (1991). Substance abuse and serious child mistreatment: Prevalence, risk, and outcome in a court sample. *Child Abuse and Neglect, 15,* 197-211.

Murphy, S., Orkow, B., & Nicola, R. (1985). Prenatal prediction of child abuse and neglect: A prospective study. *Child Abuse and Neglect, 9,* 225-235.

Murphy, S., & Rosenbaum, M. (1999). *Pregnant women on drugs: Combating stereotypes and stigma.* New Brunswick, NJ: Rutgers University Press.

Murray, L., Fiori-Cowley, A., Hooper, R., & Cooper, P. (1996). The impact of postnatal depression and associated adversity on early mother-infant interactions and later infant outcomes. *Child Development, 67*(5), 2512-2526.

Murray, L., & Cooper, P. J. (1997). Postpartum depression and child development. *Psychological Medicine, 27*(2), 253-260.

National Center on Child Abuse and Neglect. (1981). *Study findings: National study of incidence and severity of child abuse and neglect.* Washington, DC: U.S. Department of Health and Human Services.

National Center on Child Abuse and Neglect. (1993). *A report to Congress: Study of child maltreatment in alcohol abusing families.* Washington, DC: Author.

National Center on Child Abuse and Neglect. (1994). *Child maltreatment 1883: Reports from the states to the National Center on Child Abuse and Neglect.* Washington, DC: Government Printing Office.

National Center on Child Abuse and Neglect. (1995). *Child maltreatment, 1993: Reports from the states to the National Center on Child Abuse and Neglect.* Washington, DC: Government Printing Office.

National Commission on Children. (1991). *Beyond rhetoric: A new American agenda for children and families.* Washington, DC: Government Printing Office.

National Committee to Prevent Child Abuse. (1995a). *Final evaluation of nine child abuse prevention programs.* Chicago: Author.

National Committee to Prevent Child Abuse. (1995b). *Healthy Families America, third year progress report.* Chicago: Author.

National Institute of Mental Health. (1977). *Center for Epidemiologic Studies Depression Scale* (CES-D). Rockville, MD: Author.

National Institute on Drug Abuse. (1994). Outcomes of children of substance abusers. In *NIDA Second National Conference on Drug Research and Practice: An Alliance for the 21st Century: Conference highlights.* Rockville, MD: Author.

National Research Council. (1993). *Understanding child abuse and neglect.* Washington, DC: National Academy Press.

Neighbors, H. W., Braithwaite, R. L., & Thompson, E. (1995). Health promotion and African-Americans: From personal empowerment to community action. *American Journal of Health Promotion, 9*(4), 281-287.

Neighbors, H., Elliott, K. A., & Gant, L. M. (1990). Self-help and Black Americans: A strategy for empowerment. In T. J. Powell (Ed.), *Working with self-help* (pp. 189-217). Silver Spring, MD: National Association of Social Workers Press.

Nelson, E. E., & Panksepp, J. (1998). Brain substrates of infant-mother attachment. *Neuroscience & Biobehavioral Reviews, 22*(3), 437-452.

Neumaier, J. F., Petty, F., Kramer, G. L., Szot, P., & Hamblin, M. W. (1997). Learned helplessness increases 5-hydroxytryptamine1B receptor mRNA levels in the rat dorsal raphe nucleus. *Biological Psychiatry, 41*(6), 668-674.

Newberger, E. H., Reed, R. B., Hyde, J. N., & Kotelchuck, M. (1977). Pediatric social illness: Toward an etiologic classification. *Pediatrics, 60,* 178-185.

Nitz, K., Ketterlinus, R. D., & Brandt, L. J. (1995). The role of stress, social support, and family environment in adolescent mothers' parenting. *Journal of Adolescent Research, 10*(3), 358-382.

Nurius, P. S., Lovell, M., & Maggie, E. (1988). Self-appraisals of abusive parents: A contextual approach to study and treatment. *Journal of Interpersonal Violence, 3*(4), 458-467.

Oates, R. K., Forrest, D., & Peacock, A. (1985). Self-esteem of abused children. *Child Abuse and Neglect, 9,* 159-163.

O'Brian, R. A., & Baca, R. P. (1997). Application of solution-focused interventions to nurse home visitation for pregnant women and parents of young children. *Journal of Community Psychology, 25,* 47-57.

O'Connor, S., Vietze, P. M., Sherrod, K. B., Sandler, H. M., & Altemeier, W. A. (1980). Reduced incidence of parenting inadequacy following rooming-in. *Pediatrics, 66,* 176-182.

Ogawa, J. R., Sroufe, L. A., Weinfield, N. S., Carlson, E. A., & Egeland, B. (1997). Development and the fragmented self: Longitudinal study of dissociative symptamology in a nonclinical sample. *Development & Psychopathology, 9*(4), 855-879.

Okun, A., & Parker, J. G. (1994). Distinctive and interactive contributions of physical abuse, socioeconomic disadvantage, and negative life events to children's social, cognitive, and affective adjustment. *Development and Psychopathology, 6,* 77-98.

Oldershaw, L., Walters, G. C., & Hall, D. K. (1986). Control strategies and noncompliance in abusive mother-child dyads: An observational study. *Child Development, 57*(3), 722-732.

Olds, D. (1982). The prenatal/early infancy project: An ecological approach to prevention. In J. Belsky (Ed.), *In the beginning: Readings in infancy* (pp. 270-285). New York: Columbia University Press.

Olds, D. L. (1996, May 10). *Randomized clinical trials of prenatal and early childhood home visitation.* Paper presented at Fifth Annual NIMH National Conference on Prevention Research, McLean, VA.

Olds, D. (1999, April 16). *Discussant, engines of change: Understanding how early intervention programs work.* Paper presented at the Society for Research on Child Development, Albuquerque, NM.

Olds, D. L., Eckenrode, J., Henderson, C. R., Kitzman, H., Powers, J., Cole, R., Sidora, K., Morris, P., Pettitt, L. M., & Luckey, D. (1997). Long-term effects of home visitation on maternal life course and child abuse and neglect: Fifteen year follow-up of a randomized trial. *Journal of the American Medical Association, 278*(8), 637-643.

Olds, D. L., Henderson, C. R., Chamberlin, R., & Tatelbaum, R. (1986). Preventing child abuse and neglect: A randomized trial of nurse home visitation. *Pediatrics, 78,* 65-78.

Olds, D., Henderson, C. R., Cole, R., Eckenrode, J., Kitzman, H., Luckey, D., Pettitt, L., Sidora, K., Morris, P., & Powers, J. (1998). Long-term effects of nurse home visitation on children's criminal and antisocial behavior: 15-year follow-up of a randomized controlled trial. *Journal of the American Medical Association, 280*(14), 1238-1244.

Olds, D. L., Henderson, C. R., & Kitzman, H. (1994). Does prenatal and infancy nurse home visitation have enduring effects on qualities of parental caregiving and child health at 25 and 50 months of life? *Pediatrics, 93*(1), 89-98.

Olds, D., Henderson, C. R., Kitzman, H. J., Eckenrode, J. J., Cole, R. E. & Tatelbaum, R. C. (1999). Prenatal and infancy home visitation by nurses: Recent findings. *The Future of Children, 9*(1), 44-65.

Olds, D. L., Henderson, C. R., Tatelbaum, R. & Chamberlin, R. (1986). Improving the delivery of prenatal care and outcomes of pregnancy: A randomized trial of nurse home visitation. *Pediatrics, 77*(1), 16-28.

Olds, D. L., Henderson, C. R., Tatelbaum, R., & Chamberlin, R. (1988). Improving the lifecourse development of socially disadvantaged mothers: A randomized trial of nurse home visitation. *Pediatrics, 77,* 16-28.

Olds, D., Hill, P., & Rumsey, E. (1998, November). Prenatal and early childhood nurse home visitation. *Juvenile Justice Bulletin,* pp. 1-7.

Olds, D. L., & Kitzman, H. (1993). Review of research on home visiting for pregnant women and parents of young children. *The Future of Children, 3*(3), 53-92.

Olds, D., Kitzman, H., Cole, R., & Robinson, J. (1997). Theoretical foundations of a program of home visitation for pregnant women and parents of young children. *Journal of Community Psychology, 25*(1), 9-25.

Olds, D. L., & Korfmacher, J. (1998). Maternal psychological characteristics as influences on home visitation contact. *Journal of Community Psychology, 26*(1), 23-36.

Oregon Children's Services Division. (1993). *Task force report on child fatalities and critical injuries due to abuse and neglect.* Salem, OR: Oregon Department of Human Resources.

O'Shea, M., & Phelps, R. (1985). Multiple family therapy: Current status and critical appraisal. *Family Process, 24,* 555-584.

Osofsky, H. J. (1985). Transition to parenthood: Risk factors for parents and infants. *Journal of Psychosomatic Obstetrics and Gynecology, 4*(4), 303-315.

Osofsky, J. D., Culp, A. M., & Ware, L. M. (1988). Intervention challenges with adolescent mothers and their infants. *Psychiatry, 51,* 236-241.

Osofsky, J. D., Wewers, S., Hamn, D. M., & Fick, A. C. (1993). Chronic community violence: What is happening to our children? *Psychiatry, 56,* 36-45.

Owen, M. T., & Cox, M. J. (1997). Marital conflict and the development of infant-parent attachment relationships. *Journal of Family Psychology, 11*(2), 152-164.

Palinkas, L. A, Atkins, C. J., Miller, C., & Ferreira, D. (1996). Social skills training for drug prevention in high-risk female adolescents. *Preventive Medicine, 25*(6), 692-701.

Parke, R. D., & Collmer, C. W. (1975). Child abuse: An interdisciplinary analysis. In E. M. Hetherington (Ed.), *Review of child development research* (Vol. 5, pp. 509-590). Chicago: University of Chicago Press.

Parks, P. L., & Arndt, E. K. (1990). Differences between adolescent and adult mothers of infants. *Journal of Adolescent Health Care, 11*(3), 248-253.

Parks, P. L., Lenz, E. R., & Jenkins, L. S. (1992). The role of social support and stressors for mothers and infants. *Child: Care, Health, and Development, 18*(3), 151-171.

Parsons, R. (1991). Empowerment: Purpose and practice principle in social work. *Social Work With Groups, 14*(2), 7-21.

Pascoe, J., Loda, F., Jeffries, V., & Earp, J. (1981). The association between mothers' social support and provision of stimulation to their children. *Developmental and Behavioral Pediatrics, 2,* 15-19.

Patterson, G. (1982). *Coercive family process.* Eugene, OR: Castalia.

Pearlin, L. I. (1999). Stress and mental health: A conceptual overview. In A. Horwitz & T. L. Scheid (Eds.), *A handbook for the study of mental health: Social contexts, theories, and systems* (pp. 161-175). New York: Cambridge University Press.

Pecora, P. J., & Austin, J. J. (1983). Declassification of social service jobs: Issues and strategies. *Social Work, 28*(6), 421-426.

Pederson, D. R., Gleason, K. E., Moran, G., & Bento, S. (1998). Maternal attachment representations, maternal sensitivity, and infant-mother attachment. *Developmental Psychology, 34,* 925-933.

Peeters, M. C., Buunk, B. P., & Schaufeli, W. B. (1995). A micro-analysis exploration of the cognitive appraisal of daily stressful events at work: The role of controllability. *Anxiety, Stress, and Coping, 8*(2), 127-139.

Pelton, L. (1978). Child abuse and neglect: The myth of classlessness. *American Journal of Orthopsychiatry, 48*(4), 608-617.

Pelton, L. (1994). The role of material factors in child abuse and neglect. In G. B. Melton & F. D. Berry (Eds.), *Protecting children from abuse and neglect: Foundations for a new national strategy* (pp. 131-181). New York: Guilford.

Perez de Colon, M. (1999, June 2-5). *Prevention and family violence in Hispanic communities.* Paper presented at the 7th National Colloquium of the American Professional Society on the Abuse of Children, San Antonio, TX.

Perry, B. D., & Pollard, R. (1997). *Altered brain development following global neglect in childhood.* Paper presented at the Society for Neuroscience Annual Meeting, New Orleans.

Perry, B. D., Pollard, R. A., Blakeley, T. L., Baker, W. L., & Vigilante, D. (1995). Childhood trauma, the neurobiology of adaptation, and use-dependent development of the brain: How states become traits. *Infant Mental Health Journal, 16*(4), 271-291.

Perry, M. A., Doran, L. D., & Wells, E. A. (1983). Developmental and behavioral characteristics of the physically abused child. *Journal Clinical Child Psychology, 12,* 320-324.

Perry, M. A., Wells, E. A., & Doran, L. D. (1983). Parent characteristics in abusing and nonabusing families. *Journal of Clinical Child Psychology, 12,* 329-336.

Peterson, C., & Seligman, M. E. (1984). Causal explanations as a risk factor for depression: Theory and evidence. *Psychological Review, 91*(3), 347-374.

Pew Charitable Trusts. (1996). *See how we grow: A report on the status of parenting education in the U.S.* Philadelphia: Author.

Pfannenstiel, A. E., & Honig, A. S. (1995). Effects of a prenatal "Information and Insights About Infants" program on the knowledge base of first-time low-education fathers one month postnatally. *Early Child Development and Care, 111,* 87-105.

Pfiffner, L. J., Jouriles, E. N., Brown, M. M., & Etscheidt, M. A. (1990). Effects of problem-solving therapy on outcomes of parent training for single-parent families. *Child and Family Behavior Therapy, 12*(1), 1-11.

Phillips, D. A., & Cabrera, N. J. (1996). *Beyond the blueprint: Directions for research on Head Start's families.* Washington, DC: National Academy Press.

Phillips, R. B., Sharma, R., Premachandra, B. R., Vaughn, A. J., & Reyes-Lee, M. (1996). Intrauterine exposure to cocaine: Effect on neurobehavior of neonates. *Infant Behavior and Development, 91,* 71-81.

Pierce, T., Baldwin, M. W., & Lydon, J. E. (1997). A relational schema approach to social support. In G. R. Pierce, B. Lakey, I. G. Sarason, & B. R. Sarason (Eds.), *Sourcebook of social support and personality* (pp. 19-47). New York: Plenum.

Polansky, N. A., Chalmers, M. A., Buttenwieser, E., & Williams, D. P. (1981). *Damaged parents: An anatomy of child neglect.* Chicago: University of Chicago Press.

Polansky, N. A., Gaudin, J. M., Ammons, P. W., & Davis, K. B. (1985). The psychological ecology of the neglectful mother. *Child Abuse and Neglect, 9*(2), 265-275.

Polansky, N. A., Gaudin, J. M., & Kilpatrick, A. C. (1992). Family radicals. *Children and Youth Services Review, 14,* 19-26.

Pons, T. P. (1995). Lesion-induced cortical plasticity. In B. Julesz & I. Kovacs (Eds.), *Maturational windows and adult cortical plasticity* (pp. 175-178). Reading, MA: Addison-Wesley.

Portes, A. (1998). Social capital: Its origins and applications in modern sociology. *Annual Review of Sociology, 24,* 1-24.

Powell, C., & Grantham-McGregor, S. (1989). Home visiting of varying frequency and child development. *Pediatrics, 84*(1), 157-164.

Powell, D. R. (1984). Social network and demographic predictors of length of participation in a parent education program. *Journal of Community Psychology, 12,* 13-20.

Powell, D. R. (1993). Inside home visiting programs. *The Future of Children, 3*(3), 23-38.

Powell, T. J. (1990). Self-help, professional help, and informal help: Competing or complementary systems? In T. J. Powell (Ed.), *Working with self help* (pp. 31-49). Silver Spring, MD: National Association of Social Workers Press.

Prevent Child Abuse America. (1995). *Final evaluation of nine child abuse prevention programs.* Chicago: Author.

Prevent Child Abuse America. (1999). *Healthy Families America: A snapshot view.* Chicago: Author.

Prochaska, J. O., & DiClemente, C. C. (1983). Stages and processes of self-change smoking: Toward an integrative model of change. *Journal of Consulting and Clinical Psychology, 51*(3), 390-395.

Prochaska, J. O., Johnson, S., & Lee, P. (1998). The transtheoretical model of behavior change. In S. A. Shumaker & E. B. Schron (Eds.), *The handbook of health behavior change* (2nd ed., pp. 59-84). New York: Springer.

Prussia, G. E., & Kinicki, A. J. (1996). A motivational investigation of group effectiveness using social-cognitive theory. *Journal of Applied Psychology, 81*(2), 187-198.

Pursely-Crotteau, S., & Stern, P. N. (1996). Creating a new life: Dimensions of temperance in perinatal cocaine crack users. *Qualitative Health Research, 6*(3), 350-367.

Putnam, R. D. (1993). The prosperous community: Social capital and public life. *American Prospect, 13,* 35-42.

Rafael, T., & Pion-Berlin, L. (1999, April). Parents anonymous: Strengthening families. In *Juvenile Justice Bulletin.* Washington, DC: Office of Juvenile Justice and Delinquency Prevention.

Ramey, C. T., & Ramey, S. L. (1992). Effective early intervention. *Mental Retardation, 30*(6), 337-345.

Ramey, C. T., & Ramey, S. L. (1998). Early intervention and early experience. *American Psychologist, 53*(2), 109-120.

Rappaport, J. (1985, Fall). The power of empowerment language. *Social Policy,* pp. 15-21.

Rappaport, J. (1987). Terms of empowerment/exemplars of prevention: Toward a theory for community psychology. *American Journal of Community Psychology, 15,* 121-144.

Rau, V. A., Anisfeld, E., & Guterman, N. B. (1999). *Evaluation of Best Beginnings: A randomized clinical trial.* New York: Smith Richardson Foundation.

Reid, J. B., & Patterson, G. R. (1989). The development of antisocial behaviour patterns in childhood and adolescence. *European Journal of Personality, 3*(2), 107-119.

Reid, J., Taplin, P., & Loeber, R. (1981). A social interactional approach to the treatment of abusive families. In R. Stuart (Ed.), *Violent behavior: Social learning approaches to prediction, management, and treatment.* New York: Brunner/Mazel.

Reidinger, P. (1988, December 1). Why did no one protect this child? *American Bar Association Journal,* pp. 48-51.

Renken, B., Egeland, B., Marvinney, D., & Mangelsdorf, S. (1989). Early childhood ante-cedents of aggression and passive-withdrawal in early elementary school. *Journal of Personality, 57*(2), 257-281.

Resnick, G. (1985). Enhancing parental competencies for high risk mothers: An evaluation of prevention effects. *Child Abuse and Neglect, 9,* 479-489.

Rhodes, J. E., Contreras, J. M., & Mangelsdorf, S. C. (1994). Natural mentor relationships among Latina adolescent mothers: Psychological adjustment, moderating processes, and the role of early parental acceptance. *American Journal of Community Psychology, 22*(2), 211-227.

Rhodes, J. E., Ebert, L., & Fischer, K. (1992). Natural mentors: An overlooked resource in the social networks of young African American mothers. *American Journal of Community Psychology, 20*(4), 445-461.

Richey, C. A., Lovell, M. L., & Reid, K. (1991). Interpersonal skill training to enhance so-cial support among women at risk for child maltreatment. *Children and Youth Services Review, 13*(1-2), 41-59.

Richters, J. E., & Martinez, P. (1993). The NIMH Community Violence Project: I. Children as victims and witnesses to violence. *Psychiatry, 56,* 7-21.

Riger, S. (1993). What's wrong with empowerment. *American Journal of Community Psychology, 21*(3), 279-292.

Ritchie, J., & Ritchie, J. (1981). Child rearing and child abuse: The Polynesian context. In J. Korbin (Ed.), *Child abuse and neglect: Cross-cultural perspectives* (pp. 186-294). Berkeley: University of California Press.

Rivera, B., & Widom, C. S. (1990). Childhood victimization and violent offending. *Violence & Victims, 5*(1), 19-35.

Rodriguez, C. M., & Green, A. J. (1997). Parenting stress and anger expression as predic-tors of child abuse potential. *Child Abuse and Neglect, 21*(4), 367-377.

Rodriguez, G. G., & Cortez, C. P. (1988). The evaluation experience of the AVANCE par-ent-child education program. In H. B. Weiss & F. H. Jacobs (Eds.), *Evaluating family programs* (pp. 287-301). Hawthorne, NY: Aldine de Gruyter.

Rodwell, M. K., & Chambers, D. E. (1989). Promises, promises: Child abuse prevention in the 1980s. *Policy Studies Review, 8*(4), 749-773.

Rodwell, M. K., & Chambers, D. E. (1992). Primary prevention of child abuse: Is it really possible? *Journal of Sociology and Social Welfare, 19*(3), 159-176.

Rollnick, S., & Morgan, M. (1996). Motivational interviewing: Increasing readiness for change. In A. M. Washton (Ed.), *Psychotherapy and substance abuse: A practitioner's handbook* (pp. 179-191). New York: Guilford.

Rook, K. S. (1984). Research on social support, loneliness, and social isolation. In P. Shaver (Ed.), *Review of personality and social psychology: Emotions, relationships, and health* (pp. 239-264). Beverly Hills, CA: Sage.

Rosenthal, R. (1984). *Meta-analytic procedures for social research.* Beverly Hills, CA: Sage.

Rothman, J., & Thomas, E. J. (Eds.). (1994). *Intervention research: Design and develop-ment for human services.* Binghamton, NY: Haworth.

Sackett, D. L., & Rosenberg, W. M. (1995). On the need for evidence-based medicine. *Journal of Public Health Medicine, 17*(3), 330-334.

Salas, M., & Beasetsny, L. (in press). Air Force New Parent Support Program. In J. Martin (Ed.), *The military family: A practice guide for human service providers.* New York: Praeger.

Salzinger, S., Kaplan, S., & Artemyeff, C. (1983). Mothers' personal social networks and child maltreatment. *Journal of Abnormal Psychology, 92*(1), 68-76.

Salzinger, S., Kaplan, S., Pelcovitz, D., Samit, C., & Krieger, R. (1983). Parent and teacher assessment of children's behavior in child maltreating families. *Journal of the American Academy of Child Psychiatry, 23,* 458-464.

Sameroff, A. (1993). Models of development and developmental risk. In C. H. Zeanah (Ed.), *Handbook of infant mental health* (pp. 3-13). New York: Guilford.

Sampson, R. J. (1991). Linking the micro- and macrolevel dimensions of community social organization. *Social Forces, 70*(1), 43-64.

Sampson, R. J., Raudenbush, S. W., & Earls, F. (1997). Neighborhoods and violent crime: A multilevel study of collective efficacy. *Science, 277,* 918-924.

Samuels, V. J., Stockdale, D. F., & Crase, S. J. (1994). Adolescent mothers' adjustment to parenting. *Journal of Adolescence, 17*(5), 427-443.

Sanchez, L., & Thomson, E. (1997). Becoming mothers and fathers: Parenthood, gender, and the division of labor. *Gender & Society, 11*(6), 747-772.

Santisteban, D. A., Szapocznik, J., Perez-Vidal, A., Kurtines, W. M., Murray, E. J., & LaPerriere, A. (1996). Efficacy of intervention for engaging youth and families into treatment and some variables that may contribute to differential effectiveness. *Journal of Family Psychology, 10*(1), 35-44.

Sarason, I. G., Levine, H. M., Basham, R. B., & Sarason, B. R. (1983). Assessing social support: The Social Support Questionnaire. *Journal of Personality & Social Psychology, 44*(1), 127-139.

Sarason, I. G., Pierce, G. P., & Sarason, B. R. (1994). General and specific perceptions of social support. In W. R. Avison & I. H. Gotlib (Eds.), *Stress and mental health* (pp. 151-177). New York: Plenum.

Schaefer, C. E., & Briesmeister, J. M. (1989). *Handbook of parent training: Parents as cotherapists for children's behavior problems.* New York: John Wiley.

Schellenbach, C. J., Monroe, L. D., & Merluzzi, T. V. (1991). The impact of stress on cognitive components of child abuse potential. *Journal of Family Violence, 6*(1), 61.

Schilling, R. (1987). Limitations of social support. *Social Service Review, 61,* 19-31.

Schincke, S. P., Schilling, R. F., Barth, R. P., Gilchrist, L. D., & Maxwell, J. S. (1986). Stress management intervention to prevent family violence. *Journal of Family Violence, 1*(1), 13-26.

Schneider-Rosen, K., Braunwald, K. G., Carlson, V., & Cicchetti, D. (1985). Current perspectives in attachment theory: Illustration from the study of maltreated infants. *Monographs of the Society for Research in Child Development, 50*(1-2), 194-210.

Scholz, K., & Samuels, C. A. (1992). Neonatal bathing and massage intervention with fathers, behavioural effects 12 weeks after birth of the first baby: The Sunraysia Australia Intervention Project. *International Journal of Behavioral Development, 15,* 67-81.

Schorr, L. B. (1997). *Common purpose: Strengthening families and neighborhoods to rebuild America.* New York: Doubleday.

Schorr, L. B., & Schorr, D. (1988). *Within our reach: Breaking the cycle of disadvantage.* New York: Anchor Books.

Schuerman, J. R., Rzepnicki, T. L., & Littell, J. H. (1994). *Putting families first: An experiment in family preservation.* New York: Aldine de Gruyter.

Schulz, A. J., Israel, B. A., Zimmerman, M. A., & Checkoway, B. N. (1995). Empowerment as a multi-level construct: Perceived control at the individual, organizational, and community levels. *Health Education Research, 10*(3), 309-327.

Schweinhart, L. J., Barnes, H. V., & Weikart, D. P. (1993). *Significant benefits: The High/ Scope Perry Preschool Study through age 27*. Ypsilanti, MI: High/Scope Educational Research Foundation.

Scott, W. O., Baer, G., Christoff, K. A., & Kelley, J. A. (1984). The use of skills training procedures in the treatment of a child-abusive parent. *Journal of Behavior Therapy and Experimental Psychiatry, 15*(4), 329-336.

Seagull, E. (1987). Social support and child maltreatment: A review of the evidence. *Child Abuse and Neglect, 11,* 41-52.

Sedlak, A. J., & Broadhurst, D. D. (1996). *Third national incidence study of child abuse and neglect: Final report*. Washington, DC: U.S. Department of Health and Human Services.

Segal, S. P., Silverman, C., & Temkin, T. (1993). Empowerment and self-help agency practice for people with mental disabilities. *Social Work, 38*(6), 705-712.

Seitz, V., Rosenbaum, L. K., & Apfel, N. H. (1985). Effects of family support intervention: A ten-year follow-up. *Child Development, 56,* 376-391.

Seligman, M. E. P. (1975). *Helplessness: On depression, development, and death*. San Francisco: W. H. Freeman.

Sennett, R., & Cobb, J. (1972). *The hidden injuries of class*. New York: Vintage.

Shaver, P. R., Collins, N., & Clark, C. L. (1996). Attachment styles and internal working models of self and relationship partners. In G. J. O. Fletcher & J. Fitness (Eds.), *Knowledge structures in close relationships: A social psychological approach* (pp. 25-61). Mahwah, NJ: Lawrence Erlbaum.

Sherman, B. R. (1998). Measuring the self-efficacy of pregnant and postpartum women in recovery. In B. R. Sherman (Ed.), *Addiction and pregnancy: Empowering recovery through peer counseling* (pp. 77-91). Westport, CT: Praeger.

Sherman, B. R., & Donovan, B. R. (1991). Relationship of perceived maternal acceptance-rejection in childhood and social support networks of pregnant adolescents. *American Journal of Orthopsychiatry, 6,* 103-113.

Sherman, B. R., Saunders, L. M., & Trinh, C. (1998). *Addiction and pregnancy: Empowering recovery through peer counseling*. Westport, CT: Praeger.

Shields, A. M., Cicchetti, D., & Ryan, R. M. (1994). The development of emotional and behavioral self-regulation and social competence among maltreated school-age children. *Development and Psychopathology, 6,* 57-75.

Shipman, K. L., Rossman, B. R., & West, J. C. (1999). Co-occurrence of spousal violence and child abuse: Conceptual implications. *Child Maltreatment, 4,* 93-102.

Shulman, S., Elicker, J., & Sroufe, L. A. (1994). Stages of friendship growth in preadolescence as related to attachment history. *Journal of Social & Personal Relationships, 11*(3), 341-361.

Siegel, E., Bauman, K. E., Schaefer, E. S., Saunders, M. M., & Ingram, D. D. (1980). Hospital and home support during infancy: Impact on maternal attachment, child abuse and neglect, and health care utilization. *Pediatrics, 66*(2), 183-190.

Silverman, A. B., Reinherz, H. Z., & Giaconia, R. M. (1996). The long-term sequelae of child and adolescent abuse: A longitudinal community study. *Child Abuse and Neglect, 20*(8), 709-723.

Silverman, F. N. (1953). The Roentgen manifestations of unrecognized skeletal trauma in infants. *American Journal of Roentgenology, 69*(1), 413-427.

Simon, B. L. (1990). Rethinking empowerment. *Journal of Progressive Human Services, 1*(1), 27-39.

Simpson, K. R., & Knox, G. E. (1999). Strategies for developing an evidence-based approach to perinatal care. *American Journal of Maternal Child Nursing, 24*(3), 122-131.

Singer, L., Arendt, R., Farkas, K., Minnes, S., Huang, J., & Yamashita, T. (1997). Relationship of prenatal cocaine exposure and maternal postpartum psychological distress to child development outcome. *Development and Psychopathology, 9,* 473-489.

Singh, N. N., Curtis, W. J., Ellis, C. R., Wechsler, H. A., Best, A. M., & Cohen, R. (1997). Empowerment status of families whose children have serious emotional disturbance and attention-deficit/hyperactivity disorder. *Journal of Emotional & Behavioral Disorders, 5*(4), 223-229.

Skocpol, T. (1995). *Social policy in the United States: Future possibilities in historical perspective.* Princeton, NJ: Princeton University Press.

Smith, S. M., Hanson, R., & Noble, S. (1974). Social aspects of the battered baby syndrome. *British Journal of Psychiatry, 125,* 568-582.

Smolowe, J. (1995, December 11). Making the tough calls. *Time,* pp. 40-44.

Snow, D. A., Zurcher, L. A., & Elkind-Olson, S. (1980). Social networks and social movements. *American Sociological Review, 45,* 787-801.

Solheim, J. S. (1982). A cross-cultural examination of use of corporal punishment on children: A focus on Sweden and the United States. *Child Abuse and Neglect, 6*(2), 147-154.

Sommer, R. (1990). Family advocacy and the mental health system: The recent rise of the alliance for the mentally ill. *Psychiatric Quarterly, 61*(3), 205-221.

Sorenson, J. L., & Gibson, D. (1983). Community network approach to drug abuse treatment. *Bulletin of Social Psychologists and Addictive Behavior, 2,* 99-102.

Soumenkoff, G., Marneffe, C., Gerard, M., Limet, R., Beeckmans, M., & Hubinont, P. O. (1982). A coordinated attempt for prevention of child abuse at the antenatal care level. *Child Abuse and Neglect, 6,* 87-94.

Spearly, J., & Lauderdale, M. (1983). Community characteristics and ethnicity in the prediction of child maltreatment rates. *Child Abuse and Neglect, 7,* 91-105.

Spendlove, D. C., Gavelek, J. R., & MacMurray, V. (1981). Learned helplessness and the depressed housewife. *Social Work, 26,* 474-479.

Spitz, R. A. (1945). Hospitalism: An inquiry into the genesis of psychiatric conditions in early childhood. *Psychoanalytic Study of the Child, 1,* 53-74.

Spoth, R., Redmond, C., Hockaday, C., & Shin, C. Y. (1996). Family programs: Barriers to participation in family skills preventive interventions and their evaluation: A replication and extension. *Family Relations, 45*(3), 247-254.

Spreen, O., Risser, A. H., & Edgell, D. (1995). *Developmental neuropsychology.* New York: Oxford University Press.

Sroufe, L. A., Carlson, E., & Shulman, S. (1993). Individuals in relationships: Development from infancy through adolescence. In D. C. Funder, R. D. Parke, C. Tomlinson-Keasey, & K. Widaman (Eds.), *Studying lives through time, personality and development.* Washington, DC: APA Publications.

Stark, E., & Flitcraft, A. H. (1988). Women and children at risk: A feminist perspective on child abuse. *International Journal of Health Services, 18,* 97-118.

Starr, R. H. (1982). A research-based approach to the prediction of child abuse. In R. H. Starr (Ed.), *Child abuse prediction* (pp. 105-134). Cambridge, MA: Ballinger.

State of Hawaii Department of Health. (1991). *Healthy Start/family support programs evaluation results.* Unpublished document.

Steele, H., & Steele, M. (1994). Intergenerational patterns of attachment. In K. Bartholo-
mew & D. Perlman (Eds.), *Attachment processes in adulthood, advances in personal relationships* (Vol. 5, pp. 93-120). London: Jessica Kingsley.

Steffensmeier, R. H. (1982). A role model of transition to parenthood. *Journal of Marriage
and the Family, 44*(2), 319-334.

Stein, A. R., & Haggard, M. (1988). *Parent Services Project evaluation: Final report of
findings.* Fairfax, CA: Parent Services Project.

Stein, T. (1993). *Child welfare and the law.* White Plains, NY: Longman.

Stets, J. E. (1988). *Domestic violence and control.* New York: Springer-Verlag.

Stiles, J. (1995). Plasticity and development: Evidence from children with early occurring
focal brain injury. In B. Julesz & I. Kovacs (Eds.), *Maturational windows and adult cortical plasticity* (pp. 217-237). Reading, MA: Addison-Wesley.

St. Pierre, R. G., & Layzer, J. I. (1999). Using home visits for multiple purposes: The Comprehensive Child Development Program. *The Future of Children, 9*(1), 134-151.

Straus, M., & Kantor, G. (1987). Stress and child abuse. In R. Helfer & R. S. Kempe (Eds.),
The battered child (4th ed., pp. 42-59). Chicago: University of Chicago Press.

Straus, M. A., & Smith, C. (1990). Family patterns and child abuse. In M. A. Straus & R. J.
Gelles (Eds.), *Physical violence in American families: Risk factors and adaptations to
violence in 8,145 families* (pp. 245-262). New Brunswick, NJ: Transaction.

Straussner, S. L. A. (1993). Assessment and treatment of clients with alcohol and other
drug abuse problems: An overview. In S. L. A. Straussner (Ed.), *Clinical work with substance abusing clients* (pp. 3-30). New York: Guilford.

Stringer, S. A., & LaGreca, A. M. (1985). Correlates of child abuse potential. *Journal of
Abnormal Child Psychology, 13*(2), 217-226.

Substance Abuse and Mental Health Services Administration. (1994). *CSAT treatment improvement protocol No. 9: Assessment and treatment of patients with co-existing mental illness and alcohol and other drug abuse.* Rockville, MD: Author.

Substance Abuse and Mental Health Services Administration. (1996). *The national treatment improvement evaluation study.* Rockville, MD: Author.

Suess, G. J., Grossmann, K. E., & Sroufe, L. A. (1992). Effects of infant attachment to
mother and father on quality of adaptation in preschool: From dyadic to individual organization of self. *International Journal of Behavioral Development, 15*(1), 43-65.

Sussman, L. K., Robins, L. N., & Earls, F. (1987). Treatment-seeking for depression by
Black and White Americans. *Social Science & Medicine, 24*(3), 187-196.

Swift, C., & Levin, G. (1987). Empowerment: An emerging mental health technology.
Journal of Primary Prevention, 8, 71-94.

Szapocznik, J., & Kurtines, W. M. (1989). *Breakthroughs in family therapy with drug abusing and problem youth.* New York: Springer.

Szapocznik, J., Perez-Vidal, A., Hervis, O. E., Brickman, A. L., & Kurtines, W. M. (1990).
Innovations in family therapy: Strategies for overcoming resistance to treatment. In
R. A. Wells & V. Giannetti (Eds.), *Handbook of brief psychotherapies: Applied clinical
psychology* (pp. 93-114). New York: Plenum.

Tarter, R., Blackson, T., Martin, C., Loeber, R., & Moss, H. (1993). Characteristics and correlates of child discipline practices in substance abuse and normal families. *American
Journal on Addictions, 2*(1), 18-25.

Taylor, D. K., & Beauchamp, C. (1988). Hospital-based primary prevention strategy in
child abuse: A multi-level needs addressment. *Child Abuse and Neglect, 12,* 343-354.

Taylor, S. (1983). Adjustment to threatening events: A theory of cognitive adaptation. *American Psychologist, 38,* 1161-1173.

Teicher, M. H., Ito, Y., Glod, C. A., Schiffer, F., & Gelbard, H. A. (1996). Neurophysiological mechanisms of stress response in children. In C. R. Pfeffer (Ed.), *Severe stress and mental disturbance in children* (pp. 59-84). Washington, DC: American Psychiatric Press.

Telleen, S., Herzog, A., & Kilbane, T. L. (1989). Impact of a family support program on mother's social support and parenting stress. *American Journal of Orthopsychiatry, 59,* 410-419.

Teti, D. M., & Gelfand, D. M. (1991). Behavioral competence among mothers of infants in the first year: The mediational role of maternal self-efficacy. *Child Development, 62*(5), 918-929.

Thoits, P. (1983). Dimensions of life events that influence psychological distress: An evaluation and synthesis of the literature. In H. Kaplan (Ed.), *Psychosocial distress: Trends in theory and research.* New York: Academic Press.

Thompson, R. (1995). *Preventing child maltreatment through social support: A critical analysis.* Thousand Oaks, CA: Sage.

Thompson, S. C. (1981). Will it hurt less if I can control it? A complex answer to a simple question. *Psychological Bulletin, 90*(1), 89-101.

Thyen, U., Leventhal, J. M., Yazdgerdi, S. R., & Perrin, J. M. (1997). Concerns about child maltreatment in hospitalized children. *Child Abuse and Neglect, 21*(2), 187-198.

Tracy, E. (1994). Maternal substance abuse: Protecting the child, preserving the family. *Social Work, 39*(5), 534-540.

Tracy, E. M., & Whittaker, J. K. (1990). The social network map: Assessing social support in clinical practice. *Families in Society, 7,* 461-470.

Trickett, P. K., Aber, J. L., Carlson, V., & Cicchetti, D. (1991). Relationship of socioeconomic status to the etiology and developmental sequelae of physical child abuse. *Developmental Psychology, 27*(1), 148-158.

Trinh, C. (1998). The crack epidemic: Drug addiction in women. In B. Sherman, L. M. Saunders, & C. Trinh (Eds.), *Addiction and pregnancy: Empowering recovery through peer counseling* (pp. 9-28). Westport, CT: Praeger.

Tronick, E. Z., Winn, S., & Morelli, G. A. (1985). Multiple caretaking in the context of human evolution: Why don't the Efe know the Western prescription for child care? In M. Reite & T. Field (Eds.), *Psychobiology of attachment and separation* (pp. 292-322). New York: Academic Press.

Troy, M., & Sroufe, L. A. (1987). Victimization among preschoolers: Role of attachment relationship history. *Journal of the American Academy of Child and Adolescent Psychiatry, 26*(2), 166-172.

Tucker, M. B. (1982). Social support and coping: Applications for the study of female drug abuse. *Journal of Social Issues, 38*(2), 117-137.

Umberson, D., Anderson, K., Glick, J., & Shapiro, A. (1998). Domestic violence, personal control, and gender. *Journal of Marriage and the Family, 60*(2), 442-452.

U.S. Advisory Board on Child Abuse and Neglect. (1990). *Child abuse and neglect: Critical first steps in response to a national emergency.* Washington, DC: Government Printing Office.

U.S. Advisory Board on Child Abuse and Neglect. (1991). *Creating caring communities: Blueprint for an effective federal policy on child abuse and neglect.* Washington, DC: Government Printing office.

U.S. Advisory Board on Child Abuse and Neglect. (1993). *Neighbors helping neighbors: A new national strategy for the protection of children.* Washington, DC: Government Printing Office.

U.S. Bureau of the Census. (1998). *Resident population of the United States: Estimates by age and sex.* Washington, DC: Author.

U.S. Bureau of the Census. (1999). *Annual population estimates by age group and sex, selected years from 1990 to 1999.* Washington, DC: Author.

U.S. Department of Defense. (1995). *Department of Defense programs and policies that support the role of fathers in families.* Washington, DC: Author.

U.S. Department of Defense. (1999). *New parent support programs.* Washington, DC: Author.

U.S. Department of Health and Human Services, Administration on Children, Youth, and Families. (1999a). *Child maltreatment 1997: Reports from the states to the National Child Abuse and Neglect Data System.* Washington, DC: U.S. Government Printing Office.

U.S. Department of Health and Human Services. (1999b). *Blending perspectives and building common ground: A report to Congress on substance abuse and child protection.* Washington, DC: Government Printing Office.

Valzelli, L., & Bernasconi, S. (1979). Aggressiveness by isolation and brain serotonin turnover changes in different strains of mice. *Neuropsychobiology, 5*(3), 129-135.

Vandell, D. L., Hyde, J. S., Plant, E. A., & Essex, M. J. (1997). Fathers and "others" as infant-care providers: Predictors of parents' emotional well-being and marital satisfaction. *Merrill-Palmer Quarterly, 43*(3), 361-385.

Van Praag, H. M. (1982). Depression, suicide, and the metabolism of serotonin in the brain. *Journal of Affective Disorders, 4*(4), 275-290.

Vaux, A. (1988). *Social support: Theory, research, and intervention.* New York: Praeger.

Vinokur, A. D., Price, R. H., & Caplan, R. D. (1996). Hard times and hurtful partners: How financial strain affects depression and relationship satisfaction of unemployed persons and their spouses. *Journal of Personality & Social Psychology, 71*(1), 166-179.

Wagner, M. M., & Clayton, S. L. (1999). The Parents as Teachers program: Results from two demonstrations. *The Future of Children, 9*(1), 91-115.

Wahler, R. G., & Dumas, J. E. (1989). Attentional problems in dysfunctional mother-child interactions: An interbehavioral model. *Psychological Bulletin, 105*(1), 116-130.

Waldfogel, J. (1998). Rethinking the paradigm for child protection. *The Future of Children, 8*(1), 104-119.

Waldfogel, J. (1999). *The future of child protection.* Cambridge, MA: Harvard University Press.

Walker, T. B., Rodriguez, G. G., Johnson, D. L., & Cortez, C. P. (1995). AVANCE parent-child education program. In S. Smith (Ed.), *Two generation programs for families in Poverty: A new intervention strategy* (Advances in Applied Developmental Psychology, Vol. 9, pp. 67-90). Norwood, NJ: Ablex.

Wallace, B. C. (1991). Chemically dependent treatment for the pregnant crack addict: Beyond the criminal-sanctions perspective. *Psychology of Addictive Behavior, 5*(1), 23-35.

Waller, A. E., Baker, S. P., & Szocka, A. (1989). Childhood injury deaths: National analysis and geographical variations. *American Journal of Public Health, 79,* 310-315.

Wallerstein, N. (1992). Powerlessness, empowerment, and health: Implications for health promotion programs. *American Journal of Health Promotion, 6*(3), 197-205.

Wang, C. T., & Daro, D. (1997). *Current trends in child abuse reporting and fatalities: The results of the 1996 Annual Fifty State Survey.* Chicago: National Committee to Prevent Child Abuse.

Wang, C., & Daro, D. (1998). *Current trends in child abuse reporting and fatalities: The results of the 1997 Annual Fifty State Survey* (Working Paper No. 808). Chicago: National Committee to Prevent Child Abuse.

Wang, C. T., & Harding, K. (1999). *Current trends in child abuse reporting and fatalities: The results of the 1998 Annual Fifty State Survey.* Chicago: National Center on Child Abuse Prevention Research.

Warren, S., Huston, L., Egeland, B., & Sroufe, L. A. (1997). Child and adolescent anxiety disorders and early attachment. *Journal of the American Academy of Child & Adolescent Psychiatry, 36*(5), 637-644.

Washton, A. M. (1996). Clinical assessment of psychoactive substance use. In A. M. Washton (Ed.), *Psychotherapy and substance abuse: A practitioner's handbook* (pp. 23-54). New York: Guilford.

Wasik, B. H. (1993). Staffing issues for home visitors. *The Future of Children, 3*(3), 140-157.

Wasik, B. H., Bryant, D. M., & Lyons, C. M. (1990). *Home visiting: Procedures for helping families.* Thousand Oaks, CA: Sage.

Wasik, B. H., & Roberts, R. N. (1994). Survey of home visiting programs for abused and neglected children and their families. *Child Abuse and Neglect, 18*(3), 271-283.

Webster-Stratton, C. (1985). Predictors of treatment outcome in parent training for conduct disordered children. *Behavior Therapy, 16,* 223-243.

Webster-Stratton, C. (1990). Predictors of treatment outcome in parent training for conduct disordered children. *Behavior Therapy, 21,* 319-337.

Weikert, D. P., Bond, J. T., & McNeil, J. T. (1978). *The Ypsilanti Perry Preschool Project: Preschool years and longitudinal results through fourth grade.* Ypsilanti, MI: High/ Scope Educational Research Foundation.

Weiss, H. B. (1993). Home visits: Necessary but not sufficient. *The Future of Children, 3*(3), 113-128.

Wekerle, C., & Wolfe, D. A. (1993). Prevention of child physical abuse and neglect: Promising new directions. *Clinical Psychology Review, 13,* 501-540.

Westney, O. E., Cole, O. J., & Munford, T. L. (1988). The effects of prenatal education intervention on unwed prospective adolescent fathers. *Journal of Adolescent Health Care, 9,* 214-218.

Whipple, E. E., & Webster-Stratton, C. (1991). The role of parental stress in physically abusive families. *Child Abuse and Neglect, 15,* 279-291.

Whipple, E. E., & Wilson, S. R. (1996, April). Evaluation of a parent education and support program for families at risk of physical child abuse. *Families in Society: The Journal of Contemporary Human Services,* p. 227.

Widom, C. S. (1989a). The cycle of violence. *Science, 244*(4901), 160-166.

Widom, C. S. (1989b). Does violence beget violence? A critical examination of the literature. *Psychological Bulletin, 106*(1), 3-28.

Widom, C. S., & White, H. R. (1997). Problem behaviours in abused and neglected children grown up: Prevalence and co-occurrence of substance abuse, crime, and violence. *Criminal Behaviour & Mental Health, 7*(4), 287-310.

Wiehe, V. (1986). Empathy and locus of control in child abusers. *Journal of Social Service Research, 9*(2-3), 17-30.

Wiese, D. & Daro, D. (1995). *Current trends in child abuse reporting and fatalities: The results of the 1994 Annual Fifty State Survey* (Working Paper No. 808). Chicago: National Committee to Prevent Child Abuse.

Windham, A. (1998, May 11). *Comprehensive evaluation of the Hawaii Healthy Start program: Maternal outcomes at year 1.* Paper presented at the Seventh Healthy Families America Research Network Meeting, Chicago.

Winter, M. M (1999). Parents as teachers. *The Future of Children, 9*(1), 179-181.

Wolf, F. M. (1986). *Meta-analysis: Quantitative methods for research synthesis.* Beverly Hills, CA: Sage.

Wolfe, D. A. (1985). Child-abusive parents: An empirical review and analysis. *Psychological Bulletin, 97*(3), 462-482.

Wolfe, D. A., Edwards, B., Manion, I., & Koverola, C. (1988). Early intervention for parents at risk of child abuse and neglect: A preliminary investigation. *Journal of Consulting and Clinical Psychology, 56*(1), 40-47.

Wolff, R. (1983). Child abuse and neglect; Dynamics and Underlying pattern. *Victimology, 8*(1-2), 105-112.

Wolley, P. V., & Evans, W. A. (1955). Significance of skeletal lesions in infants resembling those of traumatic origin. *Journal of the American Medical Association, 181,* 17-24.

Wu, J., Kramer, G. L., Kram, M., Steciuk, M., Crawford, I. L., & Petty, F. (1999). Serotonin and learned helplessness: A regional study of 5-HT1A, 5-HT2A receptors and the serotonin transport site in rat brain. *Journal of Psychiatric Research, 33*(1), 17-22.

Wulczyn, F., Harden, A., & Goerge, R. (1997). *An update from the multistate foster care data archive: Foster care dynamics, 1983-1994.* Chicago: University of Chicago.

Yarrow, L. J. (1961). Maternal deprivation: Toward an empirical and conceptual reevaluation. *Psychological Bulletin, 58,* 459-490.

Yeich, S., & Levine, R. (1994). Political efficacy: Enhancing the construct and its relationship to mobilization of people. *Journal of Community Psychology, 22*(3), 259-271.

Young, L. (1964). *Wednesday's children: A study of child neglect and abuse.* New York: McGraw-Hill.

Zeanah, C. H., Boris, N. W., & Larrieu, J. A. (1997). Infant development and developmental risk: A review of the past 10 years. *Journal of the American Academy of Child and Adolescent Psychiatry, 36*(2), 165-178.

Zeanah, C. H., & Scheeringa, M. S. (1997). The experience and effects of violence in infancy. In J. D. Osofsky (Ed.), *Children in a violent society* (pp. 97-123). New York: Guilford.

Zeitlin, H. (1994). Children with alcohol misusing parents. *British Medical Bulletin, 50*(1), 139-151.

Zelkowitz, P., & Milet, T. H. (1995). Screening for postpartum depression in a community sample. *Canadian Journal of Psychiatry, 40*(2), 80-86.

Ziegler, E. F., & Muenchow, S. (1992). *Head Start: The inside story of America's most successful educational experiment.* New York: Basic Books.

Zigler, E. (1979). Controlling child abuse in America: An effort doomed to failure? In R. Bourne & E. H. Newberger (Eds.), *Critical perspectives on child abuse* (pp. 171-213). Lexington, MA: Lexington Books.

Zimmerman, M. A. (1990). Taking aim on empowerment research: On the distinction between individual and psychological conceptions. *American Journal of Community Psychology, 18*(1), 169-177.

Zimmerman, M. A. (1993). *Empowerment theory: Psychological, organizational, and community levels of analysis.* Unpublished manuscript, University of Michigan, Ann Arbor.

Zimmerman, M. A., Israel, B. A., Schulz, A., & Checkoway, B. (1992). Further explorations in empowerment theory: An empirical analysis of psychological empowerment. *American Journal of Community Psychology, 20,* 707-727.

Zippay, A. (1995). Expanding employment skills and social networks among teen mothers: Case study of a mentor program. *Child and Adolescent Social Work Journal, 12*(1), 51-69.

Zubrow, J. M. (1993). The pedagogy of adolescent peer relations: Searching with inner-city adolescents for critical consciousness. *Dissertation Abstracts International,* 54-03-B, 16.

Zuckerman, B. (1994). Effects on parents and children. In D. J. Besharov (Ed.), *When drug addicts have children: Reorienting child welfare's response* (pp. 49-63). Washington, DC: Child Welfare League of America.

Zuckerman, B., & Brown, E. R. (1993). Maternal substance abuse and infant development. In C. H. Zeanah (Ed.), *Handbook of infant mental health* (pp. 143-158). New York: Guilford.

Zuravin, S. J. (1989a). The ecology of child abuse and neglect: Review of the literature and presentation of data. *Violence and Victims, 4*(2), 101-120.

Zuravin, S. J. (1989b). Severity of maternal depression and three types of mother-to-child aggression. *American Journal of Orthopsychiatry, 59*(3), 377-389.

Zuravin, S., McMillen, C., DePanfilis, D., & Risley-Curtiss, C. (1996). The intergenerational cycle of child maltreatment: Continuity versus discontinuity. *Journal of Interpersonal Violence, 11*(3), 315-334.

INDEX

ABOUT THE AUTHOR

Neil B. Guterman is Associate Professor in the Columbia University School of Social Work in New York City, where he teaches courses in clinical social work practice and family and children's services. He received his MSW in 1986, and his PhD in social work and psychology in 1992 at the University of Michigan. He was awarded a Lady Davis Post Doctoral Fellowship at the Hebrew University School of Social Work (Jerusalem) in 1992-1993. Dr. Guterman has been a faculty affiliate of the Center for the Study of Social Work Practice, a joint practice-research Center of the Columbia University School of Social Work and the Jewish Board of Family and Children's Services, and he has conducted clinical practice with families and children in a wide variety of family and children's services settings, with a particular emphasis on cases of child maltreatment. He is the co-principal investigator of one of the largest randomized trials of early home visitation services in the northeastern United States, and a site co-principal investigator in a national study of engagement and retention within early home visitation services, coordinated by Prevent Child Abuse America. In addition, he is a senior investigator of a National Institutes of Health-funded longitudinal study of early childhood neglect, economic factors, and public policy (with Drs. Chris Paxton, Jane Waldfogel, and Jeanne Brooks-Gunn). In 1999, Dr. Guterman was named a Rochester Child Health Congressional Fellow, one of 50 "up-and-coming" cross-disciplinary academic leaders in the United States within the field of maternal-child health.